macromedia
FLASH™ 5

Using Flash

macromedia

Acknowledgments

Project Management: Erick Vera

Writing: Jody Bleyle, Mary Burger, Louis Dobrozensky, Stephanie Gowin, Marcelle Taylor, and Judy Walthers Von Alten

Editing: Peter Fenczik, Rosana Francescato, Ann Szabla

Multimedia: George Brown, John "Zippy" Lehnus, and Noah Zilberberg

Print and Help Design: Chris Basmajian and Noah Zilberberg

Production: Chris Basmajian and Rebecca Godbois

Special thanks: Jeremy Clark, Brian Dister and the entire Flash Development team, Margaret Dumas, Kipling Inscore, Alyn Kelley and the entire Flash QA team, Pete Santangeli, Cyn Taylor, and Eric Wittman

First Edition: July 2000

Macromedia, Inc.
600 Townsend St.
San Francisco, CA 94103

CONTENTS

CHAPTER 2

Flash Basics 65

CHAPTER 3

Drawing 113

CHAPTER 8
Using Layers...............................201

CHAPTER 9
Using Type 209

CHAPTER 10
Using Symbols and Instances.................225

CHAPTER 11

CHAPTER 12

CHAPTER 13

CHAPTER 14

Publishing and Exporting 311

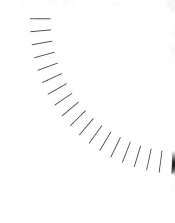

INTRODUCTION
Getting Started

Macromedia Flash is the professional standard for producing high-impact Web experiences. Whether you are creating animated logos, Web site navigation controls, long-form animations, entire Flash Web sites, or Web applications, you'll find the power and flexibility of Flash ideal for your own creativity.

System requirements for Flash authoring

- For Microsoft Windows™: An Intel Pentium® 133 Mhz or equivalent (200 recommended) processor running Windows 95 or higher (including Windows 2000), or NT version 4.0 or later; 32 MB of RAM (64 MB recommended); 40 MB of available disk space; a color monitor capable of 800 x 600 resolution; and a CD-ROM drive.

- For the Macintosh®: A Power Macintosh (G3 or higher recommended) running System 8.5 or later; 32 MB RAM free application memory, plus 40 MB of available disk space; a color monitor capable of 800 x 600 resolution; and a CD-ROM drive.

System requirements for the Flash Player

The following hardware and software are required to play Flash Player movies in a browser:

- Microsoft Windows 95, NT 4.0 or later; or a PowerPC with System 8.1 or later.

- Netscape plugin that works with Netscape 3 or later (Windows 95 and Macintosh).

- To run ActiveX controls, Microsoft Internet Explorer 3.02 or later (Windows 95) is required.

- To run Flash Player Java Edition, a Java-enabled browser is required.

Installing Flash

Follow these steps to install Flash on either a Windows or a Macintosh computer.

To install Flash on a Windows or a Macintosh computer:

1 Insert the Flash 5 CD into the computer's CD-ROM drive.

2 Do one of the following:

- In Windows, choose Start > Run. Click Browse and choose the Setup.exe file on the Flash 5 CD. Click OK in the Run dialog box to begin the installation.

- On the Macintosh, double-click the Flash 5 Installer icon.

3 Follow the onscreen instructions.

4 If prompted, restart your computer.

What's new in Flash 5

The new features in Flash 5 provide enhanced capabilities for creating artwork, streamlining your workflow, and creating interactivity. Flash 5 also includes greatly expanded capabilities for creating actions with ActionScript. See "What's New in ActionScript" in the *ActionScript Reference Guide*.

Creating artwork

Enhanced color controls, including the Mixer panel, Fill and Stroke panels, Swatches panel, and Fill and Stroke toolbox controls, provide expanded capabilities for painting artwork. See Chapter 4, "Working with Color."

New selection highlights make it easy to identify selected lines, fills, and groups as well as the color of selected objects. See "Selecting objects" on page 182.

Draggable guides aid you in arranging objects on the Stage. See "Using the grid, guides, and rulers" on page 104.

The Pen tool lets you create precise paths; it works like the Pen tool in Macromedia FreeHand or Macromedia Fireworks. See "Using the Pen tool" on page 118.

Workflow

New panels for working with color, type, actions, frames, instances, and entire movies make it easy to access options for modifying elements in Flash movies. See Chapter 2, "Flash Basics."

Shared libraries let you link to library items as external assets. You can create font symbols to include in shared libraries, as well as buttons, graphics, movie clips, and sounds. See "Using shared libraries" on page 95.

The Macromedia Dashboard provides a way for you to easily keep up with the latest information on using Flash. See "Macromedia Dashboard for Flash" on page 15.

Custom shortcut keys allow you to create your own shortcuts for Flash commands and functions to customize your workflow. See "Customizing keyboard shortcuts" on page 106.

Support for importing MP3 sound files lets you import sounds into Flash that are already compressed. This reduces the time required for publishing and exporting a movie with sound, since you don't have to compress the sounds during export. Using compressed sounds reduces the file size of completed movies and reduces memory requirements during authoring. See Chapter 6, "Adding Sound."

Interactivity

Expanded ActionScript provides greatly enhanced capabilities for creating interactivity in Flash using ActionScript. See the *ActionScript Reference Guide*.

The Movie Explorer lets you easily view the complete contents of the current movie and view the Properties panel for a selected item to modify it. See "Using the Movie Explorer" on page 98.

The Print action lets you assign actions for printing Flash movie frames from the Flash Player as vector or bitmap graphics. See the *ActionScript Reference Guide*.

Expanded cross-product integration

Support for importing FreeHand and Fireworks PNG files lets you import these files directly into Flash as editable graphics, preserving layers, text, and other elements. See "Placing artwork into Flash" on page 152.

Enhanced integration with Macromedia Generator lets you extend the Flash authoring environment to create fast-changing dynamic content. See "About Generator and Flash" on page 318.

Enhanced integration with Macromedia Fireworks lets you easily launch Fireworks to edit bitmap images imported into Flash. See "Editing bitmaps" on page 164.

Guide to instructional media

The Flash 5 package contains a variety of media to help you learn the program quickly and become proficient in creating your own Flash Player movies— including online help that appears in your Web browser, interactive lessons, a tutorial, two printed books, and a regularly updated Web site.

Flash lessons and tutorial

If you are new to Flash, or if you have used only a limited set of its features, start with the lessons. The lessons introduce you to the main features of Flash, letting you practice on isolated examples.

The tutorial introduces the workflow in Flash by showing you how to create a basic movie. The tutorial assumes an understanding of the topics covered in the lessons.

To start with the lessons, choose Help > Lessons > Introduction.

Using Flash and *ActionScript Reference Guide*

Using Flash contains instructions and information for using all Flash tools and commands. It is provided as both online help and a printed book. The online help contains a variety of Flash Player movies demonstrating effects and features.

The *ActionScript Reference Guide* contains instructions and information on ActionScript, including writing ActionScript, creating interaction with ActionScript, and a complete ActionScript dictionary. It is provided as both online help and a printed book.

Flash Help

Flash 5 contains three help systems: Using Flash, ActionScript Reference, and ActionScript Dictionary.

For the best experience when using Flash Help, Macromedia strongly recommends that you use Netscape Navigator 4.0 or later or Microsoft Internet Explorer 4.0 or later on Windows, and Netscape Navigator 4.0 or later or Microsoft Internet Explorer 4.5 or later on the Macintosh. If you use a 3.0 browser, all the content of the movies and the Flash Help is still accessible, but some features (such as Search) will not work. Running Flash and Flash Help simultaneously on a Macintosh may require up to 32 MB of memory, depending on your browser's memory needs.

To use Flash Help:

1 Choose one of the three help systems from the Help menu.

2 Navigate the help topics using any of these features:

• Contents organizes information by subject. Click top-level entries to view subtopics.

• Index organizes information like a traditional printed index. Click a term to jump to a related topic.

• Search finds any character string in all topic text. Search requires a 4.0 or later browser with Java enabled. To search for a phrase, type it into the text entry box.

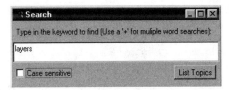

To search for files that contain two keywords (for example, **layers** and **style**), separate the words with a plus (+) sign.

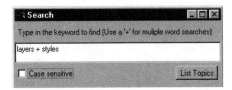

To search for files that contain a complete phrase, separate the words with a space.

• Previous and Next buttons let you move through the topics within a section.

• The Flash icon links you to the Flash Support Center Web site.

Macromedia Dashboard for Flash

The Macromedia Dashboard for Flash provides access to resources in the Flash development community directly from within the Flash application. Use the Macromedia Dashboard to get information on a variety of topics related to Flash.

Macromedia posts new content to the Macromedia Dashboard regularly. You can choose whether to manually or automatically update the contents of the Macromedia Dashboard on your computer.

To view the Macromedia Dashboard:

1 Choose Help > Macromedia Dashboard.

2 Click the Dashboard tab and choose a topic.

To specify how often the Macromedia Dashboard content is updated:

In the Macromedia Dashboard, select Auto Update to have information updated automatically on a regular basis. Deselect the option if you want to manually update Dashboard content by clicking the Update button.

Note: You must be connected to the Internet to update Dashboard content.

Flash Support Center

The Flash Support Center Web site is updated regularly with the latest information on Flash, plus advice from expert users, advanced topics, examples, tips, and other updates. Check the Web site often for the latest news on Flash and how to get the most out of the program at www.macromedia.com/support/flash/.

CHAPTER 1
Tutorial

. . . .

Overview

Imagine that once upon a time there was a kite shop with a Web site. Customers would go to this site and scroll through static images of different kites to decide on the one they wanted—at least, that was the goal. In truth, most of the customers became bored with the site and went off to do something else. While the Web page served a purpose, it didn't really capture anyone's attention.

Now imagine you can add Flash to the site. In this tutorial you'll author a Web page for Orbit Kites—an interactive site that lets users view and design their own kites. After customers decide on a kite, they click a button that displays the invoice for the selected kite while playing an animation of the kite flying.

To complete the tutorial, you'll take advantage of Flash features beyond what you learned in the lessons, and you'll learn more about creating a movie. Specifically, you will complete these tasks:

- Change Flash movie properties
- Import, create, and modify media that appear in your movie
- Add sound to a button
- Use the Stage and Timeline to assemble the movie
- Create motion-tweening and shape-tweening animations
- Use actions to add interactivity and streamline authoring
- Test the movie for download performance
- Publish the movie for Web playback

The tutorial takes approximately one hour to complete, depending upon your experience.

What you should know

Although the tutorial is designed for beginning Flash users, you need the basic Flash skills covered in seven lessons found in Flash Help. These interactive lessons, created in Flash, offer an introduction to the following topics:

- Drawing
- Symbols
- Layers
- Type
- Buttons
- Sound
- Animation

To take a lesson, choose Help > Lessons, then select from the list. To promote a greater understanding of the tutorial, be sure you're comfortable with the concepts presented in the lessons before starting the tutorial.

View the completed movie

Before you start to work on your own movie, view a completed version of the tutorial to get an idea of what you'll create. Additionally, the completed tutorial lets you examine the Timeline, Movie Explorer, Library window, and Stage to understand authoring practices.

1 In your Flash 5 application folder, open Tutorial > Finished.

2 Select the Kite.swf file and drag it to an open browser window.

Flash movies in the authoring environment have the FLA extension. A movie exported as a Flash Player movie has the SWF extension.

3 Click one of the Select a Kite buttons.

Notice that a sound plays when you click the button, and the selected kite appears.

4 Click one of the Select a Color buttons.

Notice how the kite changes to match the color you selected.

5 Click the Fly It! button.

Listen to the sound and watch the animation.

Notice that the invoice, a movie clip symbol, is tailored to the kite and color you selected.

A movie clip is a smaller movie that plays within the main Flash movie.

6 To start the movie again, you can click the Back button.

7 When you finish viewing the SWF file, you can either close the window or leave it open to serve as a reference.

Analyze the Kite.fla file

It's helpful to analyze the completed FLA file to determine just how the author put the file together. There are a variety of ways to approach this analysis. In this tutorial, you will analyze the file by completing the following steps:

1 In Flash, choose File > Open. Navigate to the Flash application folder and open Tutorial/Finished/Kite.fla.

   You now see the completed tutorial movie in the authoring environment.

2 To see more of the Stage and Timeline, choose Window > Close All Panels.

3 To resize the Timeline and Stage, drag the bar that separates the Stage from the Timeline up and down. Scroll around the Timeline to see how the layers are organized.

4 As you learned in the Animation lesson, a keyframe is a frame where you define changes in animation. As you scroll around the Timeline, note which layers and frames have keyframes.

   Beginning and intermediate keyframes appear as solid circles, while ending keyframes appear as small outlined rectangles.

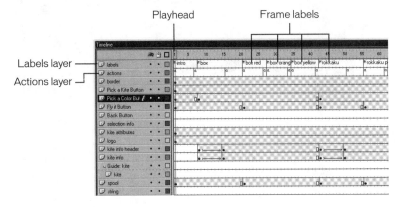

5 To view labels the author created that indicate segments of the movie, scan the labels layer, which is the first layer in the Timeline.

   In addition to using labels to create and identify movie segments, you can use labels for navigation by specifying that the playhead move to the first frame of a specific label when the user clicks a button. You'll learn more about labels and navigation later in the tutorial.

6 Look at the next layer down, which is the actions layer.

   The actions layer indicates frames where ActionScript, the Flash scripting language, is included in the movie.

   Each lowercase *a* that you see in a frame represents ActionScript.

7 Select the playhead and drag it slowly across the frames.

Watch how changes in action on the Stage correspond to changes in the Timeline. Notice, however, that as you drag the playhead, the movie plays sequentially instead of playing as it appears to users. Navigation implemented with ActionScript in the movie lets users jump to specific frames rather than moving sequentially through the Timeline.

Use the Movie Explorer

The Movie Explorer assists you with arranging, locating, and editing media and is most beneficial when you're working on a movie with numerous assets. With its hierarchical tree structure, the Movie Explorer provides insight into the organization and flow of a movie, which is especially useful when you work with a movie authored by someone else.

1 If the Movie Explorer is not already open, choose Window > Movie Explorer or click the Movie Explorer button in the Launcher bar.

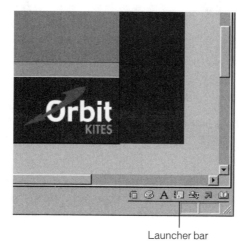

Launcher bar

2 If necessary, make the Movie Explorer larger (drag the lower right corner of the window) to view the tree structure in the pane.

The Movie Explorer filtering buttons display or hide information.

Find text box ——— 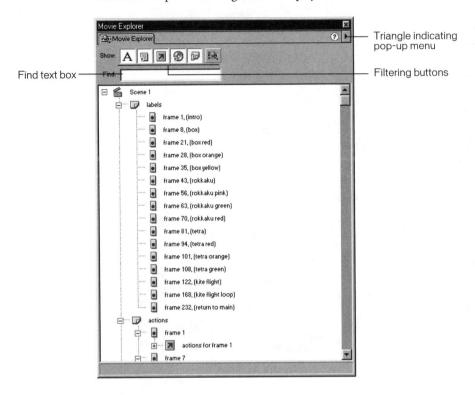 ——— Triangle indicating pop-up menu

Filtering buttons

3 Click the triangle in the upper right of the Movie Explorer, and in the pop-up menu that appears, verify that Show Movie Elements and Show Symbol Definitions are selected.

4 Along the top left of the Movie Explorer window, verify that the only filtering buttons selected are Show Text; Show Buttons, Movie Clips, and Graphics; and Show ActionScripts.

5 Scroll through the list to view some of the assets included in the movie, and to see their relationship to other assets.

If you scroll to the Rokkaku Kite button, for example, you see that it has ActionScript associated with it. Expand the icon to view the action, which plays a SWF of a rokkaku kite when the user clicks the Rokkaku Kite button.

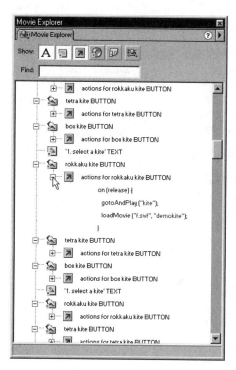

6 Deselect the Show ActionScripts filtering button and select the Show Frames and Layers filtering button.

7 Scroll up to the top of the Movie Explorer. Under the labels layer, double-click Frame 43 (rokkaku) to move the playhead in the Timeline to the first frame of the rokkaku label.

Panels associated with the frame will also appear.

To view an item listed in the hierarchical tree, you double-click the corresponding icon. If you double-click a frame icon, the playhead moves to that frame in the Timeline. If you double-click another icon type, the associated panel appears, allowing you to view or change asset properties.

8 Deselect the Show Frames and Layers filtering button.

9 In the Find text box, type **rokkaku kite BUTTON**.

The Movie Explorer displays the search results.

10 Right-click (Windows) or Control-click (Macintosh) the first Rokkaku Kite button icon on the list and select Find in Library from the pop-up menu at the upper right corner of the Movie Explorer.

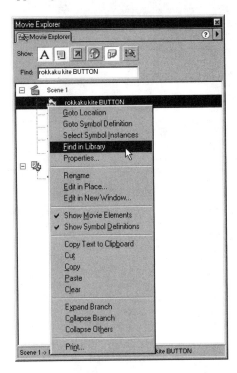

Find in Library opens the library, if it's not already open, and highlights the symbol in the Library window.

The library contains and organizes assets in your movie.

11 Close the Movie Explorer.

12 To close the movie, choose File > Close.

If you've made changes to the movie, do not save them.

Open the starting file

Now you're ready to create your own version of the tutorial movie.

1 Choose File > Open.

2 In the Flash application folder, browse to and open Tutorial/My_kite/ MyKite.fla.

You see a partially completed tutorial movie.

3 Choose File > Save As and save the movie with a new name, in the same folder as MyKite.fla.

By making a copy of the file, you allow yourself or another user to complete the tutorial again using MyKite.fla.

4 If the Library window isn't open, choose Window > Library.

Note: As you complete the tutorial, remember to save your work frequently.

Define properties to set up a Flash movie

Configuring the movie's properties is a common first step in authoring. You use the Movie Properties dialog box to specify settings that affect the entire movie, such as the frames per second (fps) playback rate, and the Stage size and background color.

Modify the default movie properties

1 Choose Modify > Movie.

2 In the Movie Properties dialog box, verify that 12 is the number in the Frame Rate text box.

   The movie will play at 12 frames per second, an optimal frame rate for playing animations on the Web.

3 Click the Background Color box to display the pop-up window, and select a dark gray.

   When you select a color, the hexadecimal value appears in a field along the top of the window. The completed tutorial uses gray with the hexadecimal value of #333333.

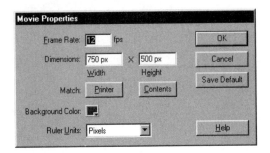

4 To apply the properties, click OK.

For additional information on movie properties, see "Creating a new movie and setting its properties" on page 74.

Create media

In addition to importing media, Flash offers a variety of tools to create high-quality graphics and text. In the completed tutorial, text appears offering background information about each selected kite. You'll create a symbol that tells customers about the inventor of the box kite.

Note: While completing the tutorial, you may find it useful to undo a change you've made. Flash can undo several of your recent changes, depending on the number of undo levels you have set in Preferences. To undo, choose Edit > Undo or press Control+Z (Windows) or Command+Z (Macintosh). Conversely, you can redo what you've undone by choosing Edit > Redo or pressing Control+Y (Windows) or Command+Y (Macintosh).

1 Choose Insert > New Symbol.

2 In the Symbol Properties dialog box, name the symbol **box TEXT**.

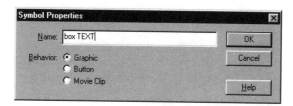

3 For Behavior, verify that Graphic is selected, then click OK.

Flash switches to symbol-editing mode. Note that the name of the symbol you're editing appears in the upper left corner of the window. The window background remains the same shade of gray that you selected in Movie Properties.

4 In the toolbox, select the Text tool.

5 If the Character panel is not open, choose Window > Panels > Character.

6 In the Font pop-up menu of the Character panel, select _sans.

Your Flash movie will replace your font with your user's default sans serif font, such as Arial or Helvetica.

7 In the Font Size pop-up menu, use the slider to select 12 pt.

8 Select the Bold button.

9 Click the color box to display the pop-up window and select white, with the hexadecimal value of # FFFFFF.

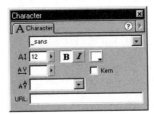

10 Click the Text tool anywhere on the left side of the window and type this text: **The box kite was invented by an Australian, Lawrence Hargrave, in 1893. He used the kite to carry weather instruments aloft.**

Although you selected white text, it appears gray so that it will show up against the white text box.

11 With the Text tool still selected, click the resizing handle—the small circle in the upper right corner of the text block—and drag it to the left so the text breaks after the word **invented.**

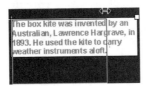

The text wraps into several lines. Once you move the sizing handle, it changes from a circle to a square to indicate that the type block now has a defined width.

Change the text block registration point

Each text block, like other elements in Flash, has a registration point that the application can use to position it. You will check the registration point of your text block to verify that it matches the registration point of the other text blocks in the movie; this ensures that all the text blocks align consistently.

1 In the toolbox, select the Arrow tool.

On the Stage, the text block is selected.

2 To open the Info panel, choose Window > Panels > Info, or click the Info Panel button in the Launcher bar.

Info Panel button

3 The Info panel contains a small grid, with a black square that indicates the registration point. If the black square is not in the upper left corner of the grid, click the upper left square to move the registration point to that position.

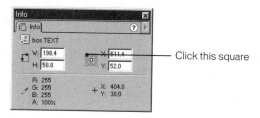

Click this square

4 Enter 0 for both the X and Y coordinates, and press Enter (Windows) or Return (Macintosh); then close the Info panel.

5 Click Scene 1 in the upper left corner of the window to return to movie-editing mode.

In Flash, you can create different scenes using the Insert > Scene command. This tutorial uses one scene only.

Test your movie

At any point during authoring, you can test how your movie will look and behave as a SWF file.

1 Save your movie and choose Control > Test Movie.

   Flash exports a SWF copy of your movie.

2 In the SWF file, click the Box Kite button and notice that, instead of seeing text about the box kite as expected, you see text about the rokkaku kite. Oops! You need to replace rokkaku TEXT with the correct text about the box kite.

3 Close the SWF file and return to the Flash authoring environment.

Replace an instance

During authoring, it is common to replace one instance with another, especially when you decide to change artwork or text. Flash simplifies the process by letting you replace one instance with another while maintaining the attributes of the original instance.

1 In the Timeline's labels layer, click the first frame of Box Red (Frame 21) to move the playhead to the section of the movie that displays information about the box kite.

   The selected frame number appears in the status display at the bottom of the Timeline.

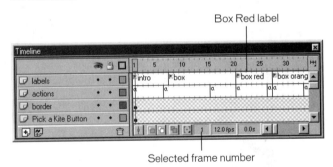

Box Red label

Selected frame number

2 With the Arrow tool selected, click the text instance on the Stage that reads "The rokkaku is a Japanese fighting kite ..."

   This is the text that you want to replace with the text you created about the box kite.

3 If the Instance panel is not visible, choose Window > Panels > Instance.

   The Instance panel appears.

 4 In the Instance panel, click the Swap Symbol button.

5 In the Swap Symbol dialog box, double-click box TEXT in the list of symbols. You might need to scroll through the list to find the symbol.

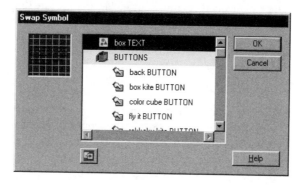

On the Stage, the new symbol replaces the previous one. Instance attributes from the previous symbol are applied to the new symbol.

Import media

In addition to creating high-quality text and graphics in Flash, you can import a variety of media types into your movie. For the kite shop, you want a sound to play when the user clicks the Fly It! button. To associate a sound with your button, you will first import an MP3 sound file. By using this compressed sound format, you're ensuring that the sound does not significantly increase the size of your movie.

1   Choose File > Import.

2   If you're using a Windows operating system, in the Import dialog box, browse to Tutorial/My_kite within your Flash application folder, and double-click wizz.mp3.

    If you're using a Macintosh operating system, browse to Tutorial/My_kite within your Flash application folder. Double-click wizz.mp3f, then click Import.

    The sound file appears in the Library window. To hear the sound, select it and click the Play button in the Library window.

Play button

Organize your library

In general, it's a good practice to organize your files in folders within your movie's library. This tutorial requires many media files, so organization is important. In this section you'll move your text file to the Text folder, and you'll create a folder for the sound files, then move all of the sound files into that folder.

1   In the Library Options menu, choose Collapse All Folders to view just the folders and items outside of folders.

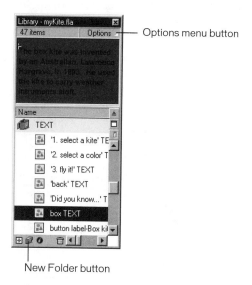

Options menu button

New Folder button

2   Select the box TEXT symbol and drag it to the Text folder.

3   Double-click the Text folder to close it.

Create a new folder for the sound files

1   In the Library Options menu, choose New Folder, and name the new folder Sound.

2   If necessary, resize the Library window to view both wizz.aif and the Sound folder.

3   To select all four sound files, Control-click (Windows) or Command-click (Macintosh) chirp.mp3, squeak.mp3, switch2.mp3, and wizz.mp3. Drag the selected files into the Sound folder.

Add sound to a button

When you create a button symbol, Flash creates keyframes for the different button states in relation to the mouse pointer. The Over keyframe, for example, represents the button's appearance when the pointer is over the button. Other button keyframes include Up, Down, and Hit. For more information about keyframes in button symbols, refer to the Buttons lesson (choose Help > Lessons > Buttons).

Now you'll add a sound to the button's Down frame, which means the sound will play when the user clicks the button. Because you're adding the sound to the button symbol in the library, not just to an instance of the symbol, the sound will play for each instance of the button.

1 In the Library window, double-click the Buttons folder to expand it.

2 Select the fly it BUTTON symbol, then choose Edit from the Library Options menu. You can also double-click the symbol's icon in the Library window.

   Flash switches to symbol-editing mode.

3 Choose Insert > Layer and name the new layer Sound.

   Remember, you can double-click a layer name to rename that layer.

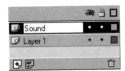

4 To insert a blank keyframe, select the Down frame (Frame 3) of the Sound layer and choose Insert > Keyframe.

5 To define the sound properties, double-click Frame 3 of the Sound layer.

   In addition to the Sound panel, other panels might appear.

6 In the Sound panel, select wizz.mp3 from the Sound pop-up menu. Then close the panel.

7 Choose Edit > Edit Movie or click Scene 1 in the upper left corner of the window to return to movie-editing mode from symbol-editing mode.

Note: Remember to save your work frequently. Also remember that you can choose Control > Test Movie to hear how the sound plays in a SWF.

Use the Stage and Timeline

Now that you've created, imported, and modified your media, use the Stage and Timeline to assemble your movie. You can create media directly on the Stage (in which case it does not appear in the library unless you decide to turn it into a symbol), or you can use the Stage to arrange imported media for individual frames. The Timeline determines when your media appears in the movie as the playhead moves through the frames.

Change the width and height of a button

On the Stage, one of the Select a Kite buttons is missing: you'll add an instance of the button, resize it, and align it on the Stage.

Since the button symbol you will add to your movie is larger than the button instances already on the Stage, you'll use the Info panel to resize the new instance.

 1   If the Info panel is not open, choose Window > Panels > Info or click the Info Panel button in the Launcher bar.

2   In the Timeline, click Frame 1 of the Pick a Kite Button layer.

3   Drag an instance of rokkaku kite BUTTON from the Library window to the Stage and place it between the other two Select a Kite buttons. When you've finished, the buttons should look like this:

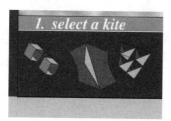

4   In the Info panel, change the width (W) to 54.2 and the height (H) to 50.0 and press Enter (Windows) or Return (Macintosh).

Align objects on the Stage

You can use the Align panel to align an object in relation to other objects. You'll use this feature now to align the three Select a Kite buttons.

1 On the Stage, select a Select a Kite button, then Shift-click to select the other two Select a Kite buttons pictured above.

The playhead should still be in Frame 1 of the Timeline.

2 If the Align panel is not visible, choose Window > Panels > Align.

3 In the Align panel, click the Vertical Align Top button, the third button from the right on the top row, to align the buttons relative to their registration points.

4 Click the Horizontal Distribute Left button, the third button from the right in the middle row, to distribute the buttons evenly apart.

Depending on where you placed the Rokkaku Kite button, the three Select a Kite buttons might require further alignment. You can align them using other alignment buttons on the Align panel until you achieve the desired result.

Vertical Align Top button

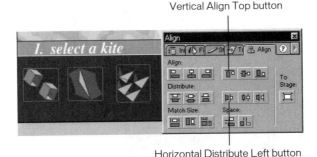

Horizontal Distribute Left button

Create a navigation action for a button instance

Flash lets you add interactivity by adding actions to your movie. The Actions panel assists you in adding ActionScript, the Flash scripting language. You can use the Actions panel to view, write, edit, or add actions to a symbol or instance.

Now you will use the Actions panel to create a navigation action that makes the playhead move to the correct frame in the Timeline when the user clicks the Rokkaku Kite button.

1 On the Stage, select just the Rokkaku Kite button (press Shift and click the other two Select a Kite buttons to deselect them).

You've selected the middle button of the three Select a Kite buttons. The Instance panel can help you identify instances by name.

The playhead should still be in Frame 1 of the Timeline.

2 Choose Window > Actions or click the Actions button in the Launcher bar.

The Object Actions panel appears.

Note: When you use the Actions panel to work with actions attached to an object, the panel is titled Object Actions. When you work with frames rather than objects, Flash displays the Frame Actions panel.

3 Click the triangle in the upper right corner of the panel to display the pop-up menu. Verify that Normal Mode, rather than Expert Mode, is selected.

Expert Mode offers features useful to those experienced with ActionScript. In Normal Mode, parameter fields and controls guide you in creating actions.

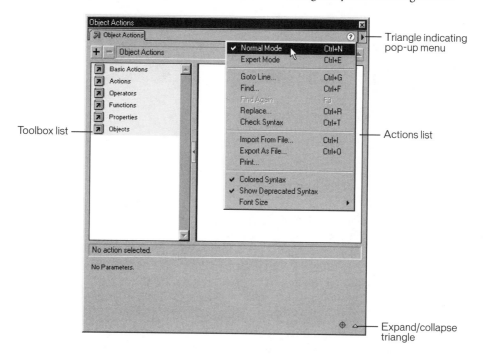

If necessary, click the triangle in the lower right corner of the Object Actions panel to open a pane that displays the parameters, and resize the window until the Toolbox list and Actions list are both visible.

4 Select the Actions icon to expand that category, then scroll down the Toolbox list and double-click `goto`.

5 In the Type pop-up menu, select Frame Label.

6 In the Frame pop-up menu, select rokkaku.

You are specifying that when users click the Rokkaku Kite button, the playhead moves to the first frame within the rokkaku label.

7 Deselect Go to and Play at the bottom of the Object Actions panel.

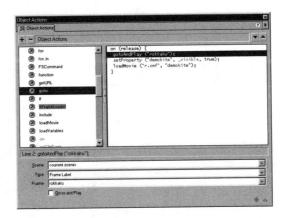

Specify that the correct kite appears

In addition to the Go To action, you will add actions to make the correct kite appear when the user clicks the Rokkaku Kite button.

1 In the Toolbox list, double-click `setProperty`.

2 In the Property pop-up menu, select _visible (Visibility)

3 In the Target text box, type **demoKite** and verify that Expression, next to the text box, is deselected.

4 In the Value text box, type **True**, and select Expression next to the text box.

5 In the Toolbox list, double-click `loadMovie`.

6 In the URL text box, type **r.swf**, which is the name of the external file with the rokkaku kite image.

7 In the Location pop-up menu, select Target.

8 In the Location text box, type **demoKite**.

9 Verify that Don't Send is selected in the Variables pop-up menu and that both Expression options are deselected, then close the Object Actions Panel.

Note: For additional information about the `setProperty` and `loadMovie` actions, refer to the *ActionScript Reference Guide.*

Lock objects

Now that you've placed and modified buttons, you'll lock the buttons to ensure that no one accidentally moves them out of alignment or makes other changes to them.

In the Timeline's Pick a Kite Button layer, click the black dot in the Lock column.

A padlock icon appears in the Lock column. (To unlock the layer, click the padlock icon again.)

Animate instances

Flash offers several different ways of animating instances using either frame-by-frame or tweening techniques. In tweening animation, you define how an instance appears in one keyframe, then define how the same instance appears in the next keyframe. Flash automatically creates the animation between the two keyframes. For this tutorial, you'll create two different types of tweening effects: motion tweening of the kite and shape tweening of the kite string.

How will you know which kite to animate if your movie has nine possible kite combinations (three kite models multiplied by three kite colors)? Will you have to animate all nine kites? Fortunately, no. Instead, you will use a kite placeholder to assist you with setting up the animation. Later in this tutorial you'll create a function that determines which kite the customer selected. Based on the information the function receives, an external SWF movie clip of the selected kite will appear in the animation instead of the placeholder.

In preparation for tweening, you need to change the registration point of the kite media.

Change the registration point

By default, the registration point of a symbol in a SWF file is in the symbol's upper left corner.

Registration point —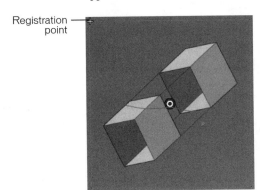

The tutorial links a kite placeholder to external SWF files of kites, which will rotate slightly in your movie. You need to move the registration point of the kite instance placeholder, so that when it's replaced by a kite SWF, the SWF will rotate around its center point rather than around its upper left corner.

The Edit Center command lets you make an instance's center of rotation different from that of the symbol.

1 In the Timeline's labels layer, locate the first frame labeled kite flight loop (Frame 168) and click the frame to move the playhead to that location.

2 Select the kite that appears on the Stage.

 3 If the Instance panel is not open, click the Instance Panel button in the Launcher bar.

Note that when the kite symbol is selected, in the Instance panel its symbol name is placeholderKite, and its instance name is demoKite. Later in the tutorial, after you add ActionScript to your movie, the kite the customer selects will replace the demoKite instance while the movie plays.

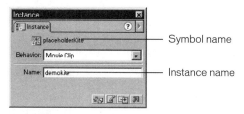

4 Choose Modify > Transform > Edit Center.

The registration point becomes visible and selected.

5 On the Stage, drag the registration point, the small cross, to the approximate center of the kite.

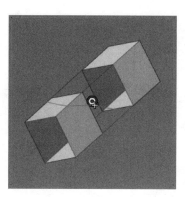

Create motion tweening for the kite

After customers select a kite, they click the Fly It! button to see the invoice while the kite flies. To achieve the effect of the kite floating around the sky, you'll add motion tweening to your movie.

For this motion tweening, you will define kite properties such as position, size, and rotation for an instance at one point on the Timeline, and then you will change those properties in keyframes that you insert in the Timeline. Flash creates the content of the frames in between the keyframes.

Add the keyframe for the end of your animation

As you add keyframes, keep in mind that you can insert the keyframes anywhere you want the animation to change; except for the first and last keyframes, you don't need to insert the keyframes in the exact frames specified in the tutorial.

1 In the Timeline's kite layer, verify that the playhead is on Frame 168.

Note the keyframe, which will indicate the start of your animation. Also notice the guideline on the Stage, which displays the path the kite will snap to. In the Timeline, this path is in the Guide:kite layer, which is a guide layer, a special layer you can create to assist in placing objects on the Stage.

Guidelines exist only to help authors assemble media along a path; they do not appear in the published Flash movie. You can recognize guide layers in the Timeline by their icon.

Guide layer icon

2 Use the pop-up menu at the lower left of the application window to increase the Stage size to 800%.

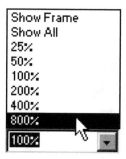

Now notice that the path is not one continuous shape—it has a small break where the animation ends.

3 In the Timeline's kite layer, move the playhead to Frame 229 and choose Insert > Keyframe.

Check the status display at the bottom of the Timeline to confirm that you selected the correct frame.

An ending keyframe appears in Frame 228, which is where the motion tween will end.

4 With the Stage still zoomed, and the playhead on Frame 229 of the kite layer, drag the kite slightly to the right, so that the registration point is on the other side of the path.

You're defining where the kite will be at the end of the animation.

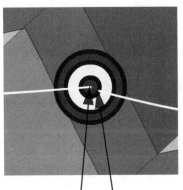

Move kite from here to here

Note: If your registration point is already on the other (right) side of the path, your animation will not work. Redo the steps to change the registration point, this time moving the point to the left of where you placed it before.

5 Resize the Stage to 100%.

Specify motion tweening

Now that you have defined the start and end of your animation, you will use the Frame panel to specify that the tween will be a motion tween.

1 In the Timeline's kite layer, click any frame between 168, the beginning of the animation, and 228, the end of the animation, so that just the frames in between those two keyframes are selected.

2 Choose Window > Panels > Frame and select Motion from the Tweening pop-up menu.

3 Verify that Snap is selected.

Snap ensures that the kite instance attaches to the guideline by its registration point.

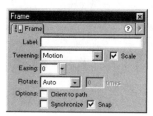

In the Timeline, you can tell that the motion tweening is implemented correctly if a solid line appears between the keyframes, and the frames have a light blue background.

A dashed line between keyframes indicates the tweening is not implemented correctly, which often occurs when a beginning or ending keyframe is accidentally deleted.

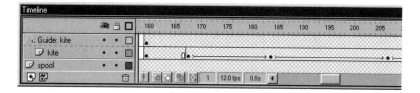

Add the intermediate keyframes

Now you'll add the intermediate keyframes that define where the animation will change.

1 In the Timeline's kite layer, with the playhead on Frame 175, press F6 to insert a keyframe.

On the Stage, the kite has moved along the path to its position relative to Frame 175.

2 Also in the kite layer, insert keyframes in Frames 184, 198, 207, and 214.

Scale and rotate the kite

The animation will be more realistic if the kite changes in size and rotates as it moves along its path. To achieve this effect, you will make the kite larger and smaller where you've added keyframes, and you'll rotate the kite.

1 With the kite layer still selected, move the playhead back to Keyframe 175.

Note: If you inserted keyframes in different frames from those specified in the tutorial, you can scale and rotate the kite wherever you inserted a keyframe.

 2 In the toolbox, select the Arrow tool and the Scale modifier. On the Stage, click and drag one of the outside corner sizing handles around the kite to make the kite slightly larger.

3 Select the Rotate modifier. On the Stage, move the mouse pointer over one of the kite's corner handles.

The pointer changes into four curved arrows.

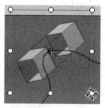

4 Click and drag the corner handle to rotate the kite approximately 30° clockwise.

5 Move the playhead to Frame 184. On the Stage, use the Rotate modifier to move the kite approximately 60° counterclockwise. Use the Scale modifier to make the kite smaller.

During the animation, the kite will appear to be flying farther away.

6 Move the playhead to Keyframe 198. On the Stage, use the Scale modifier to make the kite smaller.

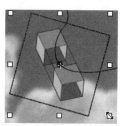

7 For Keyframes 207 and 214, use the Scale tool to make the kite larger.

8 To view the kite-flying animation, drag the playhead from Frame 168 to Frame 228.

Note: Remember to save your work frequently.

Loop the animation

The kite animation stops when the playhead reaches Frame 228. To make the kite fly continuously, you'll add a looping attribute.

1 In the Timeline's actions layer, insert a keyframe in Frame 228, and then double-click it to open the Frame Actions panel.

2 Click the Actions icon to expand that category, then double-click goto in the Toolbox list.

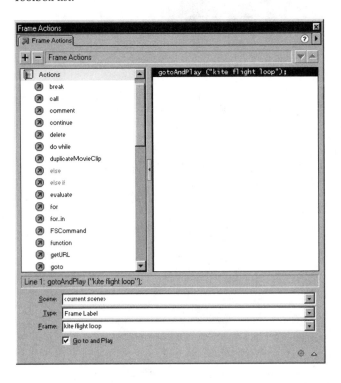

3 In the Type pop-up menu, select Frame Label.

4 In the Frame pop-up menu, select kite flight loop.

The Timeline includes a label called kite flight loop. The first frame within the kite flight loop label is Frame 168. You are specifying that the playhead loop from Frame 228, where you inserted the keyframe, back to Frame 168, the start of the animation.

5 Verify that Go to and Play is selected, then close the Frame Actions panel.

Create shape tweening for the kite string

To animate the kite, you used motion tweening. To animate the kite string, you will use shape tweening: you will draw a shape—in this case, the string—at one point in the Timeline, and you will change that shape at later points. Flash alters the shape for the frames between the beginning and ending keyframes to create the animation.

1 In the Timeline's string layer, insert a keyframe (F6) in Frame 168, which is the frame where you started the kite motion tween.

2 In the toolbox, select the Pencil tool. Click the color box to display the pop-up window, and select a pale shade of yellow.

3 From the Pencil Mode modifier, select Smooth.

4 To open the Stroke panel, choose Window > Panels > Stroke. In the Stroke Size pop-up menu, move the slider to select 2, or type **2** in the Stroke Size text box.

5 On the Stage, draw a line that curves from the spool to the target "bull's-eye" in the approximate center of the kite.

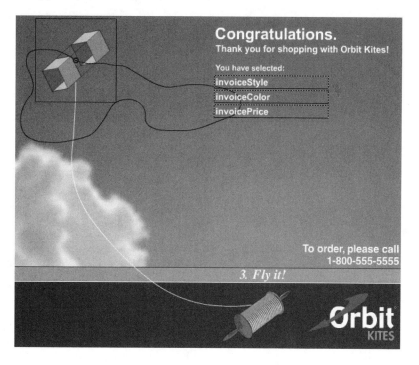

6 If necessary, use the Arrow tool to select the string on the Stage and select the Smooth modifier repeatedly until the line resembles a string.

Smooth modifier

7 In the Timeline, add a keyframe to Frame 230 of the string layer.

In addition to the keyframe in Frame 230, an end keyframe appears in Frame 229.

8 In Frame 231, choose Insert > Blank Keyframe so the string will not appear in the movie from that frame on.

Specify shape tweening

To prepare for shape tweening, you might find it helpful to lock the kite, sky, and Guide:kite layers in the Timeline to avoid accidentally moving those objects on the Stage.

1 In the Timeline's string layer, click any frame between Frames 168 and 229 so that just the frames in between those two keyframes are selected.

2 If the Frame panel is not open, choose Window > Panels > Frame and select Shape from the Tweening pop-up menu.

As with motion tweening, a solid line between keyframes tells you that you executed the tween correctly. The Timeline indicates shape tweening with a light green background.

3 Move the playhead to Frame 168. Slowly drag the playhead to the right across the Timeline until the string appears to have separated from the kite. Add another keyframe at this point in the Timeline.

Note: The gap between the kite and string can be fairly prominent before you need to add a keyframe. You do not need to add a keyframe for a small separation between the kite and string.

4 Select the Arrow tool in the toolbox. If the entire string is selected, click anywhere on the Stage to deselect it, then drag the top of the string so that it again appears to be attached to the bull's-eye.

5 Use the Arrow tool, with the Smooth modifier selected, to maintain the line's curved shape by selecting and dragging from a point around the middle of the line.

You are setting up the animation so that the kite string never looks as though it has separated from the kite.

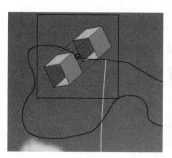 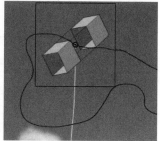

6 As you continue to move the playhead slowly to the right, add a keyframe to the string layer each time you see a prominent gap between the kite and the string, then repeat steps 4 and 5 as often as necessary until you reach the end of the animation—Frame 229.

7 To view the animation, move the playhead to Frame 168 and choose Control > Play. When you finish viewing the animation, choose Control > Stop.

Note: Remember to save your work frequently.

Use actions to streamline authoring

You're ready to add actions to your movie that determine which kite the customer selected and display the selected kite with the correct invoice. First you'll use the Frame Actions panel to create a function, a block of reusable code that performs a task. In this case, the task is to load a specific SWF movie of a kite into the Flash Player, depending on which kite the user selects.

Note: The SWFs of the different kite model and color combinations exist in your My_kite folder.

In addition to the function that you'll create, you'll also use the Include action to link to another function in an external text file.

Note: It's beyond the scope of this tutorial to teach ActionScript syntax; refer to the *ActionScript Reference Guide* for additional information about creating ActionScript.

Create a function

You will name the function that you create `refreshKite`. If you think of your movie as the store that holds the kites, think of `refreshKite` as the salesperson who retrieves a kite for the customer.

A parameter, called `currentKite`, tells the `refreshKite` function which kite the customer selected: the kite model and color. A simple definition for a parameter, therefore, is that it's a placeholder that lets you pass information to a function.

1 In the Timeline, double-click the keyframe in Frame 1 of the actions layer.

   The Frame Actions panel appears. If necessary, resize the window to view both panes. The Actions list already contains ActionScript, to which you will add new actions.

2 In the Toolbox list, click the Actions icon to expand it, then double-click `function`.

You can also drag the `function` icon to the bottom of the Actions list.

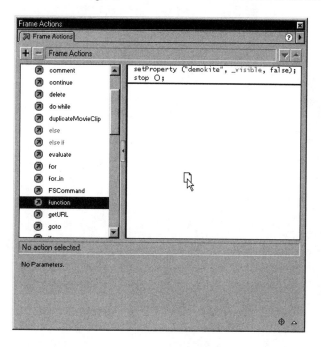

3 In the Name text box, type **refreshKite**.

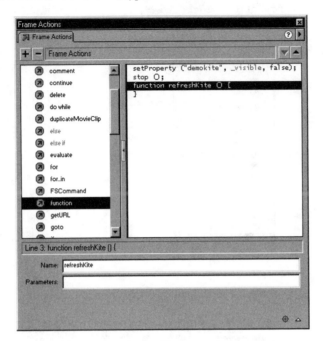

4 In the Parameters text box, type **currentKite**.

The function will use the `currentKite` (the currently selected kite) parameter to identify the correct kite to display.

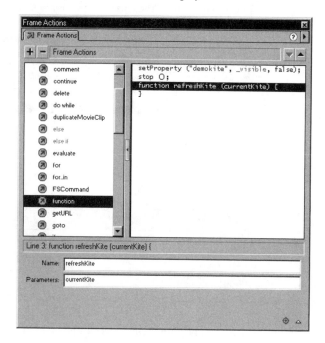

5 With the Actions category still expanded in the Toolbox list, double-click `loadMovie`.

You are telling Flash to replace the movie clip on the Stage with the SWF specified by the parameter.

6 In the URL text box, type **currentKite+".swf"**

7 Select Expression, to the right of the URL text box.

By selecting Expression, you are telling Flash that `currentKite + ".swf"` is not a literal string of characters, but rather a description. The function uses this description to determine the correct external file name.

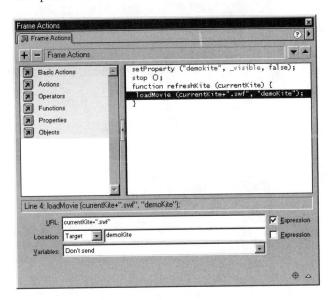

8 In the Location pop-up menu, select Target, and in the text box to the right, type **demoKite**.

The symbol name for the placeholderKite instance, remember, is demoKite.

9 Verify that Don't Send is selected in the Variables pop-up menu.

10 In the Toolbox list, double-click `set variable`, which defines a new variable.

A variable is a container that holds information, such as which kite is selected. In your movie, the variable remembers the most recent kite selected.

11 In the Variable text box, type **chosenKite**, the name of the variable. Verify that Expression, to the right of the text box, is not selected.

12 In the Value text box, type **currentKite.** Select Expression, to the right of the text box.

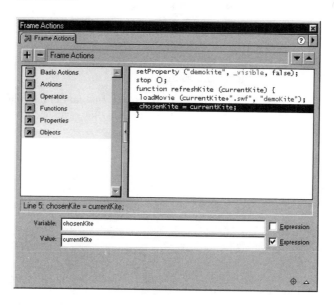

Include an external function

You have learned that a function is a set of actions that perform tasks based on the information it receives from parameters. You will now include an external function in your ActionScript that creates an invoice based on the selected kite. The external function, named kiteFunction.txt, is in a text file in the Tutorial/My_kite folder within your Flash 5 application folder. To link to the external file, you use the Include action.

One benefit of linking to an external function rather than making the function a part of your movie is that if the function changes, you do not have to update your movie.

The external function demonstrates how concise, yet powerful, ActionScript can be:

```
function generateInvoice (Style, Color, Price, currentKite) {
    _root.invoice.invoiceStyle = Style;
    _root.invoice.invoiceColor = Color;
    _root.invoice.invoicePrice = Price;
    flyingKite = currentKite;
}
```

Notice, however, that the function is not commented. It's a good idea to add comments to your ActionScript, which is like adding notes about the purpose of the script, which might otherwise take some effort to understand. Here's the same function with explanatory comments. ActionScript comments appear after double slashes (//), which indicate to Flash that it should ignore the text after the slashes on that line.

```
function generateInvoice (Style, Color, Price, currentKite) {

//Sets the invoiceStyle variable of the invoice movie clip to the
//value of the Style parameter
    _root.invoice.invoiceStyle = Style;

//Sets the invoiceColor variable of the invoice movie clip to the
//value of the Color parameter
    _root.invoice.invoiceColor = Color;

//Sets the invoicePrice variable of the invoice movie clip to the
//value of the Price parameter
    _root.invoice.invoicePrice = Price;

//Sets the variable flyingKite equal to the variable currentKite
    flyingKite = currentKite;
}
```

Now you will add the `include` script that links the internal function that you created to the external function.

1   In the Frame Actions panel Toolbox list, under the Actions category, drag the `include` icon to the end of the text in the Actions list.

2   In the Path text box, type **KiteFunction.txt**.

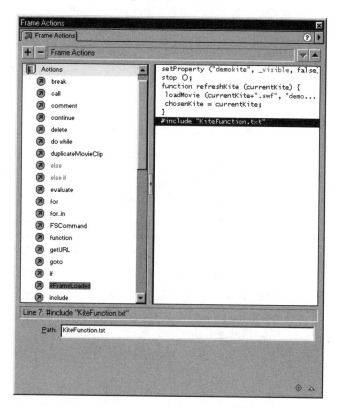

3   Close the Frame Actions panel.

Note: Remember to save your work frequently.

Publish the movie

Congratulations! You've nearly completed your movie. For the finishing touch, you will use the Publish command to create a Web-compatible version, with the SWF extension.

If you use the Publish command with the default settings, Flash prepares your file for the Web. Flash will Publish the SWF and an HTML file with the tags necessary to display the SWF.

Once you have entered all of the necessary Publish Settings options, you can repeatedly export to all selected formats at once by simply choosing File > Publish. Flash stores the publish settings you specify with the movie file, so each movie can have its own settings.

Test movie download performance

For a Flash movie to play correctly over the Internet, a frame must download before the movie reaches that frame. If the movie reaches a frame that hasn't downloaded, it pauses until the data arrives. The low bandwidth of Flash files, however, promotes fast downloads.

You can use the Bandwidth Profiler to test your movie and identify where pauses might occur. The Bandwidth Profiler graphically shows how much data is sent from each frame in the movie, according to the selected modem speed.

1 Choose Control > Test Movie.

   Flash exports the movie as a SWF file and opens it in a new window.

2 From the Debug menu, select a modem speed to determine the download rate that Flash will simulate.

   You can also choose Customize to enter a download rate.

3 Choose View > Bandwidth Profiler to see the SWF with a download performance chart.

Each shaded bar represents a frame in your movie. The height of the bar represents the frame's size in bytes and kilobytes. If a bar extends above the red line, the movie might wait for that frame to load.

Note: Although the Bandwidth Profiler does not indicate any serious download problems with the tutorial movie, you can optimize your movie for faster downloads. See "Optimizing movies" on page 313 for details.

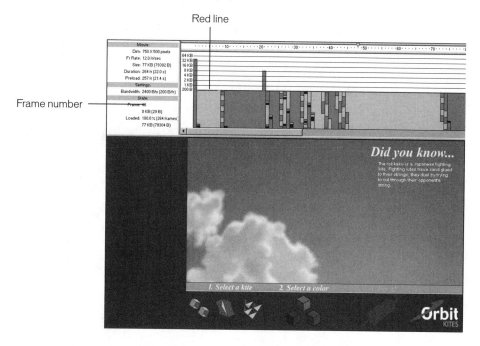

4 When you finish viewing the Bandwidth Profiler, choose View > Bandwidth Profiler to deselect it. Close the test window to return to the authoring environment.

Use the Publish command

Save your movie and choose File > Publish.

Flash publishes your movie by creating a SWF file, and possibly additional files, based on the attributes in the Publish Settings dialog box. You'll find the published files in your My_kite folder. That's how simple it is to publish your movie for Web playback.

View publish settings

Using the Publish Settings dialog box, it's easy to reconfigure the way your file publishes.

1   To view your publish settings, choose File > Publish Settings.

Flash is configured, by default, to create a supporting HTML file that displays the Flash movie or an alternate image.

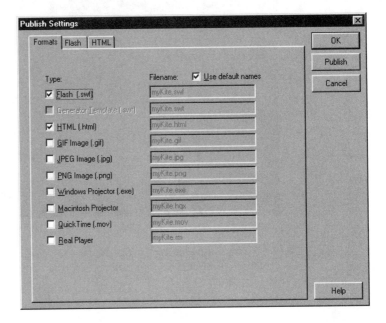

When you select a format that requires additional settings, a new tab appears.

Change publish settings

By default, Flash gives the SWF file the same name as the FLA file. Since you are creating the site for Orbit kites, you'll tell Flash to name the SWF OrbitKites.swf.

1 On the Formats tab of the Publish Settings dialog box, deselect Use Default Names.

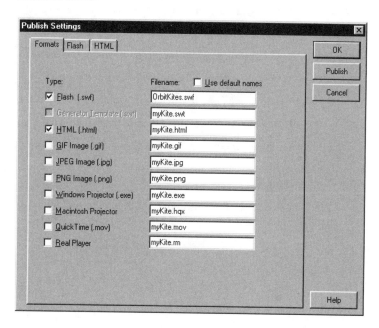

2 In the Flash (.swf) text box, select the existing text and type **OrbitKites.swf**, then click OK.

When you publish your movie again, Flash will create a file named OrbitKites.swf.

The next steps

By completing the tutorial, you've accomplished a great deal in a relatively short amount of time. You now know how to do the following:

- Change Flash movie properties
- Import, create, and modify media
- Add sound to a button
- Use the Stage and Timeline to assemble the movie
- Create motion and shape tweening animation
- Use actions to add interactivity and streamline authoring
- Test the movie for download performance
- Publish the movie for Web playback

In meeting the main objectives, you also learned how to complete a variety of related tasks.

To continue learning about Flash, browse the topics in *Using Flash* and Flash Help.

CHAPTER 2
Flash Basics

Flash movies are graphics and animation for Web sites. They consist primarily of vector graphics, but they can also contain imported bitmap graphics and sounds. Flash movies can incorporate interactivity to permit input from viewers, and you can create nonlinear movies that can interact with other Web applications. Web designers use Flash to create navigation controls, animated logos, long-form animations with synchronized sound, and even complete, sensory-rich Web sites. Flash movies are compact, vector graphics, so they download rapidly and scale to the viewer's screen size.

You've probably watched and interacted with Flash movies on many Web sites, including Disney®, The Simpsons®, and Coca-Cola®. Millions of Web users have received the Flash Player with their computers, browsers, or system software; others have downloaded it from the Macromedia Web site. The Flash Player resides on the local computer, where it plays back movies in browsers or as stand-alone applications. Viewing a Flash movie on the Flash Player is similar to viewing a videotape on a VCR—the Flash Player is the device used to display the movies you create in the Flash authoring application.

For an interactive introduction to Flash, choose Help > Lessons > Introduction.

The Flash workflow

As you work in Flash, you create a movie by drawing or importing artwork, arranging it on the Stage, and animating it with the Timeline. You make the movie interactive by using actions to make the movie respond to events in specified ways.

When the movie is complete, you export it as a Flash Player movie to be viewed in the Flash Player, or as a Flash stand-alone projector to be viewed with a self-contained Flash Player included within the movie itself.

You can play a Flash movie in the following ways:

- In Internet browsers, such as Netscape Navigator and Microsoft Internet Explorer, that are equipped with the Flash Player

- With the Flash ActiveX control in Microsoft Office, Microsoft Internet Explorer for Windows, and other ActiveX host environments

- In the Flash Player, a stand-alone application similar in operation to the Flash Player plug-in

- As a stand-alone projector, a movie file that can be played without the Flash Player software

For more information, see Chapter 14, "Publishing and Exporting."

Artwork in Flash

Flash provides a variety of methods for creating original artwork and importing artwork from other applications. You can create objects with the drawing and painting tools, and modify the attributes of existing objects. See Chapter 3, "Drawing," and Chapter 4, "Working with Color."

You can also import vector and bitmap graphics from other applications and modify the imported graphics in Flash. See Chapter 5, "Using Imported Artwork."

Note: You can also import sound files, as described in Chapter 6, "Adding Sound."

Animation in Flash

Using Flash, you can animate objects to make them appear to move across the Stage and/or change their shape, size, color, opacity, rotation, and other properties. You can create frame-by-frame animation, in which you create a separate image for each frame. You can also create tweened animation, in which you create the first and last frames of an animation and direct Flash to create the frames in between. See Chapter 11, "Creating animation."

You can also create animation in movies using the Set Property action. See the *ActionScript Reference Guide.*

Interactive movies in Flash

Flash allows you to create interactive movies, in which your audience can use the keyboard or the mouse to jump to different parts of a movie, move objects, enter information in forms, and perform many other operations.

You create interactive movies by setting up actions using ActionScript. For information on setting up the most common actions, see Chapter 12, "Creating Interactive Movies." For complete information on using ActionScript to create advanced interactivity, see the *ActionScript Reference Guide*.

Configuring a server for the Flash Player

In order for a user to view your Flash movie on the Web, the Web server must be properly configured to recognize the movie as a Flash Player file.

Your server may already be configured properly. To test server configuration, see TechNote #12696 on the Macromedia Flash Support Center, http://www.macromedia.com/support/flash/. If your server is not properly configured, follow the procedure below to configure it.

Configuring a server establishes the appropriate Multipart Internet Mail Extension (MIME) types for the server to identify files with the suffix .swf as belonging to Shockwave Flash.

A browser that receives the correct MIME type can load the appropriate plug-in, control, or helper application to process and properly display the incoming data. If the MIME type is missing or not properly delivered by the server, the browser might display an error message or a blank window with a puzzle piece icon.

Note: When you publish a Flash movie, you must configure the movie for the Flash Player in order for users to view the movie. See Chapter 14, "Publishing and Exporting."

To configure a server for the Flash Player, do one of the following:

- If your site is established through an Internet service provider, contact them and request that the MIME type application/x-shockwave-flash with the suffix .swf be added to the server.

- If you are administering your own server, consult the documentation for your Web server software for instructions on adding or configuring MIME types.

About vector and bitmap graphics

Computers display graphics in either vector or bitmap format. Understanding the difference between the two formats can help you work more efficiently. Flash lets you create and animate compact vector graphics. It also lets you import and manipulate vector and bitmap graphics that have been created in other applications.

Vector graphics

Vector graphics describe images using lines and curves, called *vectors*, that also include color and position properties. For example, the image of a leaf is described by points through which lines pass, creating the shape of the leaf's outline. The color of the leaf is determined by the color of the outline and the color of the area enclosed by the outline.

When you edit a vector graphic, you modify the properties of the lines and curves that describe its shape. You can move, resize, reshape, and change the color of a vector graphic without changing the quality of its appearance. Vector graphics are resolution-independent, meaning they can be displayed on output devices of varying resolutions without losing any quality.

Bitmap graphics

Bitmap graphics describe images using colored dots, called *pixels*, arranged within a grid. For example, the image of a leaf is described by the specific location and color value of each pixel in the grid, creating an image much in the same manner as a mosaic.

When you edit a bitmap graphic, you modify pixels, rather than lines and curves. Bitmap graphics are resolution-dependent, because the data describing the image is fixed to a grid of a particular size. Editing a bitmap graphic can change the quality of its appearance. In particular, resizing a bitmap graphic can make the edges of the image ragged as pixels are redistributed within the grid. Displaying a bitmap graphic on an output device that has a lower resolution than the image itself also degrades the quality of its appearance.

The Flash work environment

When creating and editing movies, you typically work with these key features:

- The Stage, the rectangular area where the movie plays
- The Timeline, where graphics are animated over time
- Symbols, the reusable media assets of a movie
- The Library window, where symbols are organized
- The Movie Explorer, which gives an overview of a movie and its structure
- Floating, dockable panels, which enable you to modify various elements in the movie and configure the Flash authoring environment to best suit your workflow

The Stage and the Timeline

Like films, Flash movies divide lengths of time into frames. The Stage is where you compose the content for individual frames in the movie, drawing artwork on it directly or arranging imported artwork.

The Stage is where you compose individual frames in a movie.

The Timeline is where you coordinate the timing of the animation and assemble the artwork on separate layers. The Timeline displays each frame in the movie.

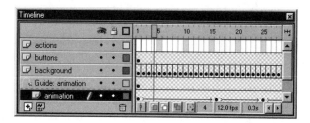

The Timeline is where you coordinate the timing of the animation and assemble separate layers.

Layers act like stacked sheets of transparent acetate, keeping artwork separate so you can combine different elements into a cohesive visual image.

Layers

The logo, chair, and navigation controls in the movie are each on separate layers.

Symbols and instances

Symbols are reusable elements that you use with a movie. Symbols can be graphics, buttons, movie clips, sound files, or fonts. When you create a symbol, the symbol is stored in the file's library. When you place a symbol on the Stage, you create an *instance* of that symbol.

Symbols reduce file size because, regardless of how many instances of a symbol you create, Flash stores the symbol in the file only once. It is a good idea to use symbols, animated or otherwise, for every element that appears more than once in a movie. You can modify the properties of an instance without affecting the master symbol, and you can edit the master symbol to change all instances.

You can edit symbols in place on the Stage. Other elements on the Stage are visible but dimmed. You can also edit a symbol in a separate window. When you edit a symbol, the Timeline window displays only the Timeline of the symbol you are editing. See "Editing symbols" on page 238.

You can locate and open a symbol in the library from within the Movie Explorer, using the Find in Library command. See "Using the Movie Explorer" on page 98.

For more information on symbols and instances, see the Symbols lesson, located under Help > Lessons > Symbols, and Chapter 10, "Using Symbols and Instances."

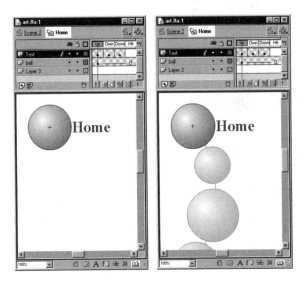

Editing a symbol in isolation (left) and editing a symbol in its context in the movie.

Symbols and interactive movies

Symbols are also an integral part of creating interactive movies; you can use instances of symbols to create interactivity in a movie. For example, you can create a button symbol that changes in response to mouse actions and place an instance of the symbol on the Stage. You use another type of symbol, called a movie clip, to create sophisticated interactive movies. See Chapter 12, "Creating Interactive Movies."

The Library window

The Library window is where you store and organize symbols created in Flash, as well as imported files, including sound files, bitmap graphics, and QuickTime movies. The Library window lets you organize library items in folders, see how often an item is used in a movie, and sort items by type. See "Using the library" on page 89.

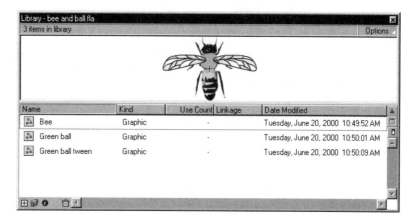

Panels

To view, organize, and modify elements in a Flash movie, you can use floating panels that contain commands and options related to each type of element. Panels enable you to modify symbols, instances, colors, type, frames, and other elements.

You can use panels to customize the Flash interface, by displaying the panels you need for a specific task and hiding other panels. See "Using panels" on page 78.

Creating a new movie and setting its properties

Each time you open Flash, the application creates a new file, with the FLA extension. You can create additional new movies as you work. To set the size, frame rate, background color, and other properties of a new movie, you use the Movie Properties dialog box.

To create a new movie and set its properties:

1 Choose File > New.

2 Choose Modify > Movie. The Movie Properties dialog box appears.

3 For Frame Rate, enter the number of animation frames to be displayed every second. For most computer-displayed animations, especially those playing from a Web site, 8 fps (frames per second) to 12 fps is sufficient. (12 fps is the default frame rate.)

4 For Dimensions, choose one of the following options:

- To specify the Stage size in pixels, enter values for Width and Height. The default movie size is 550 x 400 pixels. The minimum size is 18 pixels by 18 pixels; the maximum is 2880 x 2880 pixels.

- To set the Stage size so that there is equal space around the content on all sides, click Match Contents. To minimize movie size, align all elements to the upper left corner of the Stage before using Match Contents.

- To set the Stage size to the maximum available print area, click Match Printer. This area is determined by the paper size minus the current margin selected in the Margins area of the Page Setup dialog box (Windows) or the Print Margins dialog box (Macintosh).

5 To set the background color of your movie, choose a color from the Background color swatch.

6 Select the unit of measure from the Ruler Units pop-up menu for rulers that you can display along the top and side of the application window. See "Using the grid, guides, and rulers" on page 104. (The Ruler Units option also determines the units used in the Info panel.)

7 Click OK.

Previewing and testing movies

As you create a movie, you'll need to play it back to preview animation and test interactive controls. You can preview and test movies within the Flash authoring environment, in a separate window, or in a Web browser.

Previewing movies in the authoring environment

To preview movies, you use commands in the Control menu, buttons on the Controller, or keyboard commands.

To preview the current scene, do one of the following:

- Choose Control > Play.

- Choose Window > Toolbars > Controller (Windows) or Window > Controller (Macintosh) and click Play.

- Press Enter (Windows) or Return (Macintosh). The animation sequence plays in the Movie window at the frame rate you specified for the movie.

  To step through the frames of the animation, use the Step Forward and Step Backward buttons on the Controller, or choose those commands from the Control menu. You can also press the < and > keys on the keyboard. To go to the first or last frame in a movie, use the First Frame or Last Frame button on the Controller.

Note: You can also drag the playhead to view frames in a movie. See "Moving the playhead" on page 84.

You can modify movie playback using commands in the Control menu. Note that you must also choose Control > Play in order to preview a movie when using the following commands.

To play the movie in a continuous loop:

Choose Control > Loop Playback.

To play all the scenes in a movie:

Choose Control > Play All Scenes.

To play a movie without sound:

Choose Control > Mute Sounds.

To enable frame actions or button actions:

Choose Control > Enable Simple Frame Actions or Enable Simple Buttons.

Testing movies

Although Flash can play movies in the authoring environment, many animation and interactive functions cannot work unless the movie is exported in its final format. Using commands in the Control menu, you can export the current movie as a Flash Player movie and immediately play the movie in a new window. The exported movie uses the options set in the Publish Settings dialog box. You can also use this window to test downloading performance. See "Testing movie download performance" on page 315. In addition, you can test a movie in a Web browser.

You can also test actions in a movie using the Debugger. See "Using the Debugger" in the troubleshooting chapter of the *ActionScript Reference Guide*.

To test all interactive functions and animation:

Choose Control > Test Movie or Control > Test Scene.

Flash creates a Flash Player movie (a SWF file), opens it in a separate window, and plays it with the Flash Player. The SWF file is placed into the same folder as the FLA file.

To test the movie in a Web browser:

Choose File > Publish Preview > HTML. See "Previewing the publishing format and settings" on page 337.

Saving movie files

You can save a Flash FLA movie file using its current name and location, or save the document using a different name or location. You can revert to the last saved version of a file.

To save a document:

1 Do one of the following:

• To overwrite the current version on the disk, choose File > Save.

• To save the file in a different location or with a different name, choose File > Save As.

2 If you choose the Save As command, or if the file has never been saved before, enter the file name and location.

3 Click Save.

To revert to the last saved version of a file:

Choose File > Revert.

Using the toolbox

The tools in the toolbox let you draw, paint, select, and modify artwork, and change the view of the Stage. The toolbox is divided into four sections:

- The Tools section contains drawing, painting, and selection tools.

- The View section contains tools for zooming and panning in the application window.

- The Colors section contains modifiers for stroke and fill colors.

- The Options section displays modifiers for the selected tool, which affect the tool's painting or editing operations.

For information on using the drawing and painting tools, see "Flash drawing and painting tools" on page 114. For information on using the selection tools, see "Selecting objects" on page 182. For information on using the view modification tools, see "Viewing the Stage" on page 102.

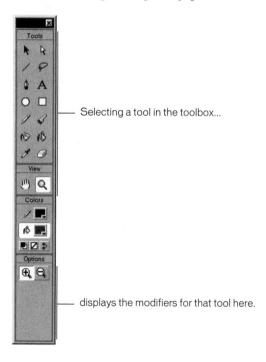

Selecting a tool in the toolbox...

displays the modifiers for that tool here.

To show or hide the toolbox:

Choose Window > Tools.

To select a tool, do one of the following:

- Click the tool you want to use. Depending on the tool you select, a set of modifiers are displayed at the bottom of the toolbox.

- Press the tool's keyboard shortcut.

Using panels

Floating panels help you view, organize, and change elements in a movie. The options available on panels control the characteristics of selected elements.

Panels in Flash let you work with objects, colors, text, instances, frames, scenes, and entire movies. For example, you use the Character panel for selecting type character attributes, and the Frame panel for entering frame labels and choosing tweening options. To view the complete list of panels available in Flash, choose Window > Panels.

You can show, hide, group, and resize panels as you work. You can also show and hide several panels, including the Info, Mixer, Instance, Frame, and Actions panels, using buttons in the Launcher bar at the bottom of the application window.

You can group panels together in custom arrangements, and you can save custom panel layouts. You can reset panel display to the default layout (displaying the Info, Mixer, Character, and Instance panels to the right of the application window) or to a custom layout that you have saved previously.

Most panels include a pop-up menu with additional options. The pop-up menu is indicated by a triangle in the panel's upper right corner. (If the triangle is dimmed, there is no pop-up menu for that panel.)

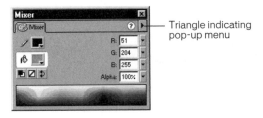 Triangle indicating pop-up menu

To open a panel:

Choose Window > Panels and select the desired panel from the list.

To close a panel, do one of the following:

- Click the Close box in the upper right corner (Windows) or upper left corner (Macintosh).

- Choose Window > Panels and select the desired panel from the list.

- Right-click (Windows) or Control-click (Macintosh) the panel's tab and choose Close Panel from the context menu.

To open or close panels using the Launcher bar:

In the Launcher bar, click the button for the Info, Color Mixer, Character, Instance, or Actions panel.

Note: You can also open or close the Library window or the Movie Explorer using the Launcher bar. See "Using the library" on page 89 or "Using the Movie Explorer" on page 98.

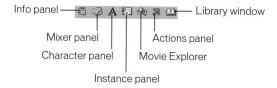

Info panel — Library window
Mixer panel / Actions panel
Character panel / Movie Explorer
Instance panel

To use a panel's pop-up options menu:

1 Click the triangle in the panel's upper right corner to view the menu.

2 Click an item in the menu.

To close all panels:

Choose Window > Close All Panels.

To group panels:

Drag a panel by its tab onto the tab of another panel.

To bring a panel within a group to the front:

Click the panel's tab.

To ungroup a panel into a separate window:

Drag the panel by its tab to the outside of its window.

To move a panel or a panel group:

Drag the panel or group by its title bar.

To save a custom panel layout:

Choose Window > Save Panel Layout. Enter a name for the layout and click OK.

To delete a custom layout:

Open the Flash 5 application folder on your hard drive and delete the
Panel Sets file.

To select a panel layout:

1 Choose Window > Panel Sets.

2 From the submenu, choose Default Layout to reset panels to the default layout,
   or choose a custom layout that you have saved previously.

To resize a panel:

Drag the panel's lower right corner (Windows) or drag the size box at the panel's
lower right corner (Macintosh).

To collapse a panel or a panel group to its title bar and tab only:

Double-click the title bar. Double-click the title bar again to return the panel or
group to its previous size.

To collapse a panel or panel group to its title bar (Macintosh only):

Click the collapse box at the right end of the title bar. Click the box again to
return the panel or group to its previous size.

Using context menus

Context menus contain commands relevant to the current selection. For example, when you select a frame in the Timeline window, the context menu contains commands for creating, deleting, and modifying frames and keyframes.

Context menu for a selected frame

To open a context menu:

Right-click (Windows) or Control-click (Macintosh) an item in the Timeline, in the Library window, or on the Stage.

Using the Timeline

The Timeline organizes and controls a movie's content over time in layers and frames. The major components of the Timeline are layers, frames, and the playhead.

Layers in a movie are listed in a column on the left side of the Timeline. Frames contained in each layer appear in a row to the right of the layer name. The Timeline header at the top of the Timeline indicates frame numbers. The playhead indicates the current frame displayed on the Stage.

The Timeline status display at the bottom of the Timeline indicates the current frame number, the current frame rate, and the elapsed time to the current frame.

Note: When an animation is played, the actual frame rate is displayed; this may differ from the movie frame rate if the computer can't display the animation quickly enough.

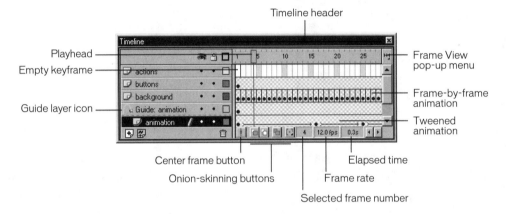

You can change the way frames are displayed, and display thumbnails of frame content in the Timeline. The Timeline shows where there is animation in a movie, including frame-by-frame animation, tweened animation, and motion paths. For more information on animation, see Chapter 11, "Creating Animation."

Controls in the layers section of the Timeline let you hide or show, lock, unlock, or display layer contents as outlines. See "Editing layers" on page 204.

You can insert, delete, select and move frames in the Timeline. You can also drag frames to a new location on the same layer or a different layer. See "Working with frames in the Timeline" on page 86.

Changing the appearance of the Timeline

By default, the Timeline appears at the top of the main application window, above the Stage. To change its position, you can dock the Timeline to the bottom or either side of the main application window, or display the Timeline as its own window. You can also hide the Timeline.

You can resize the Timeline to change the number of layers and frames that are visible. When there are more layers than can be displayed in the Timeline, you can view additional layers by using the scroll bars on the right side of the Timeline.

To move the Timeline:

Drag from the area above the Timeline header.

Drag the Timeline to the edge of the application window to dock it. Press Control (Windows or Macintosh) while dragging to prevent the Timeline from docking.

To lengthen or shorten layer name fields:

Drag the bar separating the layer names and the frames portion of the Timeline.

To resize the Timeline, do one of the following:

- If the Timeline is docked to the main application window, drag the bar separating the Timeline from the application window.

- If the Timeline is not docked to the main application window, drag the lower right corner (Windows) or the Size box in the lower right corner (Macintosh).

Moving the playhead

The playhead moves through the Timeline to indicate the current frame displayed on the Stage. The Timeline header shows the frame numbers of the animation. To display a frame on the Stage, you move the playhead to the frame in the Timeline.

When you're working with a large number of frames that can't all appear on the Timeline at once, you can center the playhead in the Timeline in order to easily locate the current frame.

To go to a frame:

Click the frame's location in the Timeline header, or drag the playhead to the desired position.

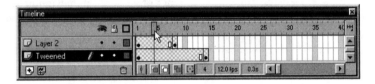

To center the playhead in the middle of the movie:

Click the Center Frame button at the bottom of the Timeline.

Changing the display of frames in the Timeline

You can change the size of frames in the Timeline, and display sequences of frames with tinted cells. You can also include thumbnail previews of frame content in the Timeline. These thumbnails are useful as an overview of the animation, but they take up extra screen space.

To change the display of frames in the Timeline:

1   Click the Frame View button in the upper right corner of the Timeline to display the Frame View pop-up menu.

2   Choose from the following options:

•   To change the width of frame cells, choose Tiny, Small, Normal, Medium, or Large. (The Large frame width setting is useful for viewing the details of sound waveforms.)

•   To decrease the height of frame cell rows, choose Short.

•   To turn tinting of frame sequences on or off, choose Tinted Frames.

•   To display thumbnails of the content of each frame scaled to fit the Timeline frames, choose Preview. This can cause the apparent content size to vary.

- To display thumbnails of each full frame (including empty space), choose Preview in Context. This is useful for viewing the way elements move within their frames over the course of the animation, but previews are generally smaller than with the Preview option.

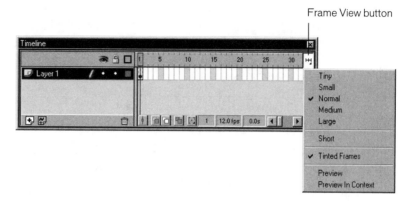

Frame View button

Frame View pop-up menu

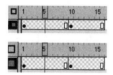

Short and Normal frame view options

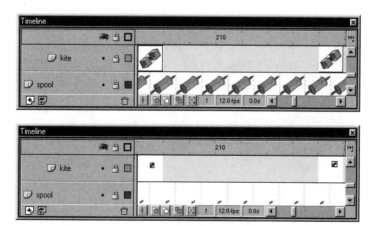

Preview and Preview in Context options

Creating frame labels and movie comments

Frame labels are useful for identifying keyframes in the Timeline and should be used instead of frame numbers when targeting frames in actions such as Go To. If you add or remove frames, the label moves with the frame it was originally attached to, whereas frame numbers can change. Frame labels are exported with movie data, so avoid long names to minimize file size.

Frame comments are useful for notes to yourself and others working on the same movie. Frame comments are not exported with movie data, so you can make them as long as you want.

To create a frame label or comment:

1 Select a frame and choose Window > Panels > Frame.

2 In the Frame panel, enter text for a frame label or comment in the Label text box. To make the text a comment, enter two slashes (//) at the beginning of each line of the text.

Working with frames in the Timeline

In the Timeline, you work with frames and keyframes. A keyframe is a frame in which you define a change in an animation or include frame actions to modify a movie. Keyframes are an important part of tweened animation. You can change the length of a tweened animation by dragging a keyframe in the Timeline.

You can perform the following modifications on frames or keyframes:

- Insert, select, delete, and move frames or keyframes

- Drag frames and keyframes to a new location on the same layer or on a different layer

- Copy and paste frames and keyframes

- Convert keyframes to frames

- Drag an item from the Library window onto the Stage to add the item to the current keyframe

The Timeline provides a view of tweened frames in an animation. For information on editing tweened frames, see Chapter 11, "Creating Animation."

To insert frames in the Timeline, do one of the following:

- To insert a new frame, choose Insert > Frame.

- To create a new keyframe, choose Insert > Keyframe, or right-click (Windows) or Control-click (Macintosh) the frame where you want to place a keyframe, and choose Insert Keyframe from the context menu.

- To create a new blank keyframe, choose Insert > Blank Keyframe, or right-click (Windows) or Control-click (Macintosh) the frame where you want to place the keyframe, and choose Insert Blank Keyframe from the context menu.

To delete or modify a frame or keyframe, do one of the following:

- To delete a frame, keyframe, or frame sequence, select the frame, keyframe, or sequence and choose Insert > Remove Frame, or right-click (Windows) or Control-click (Macintosh) the frame, keyframe, or sequence and choose Remove Frame from the context menu. Surrounding frames remain unchanged.

- To move a keyframe or frame sequence and its contents, drag the keyframe or sequence to the desired location.

- To extend the duration of a keyframe, Alt-drag (Windows) or Option-drag (Macintosh) the keyframe to the final frame of the new sequence duration.

- To copy a keyframe or frame sequence by dragging, Alt-click (Windows) or Option-click (Macintosh) and drag the keyframe to the new location.

- To copy and paste a frame or frame sequence, select the frame or sequence and choose Edit > Copy Frames. Select a frame or sequence that you want to replace, and choose Edit > Paste Frames.

- To convert a keyframe to a frame, select the keyframe and choose Insert > Clear Keyframe, or right-click (Windows) or Control-click (Macintosh) the keyframe and choose Clear Keyframe from the context menu. The cleared keyframe and all frames up to the subsequent keyframe are replaced with the contents of the frame preceding the cleared keyframe.

- To change the length of a tweened sequence, drag the beginning or ending keyframe left or right. To change the length of a frame-by-frame sequence, see "Creating frame-by-frame animations" on page 264.

- To add an item from the library to the current keyframe, drag the item from the Library window onto the Stage.

Using scenes

To organize a movie thematically, you can use scenes. For example, you might use separate scenes for an introduction, a loading message, and credits.

When you publish a Flash movie that contains more than one scene, the scenes in the SWF file play back in one sequence in the order they are listed in the Scene panel in the FLA file. Frames in the SWF file are numbered consecutively through scenes. For example, if a movie contains two scenes with ten frames each, the frames in Scene 2 are numbered 11–20.

You can add, delete, duplicate, rename, and change the order of scenes.

To stop or pause a movie after each scene, or to let users navigate the movie in a nonlinear fashion, you use actions. See Chapter 12, "Creating Interactive Movies."

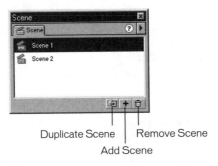

Duplicate Scene   Remove Scene

Add Scene

Scene panel

To display the Scene panel:

Choose Window > Panels > Scene.

To view a particular scene:

Choose View > Goto and then choose the name of the scene from the submenu.

To add a scene, do one of the following:

- Click the Add Scene button in the Scene panel.

- Choose Insert > Scene.

To delete a scene, do one of the following:

- Click the Delete Scene button in the Scene panel.

- Open the scene you want to delete and choose Insert > Remove Scene.

To change the name of a scene:

Double-click the scene name in the Scene panel and enter the new name.

To duplicate a scene:

Click the Duplicate Scene button in the Scene panel.

To change the order of a scene in the movie:

Drag the scene name to a different location in the Scene panel.

Using the library

A library in a Flash movie stores symbols, including those created in Flash and those imported into Flash, and allows you to view and organize these files as you work. The Library window displays a scroll list with the names of all items in the library. An icon next to an item's name in the library window indicate the item's file type.

When you select an item in the Library window, a thumbnail preview of the item appears at the top of the Library window. If the selected item is animated or is a sound file, you can use the Play button in the Library preview window or the Controller to preview the item.

You can organize library items into folders. The Library window columns list the name of an item, its type, the number of times it's used in the file, its linkage status (if the item is associated with a shared library), and the date on which it was last modified. You can sort items in the Library window by any column. The Library window also contains an Options pop-up menu with options for modifying library items.

To edit library items, including imported files, you choose options from the Library Options menu. You can update imported files after editing them in an external editor, using the Update option in the Library Options menu.

You can open the library of any Flash FLA file while you are working in Flash, to make the library items from that file available for the current movie.

You can create permanent libraries in your Flash application that will be available whenever you launch Flash. Flash also includes several built-in libraries containing buttons, graphics, movie clips, and sounds that you can add to your own Flash movies. Built-in Flash libraries, and permanent libraries that you create, are listed in the Window > Common Libraries submenu. See "Working with common libraries" on page 94.

You can export a library to a URL to create a shared library, allowing you to link to the library assets from any Flash movie. See "Using shared libraries" on page 95.

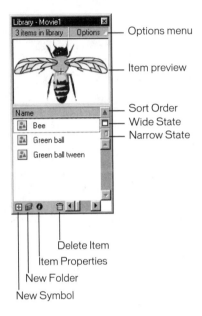

Options menu

Item preview

Sort Order
Wide State
Narrow State

Delete Item
Item Properties
New Folder
New Symbol

To display the Library window, do one of the following:

- Choose Window > Library.

- Click the Library button in the Launcher bar at the bottom of the application window.

To use a library item in the current movie:

Drag the item from the Library window onto the Stage. The item is added to the current layer.

To open the library from another Flash file:

1 Choose File > Open as Library.

2 Navigate to the Flash file whose library you want to open, and click Open.

The selected file's library opens in the current movie, with the file's name at the top of the Library window. To use items from the selected file's library in the current movie, drag the items to the current movie's Library window.

To resize the Library window, do one of the following:

- Drag the lower right corner.

- Click the Wide State button to enlarge the Library window so that it displays all the columns.

- Click the Narrow State button to reduce the width of the Library window to the Name column only.

To change the width of columns:

Position the pointer between column headers and drag to resize. You cannot change the order of columns.

To use the Library Options menu:

1 Click the triangle in the Library window's upper right corner to view the pop-up menu.

2 Click an item in the menu.

Working with folders in the Library window

You can organize items in the Library window using folders, much like in the Windows Explorer or the Macintosh Finder. When you create a new symbol, it is stored in the selected folder. If no folder is selected, the symbol is stored at the root of the library.

To create a new folder:

Click the New Folder button at the bottom of the Library window.

To move an item between folders:

Drag it from one folder to another.

To open or close a folder, do one of the following:

- Double-click the folder.

- Select the folder and choose Expand Folder or Collapse Folder from the Library Options menu.

To open or close all folders:

Choose Expand All Folders or Collapse All Folders from the Library Options menu.

Sorting items in the Library window

You can sort items in the Library window alphanumerically by any column. Sorting items lets you view related items together. Items are sorted within folders.

To sort items in the Library window:

Click the column header to sort by that column. Click the triangle button to the right of the column headers to reverse the sort order.

Editing items in the library

You can edit items in the library in Flash or, in the case of imported files, in an external editor.

To edit a library item:

1 Select the item in the Library window.

2 Choose one of the following from the Library Options menu:

• Choose Edit to edit an item in Flash.

• Choose Edit With and select an application to edit the item in an external editor.

Renaming library items

You can rename items in the library. Changing the library item name of an imported file does not change the file name.

To rename a library item, do one of the following:

• Double-click the item's name and enter the new name in the text field.

• Select the item and click the properties icon at the bottom of the Library window. Enter the new name in the Symbol Properties dialog box and click OK.

• Select the item and choose Rename from the Library Options menu, and then enter the new name in the text field.

• Right-click (Windows) or Contro+click (Macintosh) the item and choose Rename from the context menu, and then enter the new name in the text field.

Deleting library items

When you delete an item from the library, all instances or occurrences of that item in the movie are also deleted. The Use Count column in the Library window indicates whether an item is in use.

To delete a library item:

 Select the item and click the trash can icon at the bottom of the Library window.

Finding unused library items

To reduce the size of a Flash FLA file, you can locate unused library items and delete them. However, it is not necessary to delete unused library items to reduce a Flash movie's SWF file size, because unused library items are not included in the SWF file.

To find unused library items, do one of the following:

- Choose Select Unused Items from the Library Options menu.

- Sort library items by the Use Count column. See "Sorting items in the Library window" on page 92.

Updating imported files in the Library window

If you use an external editor to modify files that you have imported into Flash, such as bitmaps or sound files, you can update the files in Flash without reimporting them.

To update an imported file:

Select the imported file in the Library window and choose Update from the Library Options menu.

Working with common libraries

You can use the built-in libraries included with Flash to add symbols, buttons, or sounds to your movies. You can also create permanent libraries for your Flash application, which you can then use with any movies that you create. (The library you create when authoring a Flash movie is available only with that movie, unless you make the library a permanent library or choose File > Open As Library.)

Both of these types of libraries are listed in the Window > Common Libraries submenu.

To create a permanent library for your Flash application:

1   Create a Flash file with a library containing the symbols that you want to include in the permanent library.

2   Place the Flash file in the Libraries folder located in the Flash application folder on your hard drive.

To use an item from a common library in a movie:

1   Choose Window > Common Libraries, and select a library from the submenu.

2   Drag an item from the common library into the library for the current movie.

Using shared libraries

You can create shared libraries to use assets from one library in multiple Flash movies. To use shared libraries, you define shared library assets in a movie, and then link to those assets from other movies. When you link to an asset in a shared library, the asset is referenced as an external file, but the asset file is not added to the movie.

Using shared libraries can optimize your workflow and movie asset management in numerous ways. For example, you can use shared libraries to do the following:

- Share a sound file across a site

- Share a font symbol across multiple sites (for information on font symbols, see "Creating font symbols" on page 217)

- Provide a single source for elements in animations used across multiple scenes or movies

- Create a central resource library to use for tracking and controlling revisions

About creating and linking shared assets

To create a shared library that you can use with other movies, you define linkage properties for items in a movie's library. When you save the movie, the shared library is saved with the movie's FLA file.

To use assets from a shared library in another movie, you choose File > Open As Shared Library in the current movie, and select the shared library file that you want to use. The shared library opens as a library window in the current movie. You then add assets from the shared library to the current movie's library to create links to the assets.

You must post a shared library on the Web in order for movies that link to the shared library to display linked assets. To post a shared library on the Web, you publish the movie in which you created the shared library. This procedure posts the shared library to the URL where the movie's SWF file resides. (You can specify another location for the shared library if desired.)

When you play a Flash movie that contains links to shared assets, the movie loads the shared library from its location on the Web and displays the shared assets as specified. The movie downloads the entire shared library file when it reaches the first frame containing a linked asset. (If the movie contains linked assets from more than one shared library, each shared library will be downloaded separately, when the first asset from that shared library occurs.)

If an error occurs in downloading the shared library, the movie will not play. It is recommended that you keep shared libraries as small as possible to minimize downloading time, and that you test movies with linked assets to ensure that downloading functions properly.

Defining shared library assets

You use the Symbol Linkage dialog box to assign linkage properties to existing library items in order to specify the items as shared library assets. After you assign linkage properties to shared assets, you must save the movie file in which you defined the shared assets, to make the assets available for linking from other Flash movies.

You also use the Symbol Linkage dialog box to assign an identifier name for a movie clip or a sound file that you want to play using the attachMovie or attachSound method. For information on the attachMovie method, see "Attaching movie clips" in the movie clips chapter of the *ActionScript Reference Guide*. For information on the attachSound method, see "Creating sound controls" in the interaction chapter of the *ActionScript Reference Guide*.

To define a shared library asset:

1 With a movie file open, choose Window > Library or click the Library button in the Launcher bar (at the bottom right of the application window) to display the Library window if it is not already visible.

2 Do one of the following:

- Select an item in the Library window and choose Linkage from the Library Options menu.

- Right-click (Windows) or Control-click (Macintosh) an item in the Library window and choose Linkage from the context menu.

3 In the Symbol Linkage Properties dialog box, select Export This Symbol.

4 In the Identifier text field, enter an identifier, or name, for the symbol. (Do not include spaces in the identifier.)

5 Click OK.

6 Save the movie file.

About posting a shared library to a URL

A shared library must be posted to a URL as a SWF file in order for the shared assets to appear in movies that link to the assets. When you publish a movie that contains a shared library (that is, the movie in which you defined the shared assets), the shared library is automatically included with the movie's SWF file.

You do not need to specify a URL for a shared library to include the library with the movie's SWF file. However, you can specify a different URL for a shared library file to place the library in another location.

To specify a URL for a shared library:

1 In the Library window, choose Shared Library Properties from the Library Options menu.

2 In the Shared Library Properties dialog box, enter the URL where you want the shared library to be located.

3 Click OK.

Linking to assets in a shared library

To link to shared library assets from a Flash movie, you open the shared library and add items from the shared library to the current movie's library.

To create links to shared assets, you open the FLA file for the shared library. It is not necessary to publish the shared library as a SWF file in order to create links to the shared assets.

Note: To preview linked assets when you test a movie, or to display linked assets when you play a published movie, you must first create the SWF file for the shared library. To create the shared library's SWF file, you publish the movie in which you defined the shared library.

To link to shared library assets:

1 With a movie file open, choose File > Open As Shared Library.

2 Select the shared library that you want to open and click Open.

   The shared library opens as a Library window in the current movie. Options menu commands and buttons in the shared library window are dimmed, indicating that they are unavailable.

3 To link an asset from the shared library to the current movie, do one of the following:

• Drag the asset from the shared library into the library for the current movie.

• Drag the asset from the shared library onto the Stage.

   The shared asset name appears in the current movie's library. The asset is linked to the current movie as an external file; the asset file is not added to the current movie.

Using the Movie Explorer

The Movie Explorer provides an easy way for you to view and organize the content of a movie and select elements in the movie for modification. It offers many features to streamline the workflow for creating movies. For example, you can use the Movie Explorer to do the following:

- Search for an element in a movie by name

- Display the properties panel for a selected element to perform modifications

- Familiarize yourself with the structure of a Flash movie created by another developer

- Find all the instances of a particular symbol or action

- Replace all occurrences of a font with another font

- View name/value pairs for Macromedia Generator Objects

- Copy text to the Clipboard to paste into an external text editor for spell checking

- Print the navigable display list currently displayed in the Movie Explorer

The Movie Explorer contains a display list, a list of movie contents arranged in a navigable hierarchical tree. You can filter which categories of items in the movie are displayed in the Movie Explorer, choosing from text, graphics, buttons, movie clips, actions, imported files, and Generator Objects. You can display the selected categories as movie elements (scenes), symbol definitions, or both. You can expand and collapse the navigation tree.

The Movie Explorer has a pop-up options menu and a context menu with options for performing operations on selected items or modifying the Movie Explorer display. The pop-up options menu is indicated by a triangle in the Movie Explorer's upper right corner.

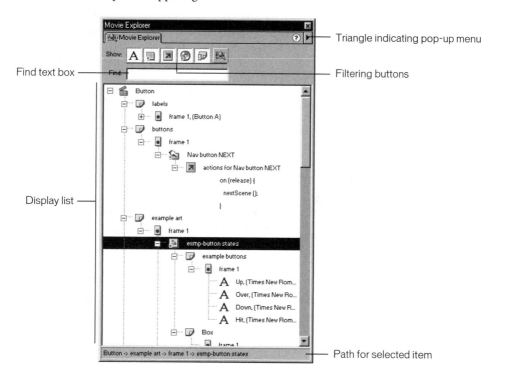

Triangle indicating pop-up menu

Find text box — Find

Filtering buttons

Display list

Path for selected item

To view the Movie Explorer:

Choose Window > Movie Explorer.

To filter the categories of items displayed in the Movie Explorer:

- Click one or more of the filtering buttons to the right of the Show option to show text, symbols, ActionScript, imported files, or frames and layers. To customize which items to show, click the Customize button. Select options in the Show area of the Movie Explorer Settings dialog box to view those elements.

- From the pop-up menu in the upper right corner of the Movie Explorer, choose Show Movie Elements to display items in scenes, and choose Show Symbol Definitions to display information about symbols. (Both options can be active at the same time.)

To search for an item using the Find text box:

In the Find text box, enter the item name, font name, ActionScript string, frame number, or Generator Object name or value pair. The Find feature searches all items currently displayed in the Movie Explorer.

To select an item in the Movie Explorer:

Click the item in the navigation tree. Shift-click to select more than one item.

The full path for the selected item appears at the bottom of the Movie Explorer. Selecting a scene in the Movie Explorer displays the first frame of that scene on the Stage. Selecting an element in the Movie Explorer selects that element on the Stage if the layer containing the element is not locked.

To use the Movie Explorer pop-up menu or context menu commands:

1 Do one of the following:

- To view the pop-up menu, click the triangle in the Movie Explorer's upper right corner.

- To view the context menu, right-click (Windows) or Control-click (Macintosh) an item in the Movie Explorer navigation tree.

2 Select an option from the menu:

- Goto Location jumps to the selected layer, scene, or frame in the movie.

- Goto Symbol Definition jumps to the symbol definition for a symbol that is selected in the Movie Elements area of the Movie Explorer. The symbol definition lists all the files associated with the symbol. (The Show Symbol Definitions option must be selected. See option definition below.)

- Select Symbol Instances jumps to the scene containing instances of a symbol that is selected in the Symbol Definitions area of the Movie Explorer. (The Show Movie Elements option must be selected. See option definition below.)

- Find in Library highlights the selected symbol in the movie's library (Flash opens the Library window if it is not already visible).

- Properties opens the appropriate panel or panels for the selected element. (Some elements may have more than one panel associated with them.)

- Rename lets you enter a new name for a selected element.

- Edit in Place lets you edit a selected symbol on the Stage.

- Edit in New Window lets you edit a selected symbol in a new window.

- Show Movie Elements displays the elements in your movie, organized into scenes.

- Show Symbol Definitions displays all the elements associated with a symbol.

- Copy Text to Clipboard copies selected text to the Clipboard. You can paste the text into an external text editor for spell checking or other editing.

- Cut, Copy, Paste, and Clear perform these common functions on a selected element. Modifying an item in the display list modifies the corresponding element in the movie.

- Expand Branch expands the navigation tree at the selected element.

- Collapse Branch collapses the navigation tree at the selected element.

- Collapse Others collapses the branches in the navigation tree not containing the selected element.

- Print prints the hierarchical display list currently displayed in the Movie Explorer.

Viewing the Stage

To change your view of the Stage, you can change the magnification level or move the Stage within the Flash work environment. You can also adjust your view of the Stage using the View commands.

Zooming

You can view the entire Stage on the screen, or a particular area of your drawing at high magnification, by changing the magnification level. The maximum magnification depends on the resolution of your monitor and the movie size.

To magnify or reduce your view of the Stage, use these techniques:

- To zoom in on a certain element, select the Zoom tool and click the element. To switch the Zoom tool between zooming in or out, use the Enlarge or Reduce modifiers or hold down the Alt key(Windows) or Option key (Macintosh).

- To zoom in on a specific area of your drawing, drag a rectangular selection marquee with the Zoom tool. Flash sets the magnification level so that the specified rectangle fills the window.

- To zoom in on or out of the entire Stage, choose View > Zoom In or View > Zoom Out.

- To zoom in or out by a specified percentage, choose View > Magnification and select a percentage from the submenu, or select a percentage from the Zoom control at the bottom left corner of the application window.

- To display the contents of the current frame, choose View > Magnification > Show All, or choose Show All from the Zoom control at the bottom left corner of the application window. If the scene is empty, the entire Stage is displayed.

- To display the entire Stage, choose View > Magnification > Show Frame or choose Show Frame from the Zoom control at the bottom left corner of the application window.

- To display the work area surrounding the Stage, choose View > Work Area. The work area is shown in light gray. Use the Work Area command to view elements in a scene that are partly or completely outside of the Stage. For example, to have a bird fly into a frame, you would initially position the bird outside of the Stage in the work area.

Moving the view of the Stage

When the Stage is magnified, you may not be able to see all of it. The Hand tool lets you move the Stage to change the view without having to change the magnification.

To move the Stage view:

1 Select the Hand tool. To temporarily switch between another tool and the Hand tool, hold down the Spacebar and click the tool in the toolbox.

2 Drag the Stage.

Using the grid, guides, and rulers

When grids are displayed in a movie, they appear as lines behind the artwork in all scenes. You can snap objects to the grid, and you can modify the grid size and grid line color.

When rulers are displayed, they appear along the top and left sides of the movie. You can select the unit of measure used in the rulers. When you move an element on the Stage with the rulers displayed, lines indicating the element's dimensions appear on the rulers.

You can drag horizontal and vertical guides from the rulers onto the Stage when the rulers are displayed. You can move guides, lock guides, hide guides, and remove guides. You can also snap objects to guides and change guide color. Draggable guides appear only in the Timeline in which they were created.

Note: To create custom guides or irregular guides, you use guide layers. See "Using guide layers" on page 206.

To display or hide rulers:

Choose View > Rulers.

To specify the rulers' unit of measure:

1 Choose Modify > Movie.

2 Select an option from the Ruler Units pop-up menu.

To display or hide the drawing grid or guides:

- Choose View > Grid > Show Grid or View > Guides > Show Guides.

- Choose View > Grid > Edit Grid or View > Guides > Edit Guides, and select Show Grid or Show Guides in the dialog box.

Note: If the grid is visible and Snap to Grid is turned on when you create guides, guides will snap to the grid.

To turn snapping to grid lines or guides on or off, do one of the following:

- Choose View > Grid > Snap to Grid or View > Guides > Snap to Guides.

- Choose View > Grid > Edit Grid or View > Guides > Edit Guides, and select Snap to Grid or Snap to Guides in the dialog box.

Note: Snapping to guides takes precedence over snapping to the grid in places where guides fall between grid lines.

To specify snapping tolerance for the grid or guides:

1 Choose View > Grid > Edit Grid or View > Guides > Edit Guides.

2 Select an option from the Snap Accuracy pop-up menu in the dialog box.

To change grid or guide line color:

1 Choose View > Grid > Edit Grid or View > Guides > Edit Guides.

2 Click the triangle next to the color box and select a color from the palette.

   The default grid line color is gray. The default guide line color is green.

To change the spacing of the grid:

1 Choose View > Grid > Edit Grid.

2 In the Grid dialog box, enter values for vertical and horizontal grid spacing, and click OK.

To move a guide:

Use the Arrow tool to click and drag the guide.

To lock guides or clear all guides:

Choose View > Guides > Edit Guides, and then choose Lock Guides or Clear All and click OK.

Note: Clear All Guides removes all guides from the current scene.

To remove a guide:

With guides unlocked, use the Arrow tool to drag the guide to the horizontal or vertical ruler.

Customizing keyboard shortcuts

You can choose keyboard shortcuts in Flash to match the shortcuts you use in other applications, or to streamline your Flash workflow. By default, Flash uses built-in keyboard shortcuts designed for the Flash application. You can also select a built-in keyboard shortcut set from one of several popular graphics applications, including Fireworks, Adobe Illustrator, and Adobe Photoshop.

To create a custom keyboard shortcut set, you duplicate an existing set, and then add or remove shortcuts from the new set. You can delete custom shortcut sets.

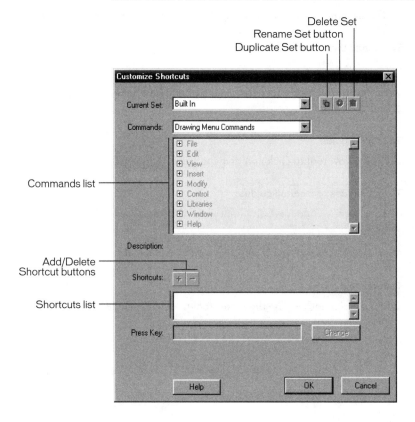

To select a keyboard shortcut set:

1 Choose Edit > Keyboard Shortcuts.

2 In the Keyboard Shortcuts dialog box, choose a shortcut set from the Current Set pop-up menu.

To create a new keyboard shortcut set:

1 Select a keyboard shortcut set as described above.

 2 Click the Duplicate Set button.

3 Enter a name for the new shortcut set and click OK.

To rename a custom keyboard shortcut set:

1 In the Customize Shortcuts dialog box, choose a shortcut set from the Current Set pop-up menu.

2 Click the Rename Set button.

3 In the Rename dialog box, enter a new name and click OK.

Note: You cannot rename built-in sets.

To add or remove a shortcut:

1 Choose Edit > Keyboard Shortcuts and select the set that you want to modify.

2 Select Drawing Menu Commands, Drawing Tools, or Test Movie Menu Commands from the Commands pop-up menu to view shortcuts for the selected category.

3 In the Commands list, select the command for which you want to add or remove a shortcut.

   An explanation of the selected command appears in the Description area in the dialog box.

4 Do one of the following:

• To add a shortcut, click the Add Shortcut (+) button.

• To remove a shortcut, click the Remove Shortcut (-) button and proceed to step 6.

5 If you are adding a shortcut, enter the new shortcut key combination in the Press Key text box.

   Note: To enter the key combination, simply press the keys on the keyboard. You do not need to spell out key names, such as Control, Option, and so on.

6 Click Change.

7 Repeat this procedure to add or remove additional shortcuts.

8 Click OK.

To delete a keyboard shortcut set:

1 Choose Edit > Keyboard Shortcuts. In the Customize Shortcuts dialog box, click the Delete Set button.

2 In the Delete Set dialog box, choose a shortcut set and click Delete.

Note: You cannot delete the built-in keyboard shortcut sets that ship with Flash.

Printing Flash files as you edit movies

You can print frames from Flash FLA files as you work, to preview and edit your movies.

You can also specify frames to be printable from the Flash Player by a viewer displaying the Flash movie. See Chapter 13, "Creating a Printable Movie."

When printing frames from a FLA file, you use the Print dialog box to specify the range of scenes or frames you want to print, as well as the number of copies. In Windows, the Page Setup dialog box specifies paper size, orientation, and various print options—including margin settings and whether all frames are to be printed for each page. On the Macintosh, these options are divided between the Page Setup and the Print Margins dialog boxes.

The Print and Page Setup dialog boxes are standard within either operating system, and their appearance depends on the printer driver selected.

To set printing options:

1 Choose File > Page Setup (Windows) or File > Print Margins (Macintosh).

2 Set page margins. Select the Center options to print the frame in the center of the page.

3 In the Frames pop-up menu, choose to print all frames in the movie or only the first frame of each scene.

4 In the Layout pop-up menu, choose one of the following options:

- Actual Size prints the frame at full size. Enter a value in the Scale option to reduce or enlarge the printed frame.

- Fit on One Page reduces or enlarges each frame so it fills the print area of the page.

- Storyboard options print several thumbnails on one page. Enter the number of thumbnails per page in the Frames text box. Set the space between the thumbnails in the Story Margin text box. Select Label to print the frame label as a thumbnail.

To preview how your scene is arranged on the printer paper:

Choose File > Print Preview.

To print frames:

Choose File > Print.

Solving printing problems

If you experience problems printing Flash files on your PostScript printer, one of the filled areas in your drawing may be too complex. (This is more common with older PostScript Level 1 printers.) There are two solutions to this problem:

- Choose Disable PostScript in the Print Margins dialog box (Macintosh) or in Preferences (Windows), and try printing again. This can slow down printing considerably, but it should solve the problem. (For information on setting preferences, see "Flash preferences" on page 111.)

- Simplify your drawing. Printing problems are typically caused by a single large area of color with complex borders. You can solve this problem by dividing the complex area into several simpler areas. Use Modify > Curves > Optimize to reduce the complexity of such areas.

Also note that Flash cannot print transparency (alpha channel) effects or mask layers.

Speeding up movie display

To speed up the movie display, you can use commands on the View menu to turn off rendering-quality features that require extra computing and slow down movies.

None of these commands have any effect on how Flash exports a movie. To specify the display quality of Flash movies in a Web browser, you use the OBJECT and EMBED parameters. The Publish command can do this for you automatically. For more information, see "Publishing Flash movies" on page 319.

To change the display speed:

Choose View and select from the following options:

- Outlines displays only the outlines of the shapes in your scene and causes all lines to appear as thin lines. This makes it easier to reshape your graphic elements and to display complex scenes faster.

- Fast turns off anti-aliasing and displays all the colors and line styles of your drawing.

- Antialias turns on anti-aliasing for lines, shapes, and bitmaps. It displays shapes and lines so that their edges appear smoother on the screen. This option draws more slowly than the Fast option. Anti-aliasing works best on video cards that provide thousands (16-bit) or millions (24-bit) of colors. In 16- or 256-color mode, black lines are smoothed, but colors might look better in Fast mode.

- Antialias Text smooths the edges of any text. This command works best with large font sizes and can be slow with large amounts of text. This is the most common mode in which to work.

Flash preferences

Flash allows you to set preferences for general application operations, editing operations, and Clipboard operations.

To set Flash preferences, you use the Edit > Preferences submenu. See also "Choosing drawing settings" on page 133.

To set preferences:

1 Choose Edit > Preferences.

2 Click the General, Editing, or Clipboard tab, and choose from the respective options.

To set general preferences, choose from the following options:

- For Undo Levels, enter a value from 0 to 200 to set the number of undo/redo levels. Undo levels require memory; the more undo levels you use, the more system memory is taken up.

- For Printing Options (Windows only), select Disable PostScript to disable PostScript output when printing to a PostScript printer. By default, this option is deselected. Select this option if you have problems printing to a PostScript printer. Selecting this option will slow down printing to a PostScript printer.

- For Selection Options, select Shift Select to control how Flash handles selection of multiple elements. When Shift Select is off, clicking additional elements adds them to the current selection. When Shift Select is on, clicking additional elements deselects other elements unless you hold down the Shift key.

- Select Show Tooltips to display tooltips when the pointer pauses over a window emblem. Deselect this option if you don't want to see the tooltips.

- For Timeline Options, select Disable Timeline Docking to keep the Timeline from attaching itself to the application window once it has been separated into its own window. See also "Using the Timeline" on page 82.

- Select Use Flash 4 Selection Style to display selected frames with the highlighting style used in Flash 4.

- Select Show Blank Keyframes to indicate blank keyframes with hollow circles.

- For Highlight Color, select Use This Color and select a color from the color box control, or select Use Layer Color to use the current layer's outline color.

- For Actions Panel, select Normal Mode to create actions using controls in the panel, or select Expert Mode to create actions by entering ActionScript in the text box in the panel.

To set editing preferences, choose from the following options:

- For Pen Tool Options, see "Setting Pen tool preferences" on page 118.

- For Drawing Settings, see "Choosing drawing settings" on page 133.

To set Clipboard preferences, choose from the following options:

- For Bitmaps (Windows only), select options for Color Depth and Resolution to specify these parameters for bitmaps copied to the Clipboard. Select Smooth to apply anti-aliasing. Enter a value for Size Limit to specify the amount of RAM that is used when putting a bitmap image on the Clipboard. Increase this value when working with large or high-resolution bitmap images. If your computer has limited memory, choose None.

- For Gradients (Windows only), choose an option to specify the quality of gradient fills placed in the Windows Metafile. Choosing a higher quality increases the time required to copy artwork. Use this setting to specify gradient quality when pasting items to a location outside of Flash. When you are pasting within Flash, the full gradient quality of the copied data is preserved regardless of the Gradients on Clipboard setting.

- For PICT Settings (Macintosh only), for Type, select Objects to preserve data copied to the Clipboard as vector artwork, or select one of the bitmap formats to convert the copied artwork to a bitmap. Enter a value for Resolution. Select Include Postscript to include PostScript data. For Gradients, choose an option to specify gradient quality in the PICT. Choosing a higher quality increases the time required to copy artwork. Use the Gradients setting to specify gradient quality when pasting items to a location outside of Flash. When you are pasting within Flash, the full gradient quality of the copied data is preserved regardless of the Gradient setting.

- For FreeHand Text, select Maintain Text as Blocks to keep text editable in a pasted FreeHand file.

CHAPTER 3
Drawing

The drawing tools in Flash let you create and modify shapes for the artwork in your movies. For an interactive introduction to drawing in Flash, choose Help > Lessons > Drawing.

Before you draw and paint in Flash, it is important to understand how Flash drawing tools work and how drawing, painting, and modifying shapes can affect other shapes on the same layer.

Flash drawing and painting tools

Flash provides various tools for drawing freeform or precise lines, shapes, and paths, and painting filled objects.

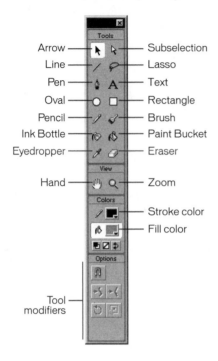

Arrow — Subselection
Line — Lasso
Pen — Text
Oval — Rectangle
Pencil — Brush
Ink Bottle — Paint Bucket
Eyedropper — Eraser

Hand — Zoom

Stroke color
Fill color

Tool modifiers

- To draw freeform lines and shapes as if drawing with a real pencil, you use the Pencil tool. See "Drawing with the Pencil tool" on page 116.

- To draw precise paths as straight or curved lines, you use the Pen tool. See "Using the Pen tool" on page 118.

- To draw basic geometric shapes, you use the Line, Oval, and Rectangle tools. See "Drawing straight lines, ovals, and rectangles" on page 117.

- To create brushlike strokes as if painting with a brush, you use the Brush tool. See "Painting with the Brush tool" on page 125.

When you use a drawing or painting tool to create an object, the tool applies the current stroke and fill attributes to the object. To change the stroke and fill attributes of existing objects, you can use the Paint Bucket and Ink Bottle tools. See "Specifying stroke and fill attributes" on page 136.

You can reshape lines and shape outlines in a variety of ways after you create them. Fills and strokes are treated as separate objects. You can select fills and strokes separately to move or modify them. See "Reshaping lines and shape outlines" on page 126.

You can use snapping to automatically align elements with each other and with the drawing grid or guides. See "Using the grid, guides, and rulers" on page 104.

About overlapping shapes in Flash

When you use the Pencil, Line, Oval, Rectangle, or Brush tool to draw a line across another line or painted shape, the overlapping lines are divided into segments at the intersection points. You can use the Arrow tool to select, move, and reshape each segment individually.

Note: Overlapping lines that you create with the Pen tool do not divide into segments at intersection points, but remain intact. See "Using the Pen tool" on page 118.

A fill; the fill with a line drawn through it; and the two fills and three line segments created by segmentation

When you paint on top of shapes and lines, the portion underneath is replaced by whatever is on top. Paint of the same color merges together. Paint of different colors remains distinct. You can use these features to create masks, cutouts, and other negative images. For example, the cutout below was made by moving the ungrouped kite image onto the green shape, deselecting the kite, and then moving the filled portions of the kite away from the green shape.

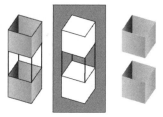

To avoid inadvertently altering shapes and lines by overlapping them, you can group the shapes or use layers to separate them. See "Grouping objects" on page 186 and Chapter 8, "Using Layers."

Drawing with the Pencil tool

To draw lines and shapes, you use the Pencil tool, in much the same way that you would use a real pencil to draw. To apply smoothing or straightening to the lines and shapes as you draw, you select a drawing mode for the Pencil tool.

To draw with the Pencil tool:

1 Select the Pencil tool.

2 Select a stroke color, line weight, and style. See "Specifying stroke and fill attributes" on page 136.

3 Choose a drawing mode under Options in the toolbox:

• Choose Straighten to draw straight lines and convert approximations of triangles, ovals, circles, rectangles, and squares into these common geometric shapes.

• Choose Smooth to draw smooth curved lines.

• Choose Ink to draw freehand lines with no modification applied.

Lines drawn with Straighten, Smooth, and Ink mode, respectively

4 Drag on the Stage to draw with the Pencil tool. Shift-drag to constrain lines to vertical or horizontal directions.

Drawing straight lines, ovals, and rectangles

You can use the Line, Oval, and Rectangle tools to easily create these basic geometric shapes. The Oval and Rectangle tools create stroked and filled shapes. You can use the Rectangle tool to create rectangles with square or rounded corners.

To draw a straight line, oval, or rectangle:

1 Select the Line, Oval, or Rectangle tool.

2 Select stroke and fill attributes. See "Specifying stroke and fill attributes" on page 136.

   Note: You cannot set fill attributes for the Line tool.

3 For the Rectangle tool, specify rounded corners by clicking the Round Rectangle modifier and entering a corner radius value. A value of zero creates square corners.

4 Drag on the Stage. If you are using the Rectangle tool, press the Up and Down Arrow keys while dragging to adjust the radius of rounded corners.

   For the Oval and Rectangle tools, Shift-drag to constrain the shapes to circles and squares.

   For the Line tool, Shift-drag to constrain lines to multiples of 45°.

Using the Pen tool

To draw precise paths as straight lines or smooth, flowing curves, you can use the Pen tool. You can create straight or curved line segments and adjust the angle and length of straight segments and the slope of curved segments.

When you draw with the Pen tool, you click to create points on straight line segments, and click and drag to create points on curved line segments. You can adjust straight and curved line segments by adjusting points on the line. You can convert curves to straight lines and the reverse. You can also display points on lines that you create with other Flash drawing tools, such as the Pencil, Brush, Line, Oval, or Rectangle tool, to adjust those lines. See "Reshaping lines and shape outlines" on page 126.

Setting Pen tool preferences

You can specify preferences for the appearance of the Pen tool pointer, for previewing line segments as you draw, or for the appearance of selected anchor points. Selected line segments and anchor points are displayed using the outline color of the layer on which the lines and points appear.

To set Pen tool preferences:

1 Choose Edit > Preferences and click the Editing tab.

2 Under Pen Tool, set the following options:

- Select Show Pen Preview to preview line segments as you draw. Flash displays a preview of the line segment as you move the pointer around the Stage, before you click to create the end point of the segment. If this option is not selected, Flash does not display a line segment until you create the end point of the segment.

- Select Show Solid Points to specify that unselected anchor points appear as solid points and selected anchor points appear as hollow points (this option is selected by default). Deselect this option to display unselected anchor points as hollow points and selected anchor points as solid points.

- Select Show Precise Cursors to specify that the Pen tool pointer appear as a cross-hair pointer, rather than the default Pen tool icon, for more precise placement of lines. Deselect the option to display the default Pen tool icon with the Pen tool.

   Note: Press the Caps Lock key when working to toggle between cursors.

3 Click OK.

Drawing straight lines with the Pen tool

To draw straight line segments with the Pen tool, you create anchor points, points on the line that determine the length of individual line segments.

To draw straight lines with the Pen tool:

1 Select the Pen tool.

2 Select stroke and fill attributes. See "Specifying stroke and fill attributes" on page 136.

3 Position the pointer on the Stage where you want the straight line to begin, and click to define the first anchor point.

4 Click again where you want the first segment of the straight line to end. Shift-click to constrain the tool to multiples of 45°.

5 Continue clicking to create additional straight segments.

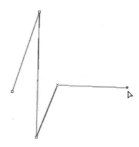

6 To complete the path as an open or closed shape, do one of the following:

- To complete an open path, double-click the last point, click the Pen tool in the toolbox, or Control-click (Windows) or Command-click (Macintosh) anywhere away from the path.

- To close a path, position the Pen tool over the first anchor point. A small circle appears next to the pen tip when it is positioned correctly. Click or drag to close the path.

- To complete the shape as is, choose Edit > Deselect All or select a different tool in the toolbox.

Drawing curved paths with the Pen tool

You create curves by dragging the Pen tool in the direction you want the curve to go to create the first anchor point, and then dragging the Pen tool in the opposite direction to create the second anchor point.

When you use the Pen tool to create a curved segment, the anchor points of the line segment display tangent handles. The slope and length of each tangent handle determine the slope and the height, or depth, of the curve. Moving the tangent handles reshapes the curves of the path. See "Adjusting segments" on page 124.

To draw a curved path:

1 Select the Pen tool.

2 Position the Pen tool on the Stage where you want the curve to begin. Hold down the mouse button. The first anchor point appears, and the pen tip changes to an arrowhead.

3 Drag in the direction you want the curve segment to be drawn. As you drag, the tangent handles of the curve appear. Shift-drag to constrain the tool to multiples of 45°.

4 Release the mouse button.

   The length and slope of the tangent handle determine the shape of the curve segment. You can move the tangent handle later to adjust the curve.

5 Position the pointer where you want the curve segment to end, hold down the mouse button, and drag in the opposite direction to complete the segment. Shift-drag to constrain the tool to multiples of 45°.

6 To draw the next segment of a curve, position the pointer where you want the next segment to end, and drag away from the curve.

Adjusting anchor points on paths

When you draw a curve with the Pen tool, you create curve points, anchor points on a continuous curved path. When you draw a straight line segment, or a straight line connected to a curved segment, you create corner points, anchor points on a straight path or at the juncture of a straight and a curved path.

By default, selected curve points appear as hollow circles, and selected corner points appear as hollow squares.

To convert segments in a line from straight segments to curve segments or the reverse, you convert corner points to curve points or the reverse.

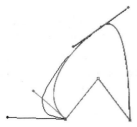

You can also move, add, or delete anchor points on a path. You move anchor points using the Subselection tool to adjust the length or angle of straight segments or the slope of curved segments. You can nudge selected anchor points to make small adjustments.

Deleting unneeded anchor points on a curved path optimizes the curve and reduces the file size.

To move an anchor point:

Drag it with the Subselection tool.

To nudge an anchor point or points:

Select the point or points with the Subselection tool and use the Arrow keys to move the point or points.

To convert an anchor point, do one of the following:

- To convert a corner point to a curve point, use the Subselection tool to Alt-drag (Windows) or Option-drag (Macintosh) the point.

- To convert a curve point to a corner point, use the Pen tool to click on the point.

To add an anchor point:

Click with the Pen tool on a line segment.

To delete an anchor point, do one of the following:

- To delete a corner point, click the point once with the Pen tool.

- To delete a curve point, click the point twice with the Pen tool. (Click once to convert the point to a corner point, and once more to delete the point.)

- Select the point with the Subselection tool and press Delete.

Adjusting segments

You can adjust straight segments to change the angle or length of the segment, or adjust curved segments to change the slope or direction of the curve.

When you move a tangent handle on a curve point, the curves on both sides of the point adjust. When you move a tangent handle on a corner point, only the curve on the same side of the point as the tangent handle adjusts.

To adjust a straight segment:

1 Select the Subselection tool, and select a straight segment.

2 Use the Subselection tool to drag an anchor point on the segment to a new position.

To adjust a curve segment:

Select the Subselection tool and drag the segment.

Note: Anchor points are hidden when you click the path with the Subselection tool. To view the anchor points after adjustment, click the path with the Subselection tool or the Pen tool. Also, adjusting a segment with the Subselection tool may add points to the path.

To adjust points or tangent handles on a curve:

1 Select the Subselection tool, and select a curved segment. Tangent handles appear for that segment.

2 Do one of the following:

• To adjust the location of the curve's anchor point, drag the anchor point.

• To adjust the shape of the curve on either side of the anchor point, drag the anchor point, or drag the tangent handle. Shift-drag to constrain the tool to multiples of 45°.

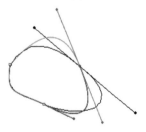

Painting with the Brush tool

The Brush tool draws brushlike strokes, as if you were painting. It lets you create special effects, including calligraphic effects. On most pressure-sensitive tablets, you can vary the width of the brush stroke by varying pressure on the stylus.

You can use an imported bitmap as a fill when painting with the Brush tool. See "Breaking apart a bitmap" on page 163.

A variable-width brush stroke drawn with a stylus

To paint with the Brush tool:

1 Select the Brush tool.

2 Select a fill color. See "Specifying stroke and fill attributes" on page 136.

3 Click the Brush mode modifier and choose a painting mode:

- Paint Normal paints over lines and fills on the same layer.

- Paint Behind paints in blank areas of the Stage on the same layer, leaving lines and fills unaffected.

- Paint Selection applies a new fill to the selection when you select a fill in the Fill modifier or the Fill panel. (This option is the same as simply selecting a filled area and applying a new fill.)

- Paint Fills paints fills and empty areas, leaving lines unaffected.

- Paint Inside paints the fill in which you start a brush stroke and never paints lines. This works much like a smart coloring book that never allows you to paint outside the lines. If you start painting in an empty area, the fill doesn't affect any existing filled areas.

Original image, Paint Normal, Paint Behind, Paint Selection, Paint Fills, and Paint Inside

4 Choose a brush size, brush shape, and paint color from the Brush tool modifiers.

5 If a pressure-sensitive tablet is attached to your computer, you can select the Pressure modifier to vary the width of your brush strokes by varying the pressure on your stylus.

6 Drag on the Stage. Shift-drag to constrain brush strokes to horizontal and vertical directions.

Reshaping lines and shape outlines

You can reshape lines and shape outlines created with the Pencil, Brush, Line, Oval, or Rectangle tools by dragging with the Arrow tool, or by optimizing their curves.

You can also use the Subselection tool to display points on lines and shape outlines and modify the lines and outlines by adjusting the points. For information on adjusting anchor points, see "Using the Pen tool" on page 118.

To display anchor points on a line or shape outline created with the Pencil, Brush, Line, Oval, or Rectangle tools:

1 Select the Subselection tool.

2 Click on the line or shape outline.

Reshaping using the Arrow tool

To reshape a line or shape outline, you can drag on any point on a line using the Arrow tool. The pointer changes to indicate what type of reshaping it can perform on the line or fill.

Flash adjusts the curve of the line segment to accommodate the new position of the moved point. If the repositioned point is an end point, you can lengthen or shorten the line. If the repositioned point is a corner, the line segments forming the corner remain straight as they become longer or shorter.

When a corner appears next to the pointer, you can change an end point. When a curve appears next to the pointer, you can adjust a curve.

Some brush stroke areas are easier to reshape if you view them as outlines.

If you are having trouble reshaping a complex line, you can smooth it to remove some of its details, making reshaping easier. Increasing the magnification can also make reshaping easier and more accurate; see "Optimizing curves" on page 129 or "Viewing the Stage" on page 102.

To reshape a line or shape outline using the Arrow tool:

1   Select the Arrow tool.

2   Do the following:

• Drag from any point on the segment to reshape it.

• Control-drag (Windows) or Option-drag (Macintosh) a line to create a new corner point.

Straightening and smoothing lines

You can reshape lines and shape outlines by straightening or smoothing them.

Note: Adjust the degree of automatic smoothing and straightening by choosing drawing settings in Preferences. See "Choosing drawing settings" on page 133.

Straightening makes small straightening adjustments to lines and curves you have already drawn. It has no effect on already straight segments.

You can also use the straightening technique to make Flash recognize shapes. If you draw any oval, rectangular, or triangular shapes with the Recognize Shapes option turned off, you can use the Straightening option to make the shapes geometrically perfect. (See "Choosing drawing settings" on page 133 for information on the Recognize Shapes option.) Shapes that are touching, and thus connected to other elements, are not recognized.

Shape recognition turns the top shapes into the bottom shapes.

Smoothing softens curves and reduces bumps or other variations in a curve's overall direction. It also reduces the number of segments in a curve. Smoothing is relative, however, and has no effect on straight segments. It is particularly useful when you are having trouble reshaping a number of very short curved line segments. Selecting all the segments and smoothing them reduces the number of segments, producing a gentler curve that is easier to reshape.

Repeated application of smoothing or straightening makes each segment smoother or straighter, depending on how curved or straight each segment was originally.

To smooth the curve of each selected fill outline or curved line:

Select the Arrow tool and click the Smooth modifier in the Options section of the toolbox, or choose Modify > Smooth.

To make small straightening adjustments on each selected fill outline or curved line:

Select the Arrow tool and click the Straighten modifier in the Options section of the toolbox, or choose Modify > Straighten.

To use shape recognition:

Select the Arrow tool and click the Straighten modifier, or choose Modify > Straighten.

Optimizing curves

Another way to smooth curves is to optimize them. This refines curved lines and fill outlines by reducing the number of curves used to define these elements. Optimizing curves also reduces the size of the Flash movie and the exported Flash Player movie. As with the Smooth or Straighten modifiers or commands, you can apply optimization to the same elements multiple times.

To optimize curves:

1   Select the drawn elements to be optimized and choose Modify > Optimize.

2   In the Optimize Curves dialog box, drag the Smoothing slider to specify the degree of smoothing.

    The exact results depend on the curves selected. Generally, optimizing produces fewer curves, with less resemblance to the original outline.

3   Set the additional options:

•   Select Use Multiple Passes to repeat the smoothing process until no further optimization can be accomplished; this is the same as repeatedly choosing Optimize with the same elements selected.

•   Select Show Totals Message to display an alert box that indicates the extent of the optimization when smoothing is complete.

4   Click OK.

Erasing

Erasing with the Eraser tool removes strokes and fills. You can quickly erase everything on the Stage, erase individual stroke segments or filled areas, or erase by dragging.

You can customize the Eraser tool to erase only strokes, only filled areas, or only a single filled area. The Eraser tool can be either round or square, and it can have one of five sizes.

To quickly delete everything on the Stage:

 Double-click the Eraser tool.

To remove stroke segments or filled areas:

1 Select the Eraser tool and then click the Faucet modifier.

2 Click the stroke segment or filled area that you want to delete.

To erase by dragging:

1 Select the Eraser tool.

2 Click the Eraser Mode modifier and choose an erasing mode:

• Erase Normal erases strokes and fills on the same layer.

• Erase Fills erases only fills; strokes are not affected.

• Erase Lines erases only strokes; fills are not affected.

• Erase Selected Fills erases only the currently selected fills and does not affect strokes, selected or not. (Select the fills you want to erase before using the Eraser tool in this mode.)

• Erase Inside erases only the fill on which you begin the eraser stroke. If you begin erasing from an empty point, nothing will be erased. Strokes are unaffected by the eraser in this mode.

3 Click the Eraser Shape modifier and choose an eraser shape and size. Make sure that the Faucet modifier is not selected.

4 Drag on the Stage.

Modifying shapes

You can modify shapes by converting lines to fills, expanding the shape of a filled object, or softening the edges of a filled shape by modifying the curves of the shape.

The Lines to Fills feature changes lines to fills, which allows you to fill lines with gradients or to erase a portion of a line. The Expand Shape and Soften Edges features allow you to expand filled shapes and blur the edges of shapes.

Expand Shape and Soften Edges work best on small shapes that do not contain many small details. Applying Soften Edges to shapes with extensive detail can increase the file size of a Flash Player movie.

To convert lines to fills:

1 Select a line or multiple lines.

2 Choose Modify > Shape > Convert Lines to Fills.

   Selected lines are converted to filled shapes. Converting lines to fills can make file sizes larger, but it can also speed up drawing for some animations.

To expand the shape of a filled object:

1 Select a filled shape. This command works best on a single filled color shape with no stroke.

2 Choose Modify > Shape > Expand Fill.

3 In the Expand Path dialog box, enter a value in pixels for Distance and select Expand or Inset for Direction. Expand enlarges the shape, and Inset reduces it.

To soften the edges of an object:

1 Select a filled shape. This command works best on a single filled shape that has no stroke.

2 Choose Modify > Shape > Soften Fill Edges.

3 Set the following options:

• Distance is the width in pixels of the soft edge.

• Number of Steps controls how many curves will be used for the soft edge effect. More steps will provide a smoother effect but will also create larger files and be slower to draw.

• Expand or Inset controls whether the shape will be enlarged or reduced to soften the edges.

Snapping

To automatically align elements with one another, you can use snapping. Snapping can be turned on using the Snap modifier for the Arrow tool, or the Snap to Objects command in the View menu.

Note: You can also snap to the grid or to guides. For more information, see "Using the grid, guides, and rulers" on page 104.

If the Snap modifier for the Arrow tool is on, a small black ring appears under the pointer when you drag an element. The small ring changes to a larger ring when the object is within snapping distance of a grid line.

To turn snapping on or off, do one of the following:

- Select the Arrow tool and click the Snap modifier in the toolbox.

- Choose View > Snap to Objects. A check mark is displayed next to the command when it is on.

When you move or reshape an object, the position of the Arrow tool on the object provides the reference point for the snap ring. For example, if you move a filled shape by dragging near its center, the center point snaps to other objects. This is particularly useful for snapping shapes to motion paths for animating.

To adjust snapping tolerances:

Adjust the Connect Lines setting under Drawing Settings in Editing Preferences. See the next section.

Note: For better control of object placement when snapping, begin dragging from a corner or center point.

Choosing drawing settings

You can set drawing settings to specify snapping, smoothing, and straightening behaviors when you use Flash drawing tools. You can change the Tolerance setting for each option, and turn each option off or on. Tolerance settings are relative, depending on the resolution of your computer screen and the current magnification of the scene. By default, each option is turned on and set to Normal tolerance.

To set drawing settings:

1 Choose Edit > Preferences and click the Editing tab.

2 Under Drawing Settings, choose from the following options:

• Connect Lines determines how close the end of a line being drawn must be to an existing line segment before the end point snaps to the nearest point on the other line. The available options are Must Be Close, Normal, and Can Be Distant. This setting also controls horizontal and vertical line recognition—that is, how nearly horizontal or vertical a line must be drawn before Flash makes it exactly horizontal or vertical. When Snap to Objects is turned on, this setting controls how close objects must be to snap to one another.

• Smooth Curves specifies the amount of smoothing applied to curved lines drawn with the Pencil tool when the drawing mode is set to Straighten or Smooth. (Smoother curves are easier to reshape, while rougher curves match more closely the original line strokes.) The selections are Off, Rough, Normal, and Smooth.

   Note: You can further smooth existing curved segments using Modify > Smooth and Modify > Optimize.

• Recognize Lines defines how nearly straight a line segment drawn with the Pencil tool must be before Flash recognizes it and makes it perfectly straight. The selections are Off, Strict, Normal, and Tolerant. If Recognize Lines is off while you draw, you can straighten lines later by selecting one or more line segments and choosing Modify > Straighten.

• Recognize Shapes controls how precisely you must draw circles, ovals, squares, rectangles, and 90° and 180° arcs for them to be recognized as geometric shapes and redrawn accurately. The options are Off, Strict, Normal, and Tolerant. If Recognize Shapes is off while you draw, you can straighten lines later by selecting one or more shapes (for example, connected line segments) and choosing Modify > Straighten.

• Click Accuracy specifies how close to an item the pointer must be before Flash recognizes the item. The options are Strict, Normal, and Tolerant.

CHAPTER 4
Working with Color

Flash provides a variety of ways to apply, create, and modify colors. Using the default palette or a palette you create, you can choose colors to apply to an object's stroke or fill. Applying a stroke color to a shape paints the outline of the shape with that color. Applying a fill color to a shape paints the interior space of the shape with that color.

When applying a stroke color to a shape, you can select any solid color, and you can select the style and weight of the stroke. For a shape's fill, you can apply a solid color, gradient, or bitmap. To apply a bitmap fill, you must import a bitmap into the current file. You can also apply a transparent stroke or fill to create an outlined object with no fill, or a filled object with no outline. And you can apply a solid color fill to type. See "Setting type attributes" on page 212.

The Mixer panel allows you to create and edit solid colors. To create and edit gradient fills, you use the Fill panel. You can import, export, delete, and otherwise modify the color palette for a file using the Swatches panel.

Specifying stroke and fill attributes

To specify stroke or fill color, you can use the Stroke and Fill controls in the toolbox, the Ink Bottle and Paint Bucket tools, or the Stroke panel and Fill panel. To modify stroke style or line weight, you use the Stroke panel. To create or edit gradient fills or apply bitmap fills, you use the Fill panel.

When you create new objects with the drawing and painting tools, the objects are painted with the attributes specified in the tools' Stroke and Fill controls. You can also change the stroke and fill attributes of existing objects.

You can copy stroke or fill attributes from one object to another using the Eyedropper tool.

Using the Stroke and Fill controls in the toolbox

To select a solid stroke color or a solid or gradient fill color, switch the stroke and fill colors, or select the default stroke and fill colors (black stroke and white fill), you can use the Stroke and Fill controls in the toolbox.

The toolbox Stroke and Fill controls set the painting attributes of new objects you create with the drawing and painting tools. To use the Stroke and Fill controls to change the painting attributes of existing objects, you must first select the objects.

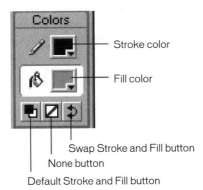

Stroke color
Fill color

Swap Stroke and Fill button
None button
Default Stroke and Fill button

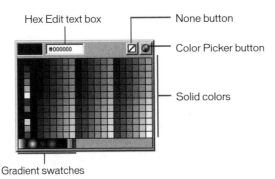

Hex Edit text box
None button
Color Picker button
Solid colors

Gradient swatches

To apply stroke and fill colors using the toolbox controls, do one of the following:

- Click the triangle next to the Stroke or Fill color box and choose a color swatch from the pop-up window. Gradients can be selected for fill color only.

- Type a color's hexadecimal value in the text box in the color pop-up window.

- Click the None button in the color pop-up window to apply a transparent stroke or fill.

  Note: You can apply a transparent stroke or fill to a new object, but you cannot apply a transparent stroke or fill to an existing object. Instead, select the existing stroke or fill and delete it.

- Click the Color Picker button in the color pop-up window and choose a color from the Color Picker.

- Click the Swap Fill and Stroke button in the toolbox to swap colors between the fill and the stroke.

- Click the Default Fill and Stroke button in the toolbox to return to the default color settings (white fill and black stroke).

Specifying stroke color, style, and weight in the Stroke panel

To change the stroke color, style, and line weight for a selected object, you can use the Stroke panel. For stroke style, you can choose from styles that are preloaded with Flash, or create a custom style.

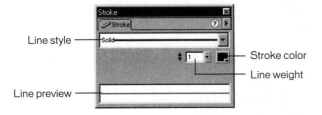

Line style

Stroke color

Line weight

Line preview

To select a stroke color, style, and weight with the Stroke panel:

1 Choose Window > Panels > Stroke.

2 To select a color, click the triangle next to the Stroke color box and do one of the following:

- Choose a color swatch from the palette.

- Type a color's hexadecimal value in the text box.

- Click the None button to apply a transparent stroke.

  Note: You can apply a transparent stroke to a new object, but not to an existing object. Instead, select the existing stroke and delete it.

- Click the Color Picker button and choose a color from the Color Picker.

3 To select a stroke style, click the triangle next to the Style pop-up menu and choose an option from the menu. To create a custom style, choose Custom from the pop-up menu in the upper right corner of the Stroke panel, then choose options in the Line Style dialog box and click OK.

  Note: Choosing a stroke style other than Solid can increase file size.

4 To select a stroke weight, click the triangle next to the Weight pop-up menu and set the slider at the desired weight.

Working with solid, gradient, and bitmap fills in the Fill panel

To select a transparent or solid color fill, a gradient fill, or a bitmap fill, you can use the Fill panel. The Fill panel also allows you to create and edit gradient fills. You can apply bitmap fills using bitmaps that you have imported into the current file. For information on creating a bitmap fill, see "Breaking apart a bitmap" on page 163.

To apply a transparent fill using the Fill panel:

1 Choose Window > Panels > Fill.

2 Choose None from the Fill menu.

   Note: You can apply a transparent fill to a new object, but not to an existing object. Instead, select the existing fill and delete it.

To apply a solid color fill using the Fill panel:

1 Choose Window > Panels > Fill.

2 Choose Solid from the Fill menu.

3 Click the triangle next to the Fill color box and do one of the following:

• Drag to select a color from the palette.

• Type a color's hexadecimal value in the text box.

• Click the Color Picker button in the color pop-up window and choose a color from the Color Picker.

To apply, create, or edit a gradient fill using the Fill panel:

1 Choose Window > Panels > Fill.

2 Choose one of the following from the Fill menu:

- Linear Gradient creates a gradient that shades from the starting point to the ending point in a straight line

- Radial Gradient creates a gradient that shades from the starting point to the ending point in a circular pattern

Fill menu —
Gradient preview —
Pointer —
Pointer color
Gradient definition bar

3 Click the Fill color box in the toolbox and select a gradient from the palette.

4 To change a color in the selected gradient, click one of the pointers below the gradient definition bar and click on the color box that appears next to the gradient definition bar to select a color.

5 To add a pointer to the gradient, click below the gradient definition bar. Select a color for the new pointer as described in step 4.

6 To remove a pointer from the gradient, drag the pointer off of the gradient definition bar.

7 To save a gradient, click the triangle in the upper right corner of the Fill panel and choose Add Gradient from the pop-up menu. The gradient is added to the Swatches palette for the current document.

To apply a bitmap fill using the Fill panel:

1 Choose Window > Panels > Fill.

2 Choose Bitmap from the Fill menu.

Fill menu ——
Bitmap preview ——

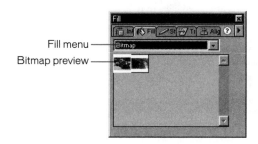

3 Click a bitmap in the Bitmap Fill window that appears in the Fill panel.

You can modify a bitmap fill using the Paint Bucket tool. See the next section.

Using the Paint Bucket tool

The Paint Bucket tool fills enclosed areas with color. It can both fill empty areas and change the color of already painted areas. You can paint with solid colors, gradient fills, and bitmap fills. You can use the Paint Bucket tool to fill areas that are not entirely enclosed, and you can specify that Flash close gaps in shape outlines when you use the Paint Bucket tool.

You can also use the Paint Bucket tool to adjust the size, direction, and center of gradient and bitmap fills. For information on creating a bitmap fill, see "Breaking apart a bitmap" on page 163.

Note: When you modify a bitmap fill with the Paint Bucket tool, all instances of the bitmap fill are modified, not just the fill in the current selection.

The left shape is not fully enclosed but can still be filled. The star shape consists of individual lines that enclose an area that can be filled.

To use the Paint Bucket tool to fill an area:

 1 Select the Paint Bucket tool.

2 Choose a fill color and style, as described in "Working with solid, gradient, and bitmap fills in the Fill panel" on page 139.

3 Click the Gap Size modifier and choose a gap size option:

• Choose Don't Close Gaps if you want to close gaps manually before filling the shape. Closing gaps manually can be faster for complex drawings.

• Choose a Close option to have Flash fill a shape that has gaps.

4 Click the shape or enclosed area that you want to fill.

Note: Zooming in or out changes the apparent, but not the actual, size of gaps. If gaps are too large, you may have to close them manually.

To adjust a gradient or bitmap fill with the Paint Bucket tool:

1 Select the Paint Bucket tool.

 2 Click the Transform Fill modifier.

3 Click an area filled with a gradient or bitmap fill.

When you select a gradient or bitmap fill for editing, its center point appears and its bounding box is displayed with editing handles. When the pointer is over any one of these handles, it changes to indicate the function of the handle.

Press Shift to constrain the direction of a linear gradient fill to multiples of 45°.

4 Reshape the gradient or fill in any of the following ways:

- To reposition the center point of the gradient or bitmap fill, drag the center point.

- To change the width of the gradient or bitmap fill, drag the square handle on the side of the bounding box. (This option resizes only the fill, not the object containing the fill.)

- To change the height of the gradient or bitmap fill, drag the square handle at the bottom of the bounding box.

- To rotate the gradient or bitmap fill, drag the circular rotation handle at the corner. You can also drag the lowest handle on the bounding circle of a circular gradient or fill.

- To scale a linear gradient or a fill, drag the square handle at the center of the bounding box.

- To change the radius of a circular gradient, drag the middle circular handle on the bounding circle.

- To skew or slant a fill within a shape, drag one of the circular handles on the top or right side of the bounding box.

- To tile a bitmap inside a shape, scale the fill.

Note: To see all of the handles when working with large fills or fills close to the edge of the Stage, choose View > Work Area.

Using the Ink Bottle tool

To change the stroke color, line width, and style of lines or shape outlines, you can use the Ink Bottle tool. You can apply only solid colors, not gradients or bitmaps, to lines or shape outlines.

Using the Ink Bottle tool, rather than selecting individual lines, makes it easier to change the stroke attributes of multiple objects at one time.

To use the Ink Bottle tool:

 1   Select the Ink Bottle tool.

2   Choose a stroke color as described in "Using the Stroke and Fill controls in the toolbox" on page 136.

3   Choose line style and line width from the Stroke panel. See "Specifying stroke color, style, and weight in the Stroke panel" on page 138.

4   Click an object on the Stage to apply the stroke modifications.

Using the Eyedropper tool

You can use the Eyedropper tool to copy fill and stroke attributes from one object and immediately apply them to another object. The Eyedropper tool also lets you sample the image in a bitmap to use as a fill. See "Breaking apart a bitmap" on page 163.

To use the Eyedropper tool to copy and apply stroke or fill attributes:

 1   Select the Eyedropper tool and click the stroke or filled area whose attributes you want to apply to another stroke or filled area.

When you click a stroke, the tool automatically changes to the Ink Bottle tool. When you click a filled area, the tool automatically changes to the Paint Bucket tool and the Lock Fill modifier is turned on. See "Locking a gradient or bitmap to fill the Stage" on page 146.

2   Click another stroke or filled area to apply the new attributes.

Locking a gradient or bitmap to fill the Stage

You can lock a gradient or bitmap fill to make it appear that the fill extends over the entire Stage and that the objects painted with the fill are masks revealing the underlying gradient or bitmap.

When you select the Lock Fill modifier with the Brush or Paint Bucket tool and paint with the tool, the bitmap or gradient fill extends across the objects you paint on the Stage.

Using the Lock Fill modifier creates the appearance of a single gradient or bitmap fill being applied to separate objects on the Stage.

To use a locked gradient or bitmap fill:

1 Select the Brush or Paint Bucket tool and choose a gradient or bitmap as a fill.

To use a bitmap as a fill, break the bitmap apart and use the Eyedropper tool to select the bitmap before selecting the Brush or Paint Bucket tool. See "Breaking apart a bitmap" on page 163.

2 Click the Lock Fill modifier.

3 First paint the areas where you want to place the center of the fill, and then move to other areas.

Creating and editing solid colors with the Mixer panel

To create and edit solid colors, you can use the Mixer panel. If an object is selected on the Stage, the color modifications you make in the Mixer panel are applied to the selection.

You can select a color from the existing color palette or create a new color. You can choose colors in RGB or hexadecimal mode, or specify Alpha value to define the degree of transparency for a color.

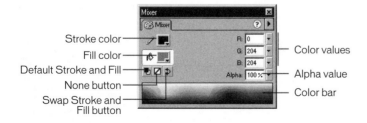

To create or edit a solid color with the Mixer panel:

1   Choose Window > Panels > Mixer.

2   To select a color mode display, choose RGB (the default setting), HSB, or Hex from the pop-up menu in the upper right corner of the Mixer panel.

3   Click the Stroke or Fill color box to specify which attribute is to be modified.

If you have selected an object with a gradient fill, the Fill color box displays the gradient. To replace the gradient in the selection with a solid color, click the Fill color box and select a solid color fill as described in step 4.

If you are currently editing a gradient fill with the Fill panel, the Mixer panel displays a color proxy box and color bulb with the currently selected color from the Fill gradient editor. To end the gradient editing session, click the color bulb in the Mixer panel.

4   Do one of the following:

•   Click the Stroke or Fill color box and choose a color from the pop-up window.

•   Click in the color bar at the bottom of the Mixer panel to select a color.

•   Enter values in the color value boxes: Red, Green, and Blue values for RGB display; Hue, Saturation, and Brightness values for HSB display; or hexadecimal values for hexadecimal display. Enter an Alpha value to specify the degree of transparency, from 0 for complete transparency to 100 for complete opacity.

•   Click the Default Stoke and Fill button to return to the default color settings (white fill and black stroke).

•   Click the Swap Stoke and Fill button to swap colors between the fill and the stroke.

•   Click the None button to apply a transparent fill or stroke.

    Note: You can apply a transparent stroke or fill to a new object but not to an existing object. Instead, select the existing stroke or fill and delete it.

5   To add the color defined in step 4 to the color swatch list for the current file, choose Add Swatch from the pop-up menu in the upper right corner of the Mixer panel.

Modifying color palettes

Each Flash file contains its own color palette, stored in the Flash file. Flash displays a file's palette as swatches in the modifiers for fill, stroke, and type color, and in the Swatches panel. The default color palette is the Web-safe palette of 216 colors. You can add colors to the current color palette using the Mixer panel. See "Creating and editing solid colors with the Mixer panel" on page 146.

To import, export, and modify a file's color palette, you use the Swatches panel. You can duplicate colors, remove colors from the palette, change the default palette, reload the Web-safe palette if you have replaced it, or sort the palette according to hue.

You can import and export both solid and gradient color palettes between Flash files, as well as between Flash and other applications, such as Macromedia Fireworks and Adobe Photoshop.

Duplicating or removing colors from the palette

You can duplicate or delete individual colors, or clear all colors from the palette.

To duplicate a color or delete a color from the color palette:

1   Choose Window > Panels > Swatches.

2   Click the color that you want to duplicate or delete.

3   Choose Duplicate Swatch or Delete Swatch from the pop-up menu in the upper right corner.

To clear all colors from the color palette:

In the Swatches panel, choose Clear Colors from the pop-up menu in the upper right corner. All colors are removed from the palette except black and white.

Using the default palette and the Web-safe palette

You can save the current palette as the default palette, replace the current palette with the default palette defined for the file, or load the Web-safe palette to replace the current palette.

To load or save the default palette:

In the Swatches panel, choose one of the following commands from the pop-up menu in the upper right corner.

- Load Default Colors replaces the current palette with the default palette.

- Save as Default saves the current color palette as the default palette. The new default palette is used when you create new files.

To load the Web-safe 216 color palette:

In the Swatches panel, choose Web 216 from the pop-up menu in the upper right corner.

Sorting the palette

To make it easier to locate a color, you can sort colors in the palette by hue.

To sort colors in the palette:

In the Swatches panel, choose Sort by Color from the pop-up menu in the upper right corner.

Importing and exporting color palettes

To import and export both RGB colors and gradients between Flash files, you use Flash Color Set files (CLR files). You can import and export RGB color palettes using Color Table files (ACT files) that can be used with Macromedia Fireworks and Adobe Photoshop. You can also import color palettes, but not gradients, from GIF files. You cannot import or export gradients from ACT files.

To import a color palette:

1 In the Swatches panel, choose one of the following commands from the pop-up menu in the upper right corner:

• To append the imported colors to the current palette, choose Add Colors.

• To replace the current palette with the imported colors, choose Replace Colors.

2 Navigate to the desired file and select it.

3 Click OK.

To export a color palette:

1 In the Swatches panel, choose Save Colors from the pop-up menu in the upper right corner.

2 In the dialog box that appears, enter a name for the color palette.

3 For Save As Type (Windows) or Format (Macintosh), choose Flash Color Set or Color Table. Click Save.

CHAPTER 5
Using Imported Artwork

Your Flash movie can use artwork created in other applications. You can import vector graphics and bitmaps in a variety of file formats. If you have QuickTime 4 or later installed on your system, you can import additional file formats. For more information, see "Import file formats" on page 154.

You can import FreeHand files (versions 7 or later) and Fireworks PNG files directly into Flash, preserving attributes from those formats.

To import sound files in WAV (Windows), AIFF (Macintosh), and MP3 (both platforms) formats, see "Importing Sounds" on page 168.

Placing artwork into Flash

Flash recognizes a variety of vector and bitmap formats. You can place artwork into Flash by importing or pasting. Flash imports vector graphics, bitmaps, and sequences of images as follows:

- Vector images from FreeHand are imported directly into a Flash movie. You can choose options for preserving FreeHand layers, pages, and text blocks. To import a FreeHand file, see "Importing FreeHand files" on page 157.

- PNG images from Fireworks can be imported directly into a Flash movie with vector and bitmap data preserved as editable objects. You can choose options for preserving images, text and guides. To import a Fireworks PNG file, see "Importing Fireworks PNG files" on page 156.

  Note: If you import a PNG file from Fireworks by cutting and pasting, the file is converted to a bitmap.

- Vector images from SWF, Adobe Illustrator, and Windows Metafile Format (WMF) files are imported as a group in the current layer. See "Import file formats" on page 154 and "Adobe Illustrator files" on page 159.

- Bitmaps (scanned photographs, BMP files) are imported as single objects in the current layer. Flash preserves the transparency settings of imported bitmaps. Because importing a bitmap can increase a movie's file size, you may want to compress imported bitmaps. See "Setting bitmap properties" on page 165.

  Note: Bitmap transparency may not be preserved when bitmaps are imported by dragging and dropping. To preserve transparency, use the File › Import command for importing.

- Any sequence of images (for example, a PICT and BMP sequence) is imported as successive frames of the current layer.

For information on specific file formats, see "Import file formats" on page 154.

To import a file into Flash:

1 Choose File > Import.

2 In the Import dialog box, choose a file format from the Show pop-up menu.

3 Navigate to the desired file and select it.

If an imported file has multiple layers, Flash might create new layers. Be sure the Timeline is visible when importing a file with multiple layers.

Note: If you are importing a Fireworks PNG file, see "Importing Fireworks PNG files" on page 156. If you are importing a FreeHand file,see "Importing FreeHand files" on page 157.

4 Do one of the following:

• In Windows, click Open.

• On a Macintosh, click Add to add the selected file to the Import list, and click Import to import the file or files in the Import list.

5 If the name of the file you are importing ends with a number, and there are additional sequentially numbered files in the same folder, Flash asks you whether to import the sequence of files:

• Click Yes to import all of the sequential files.

• Click No to import only the specified file.

The following are examples of file names that can be used as a sequence:

```
Frame001.gif, Frame002.gif, Frame003.gif
Bird 1, Bird 2, Bird 3
Walk-001.ai, Walk-002.ai, Walk-003.ai
```

To paste a bitmap from another application into Flash:

1 Copy the image in the other application.

2 In Flash, choose Edit > Paste.

Import file formats

Flash 5 can import different file formats depending on whether QuickTime 4 or later is installed. Using Flash with QuickTime 4 installed is especially useful for collaborative projects in which authors work on both Windows and Macintosh platforms. QuickTime 4 extends support for certain file formats (including Adobe Photoshop, PICT, QuickTime Movie, and others) to both platforms.

The following file formats can be imported into Flash 5, regardless of whether QuickTime 4 is installed:

File type	Extension	Windows	Macintosh
Adobe Illustrator (version 6.0 or earlier; see "Adobe Illustrator files" on page 159)	.eps, .ai	✔	✔
AutoCAD DXF (see "AutoCAD DXF files" on page 161)	.dxf	✔	✔
Bitmap	.bmp	✔	
Enhanced Windows Metafile	.emf	✔	
FreeHand	.fh7, .ft7, .fh8, .ft8, .fh9, .ft9	✔	✔
FutureSplash Player	.spl	✔	✔
GIF and animated GIF	.gif	✔	✔
JPEG	.jpg	✔	✔
PICT	.pct, .pic		✔
PNG	.png	✔	✔
Flash Player	.swf	✔	✔
Windows Metafile	.wmf	✔	

The following file formats can be imported into Flash 5 only if QuickTime 4 or later is installed:

File type	Extension	Windows	Macintosh
MacPaint	.pntg	✔	✔
Photoshop	.psd	✔	✔
PICT	.pct, .pic	✔ (As bitmap)	
QuickTime Image	.qtif	✔	✔
QuickTime Movie	.mov	✔	✔
Silicon Graphics	.sai	✔	✔
TGA	.tgf	✔	✔
TIFF	.tiff	✔	✔

Importing Fireworks PNG files

You can import Fireworks PNG files into Flash as flattened images or as editable objects. When you import a PNG file as a flattened image, the entire file (including any vector artwork) is *rasterized*, or converted to a bitmap image. When you import a PNG file as editable objects, vector artwork in the file is preserved in vector format. You can choose to preserve placed bitmaps, text, and guides in the PNG file when you import it as editable objects.

If you import the PNG file as a flattened image, you can launch Fireworks from within Flash and edit the original PNG file (with vector data). See "Editing bitmaps" on page 164.

Note: You can edit bitmap images in Flash by convert the bitmap images to vector artwork or by breaking apart the bitmap images. See "Converting bitmaps to vector graphics" on page 161 and "Breaking apart a bitmap" on page 163.

To import a Fireworks PNG file:

1   Choose File > Import.

2   In the Import dialog box, choose PNG Image from the Show pop-up menu.

3   Navigate to a Fireworks PNG image and select it.

4   Do one of the following:

- Click Open (Windows).

- Click Add (Macintosh) to add the selected file to the Import list and click Import to import the file or files in the Import list.

5   In the PNG Import Settings dialog box, select one of the following:

- Import Editable Elements imports the PNG file as separate elements, preserving vector artwork. Select Include Images to preserve bitmap images in the imported file. (Bitmap images are placed in the library for the current movie, but they cannot be edited with an external image editor.) Select Include Text to preserve text as editable text blocks. Select Include Guides to import Fireworks guides as draggable guides.

- Flatten Image imports the PNG file as a bitmap image in the current layer. The bitmap is placed in the library for the current movie, and can be edited with Fireworks or another external image editor. See "Editing bitmaps" on page 164.

6   Click OK.

Importing FreeHand files

You can import FreeHand files (version 7 or later) directly into Flash. FreeHand is the best choice for creating vector graphics for import into Flash, because you can preserve FreeHand layers, text blocks, library symbols, and pages, and choose a page range to import. If the imported FreeHand file is in CMYK color mode, Flash converts the file to RGB.

Keep the following guidelines in mind when importing FreeHand files:

- When importing a file with overlapping objects that you want to preserve as separate objects, place the objects on separate layers in FreeHand, and choose Layers in the FreeHand Import dialog box in Flash when importing the file. (If overlapping objects on a single layer are imported into Flash, the overlapping shapes will be divided at intersection points, just as with overlapping objects that you create in Flash.)

- When you import files with gradient fills, Flash can support up to eight colors in a gradient fill. If a FreeHand file contains a gradient fill with more than eight colors, Flash creates clipping paths to simulate the appearance of a gradient fill. Clipping paths can increase file size. To minimize file size, use gradient fills with eight colors or fewer in FreeHand.

- When you import files with blends, Flash imports each step in a blend as a separate path. Thus, the more steps a blend has in a FreeHand file, the larger the imported file size will be in Flash.

- When you import files with strokes that have square caps, Flash converts the caps to round caps.

- When you import files with placed grayscale images, Flash converts the grayscale images to RGB images. This conversion can increase the imported file's size.

- When importing files with placed EPS images, you must first select the Convert Editable EPS when Imported option in FreeHand Import Preferences before you place the EPS into FreeHand. If you do not select this option, the EPS image will not be viewable when imported into Flash. In addition, Flash does not display information for an imported EPS image (regardless of the Preferences settings used in FreeHand).

To import a FreeHand file:

1 Choose File > Import.

2 In the Import dialog box, choose FreeHand from the Show pop-up menu.

3 Navigate to a FreeHand file and select it.

4 Do one of the following:

- In Windows, click Open.

- On the Macintosh, click Add to add the selected file to the Import list, and click Import to import the file or files in the Import list.

5 In the FreeHand Import Settings dialog box, for Mapping Pages, choose a setting:

- Scenes converts each page in the FreeHand document to a scene in the Flash movie.

- Keyframes converts each page in the FreeHand document to a keyframe in the Flash movie.

6 For Layers, select one of the following:

- Layers converts each layer in the FreeHand document to a layer in the Flash movie.

- Keyframes converts each layer in the FreeHand document to a keyframe in the Flash movie.

- Flatten converts all layers in the FreeHand document to a single flattened layer in the Flash movie.

7 For Pages, choose one of the following:

- All imports all pages from the FreeHand document.

- From (page number) To (page number) a page range to import from the FreeHand document.

8 For Options, choose any of the following options:

- Include Visible Layers imports only visible layers (not hidden layers) from the FreeHand document.

- Include Background Layer imports the background layer with the FreeHand document.

- Maintain Text Blocks preserves text in the FreeHand document as editable text in the Flash movie.

9 Click OK.

Adobe Illustrator files

Flash supports importing and exporting Adobe Illustrator 88, 3.0, 5.0, and 6.0 formats. (For information on exporting Illustrator files, see "Adobe Illustrator" on page 341.)

When you import an Illustrator file into Flash, you must ungroup all the Illustrator objects on all layers. Once all the objects are ungrouped, they can be manipulated like any other Flash object.

About imported bitmap images

Importing bitmap images into a movie can increase the movie's file size. To reduce the file size of a bitmap image, you can choose a compression option in the Bitmap Properties dialog box. See "Setting bitmap properties" on page 165.

You can edit an imported bitmap by launching Fireworks or another external image editor from within Flash.

You can trace a bitmap to convert its image to a vector graphic. Performing this conversion enables you to modify the graphic as you do other vector artwork in Flash, and it also reduces file size. See "Converting bitmaps to vector graphics" on page 161.

You can break apart a bitmap into editable areas. The bitmap retains its original detail but is broken into discrete areas of color that you can select and modify separately with the Flash drawing and painting tools. Breaking apart a bitmap also lets you use a bitmap as a fill to paint objects. See "Breaking apart a bitmap" on page 163.

If a Flash movie displays an imported bitmap at a larger size than the original, the image may be distorted. Preview imported bitmaps to be sure that images display properly.

Using QuickTime movies

If you have QuickTime 4 or later installed on your system, you can import a QuickTime movie into Flash in order to modify the movie. However, in order to display the QuickTime movie, you must export it in QuickTime format. You cannot display a QuickTime movie in SWF format. For more information on publishing your Flash file as a QuickTime movie, see "Publishing QuickTime 4 movies" on page 336.

You can scale, rotate, and animate a QuickTime movie in Flash, and you can play and set the directory path of the movie in the library. However, you cannot tween QuickTime movie content in Flash. You can apply any of the actions listed in the Basic Actions category in the Actions panel to an imported QuickTime movie.

When you import a QuickTime movie, only the first frame of the movie is displayed. You must add frames to the imported movie's Timeline in order to view additional frames in the movie in Flash. A QuickTime movie imported into Flash does not become part of the Flash file. Instead, Flash maintains a pointer to the source file.

To preview a QuickTime movie:

1   Add the number of frames to the Timeline that correspond to the length of the QuickTime movie you want to play.

2   Choose Control > Play.

Note: You cannot preview QuickTime movie content using the Control > Test Movie command.

To set the directory path of a QuickTime movie file:

1   Choose Window > Library and select the QuickTime movie you want to edit.

2   In the Options menu in the upper right corner of the Library window, choose Properties and click Set Path in the Video Properties dialog box.

AutoCAD DXF files

Flash supports the AutoCAD DXF format in the release 10 version.

DXF files do not support the standard system fonts. Flash tries to map fonts appropriately, but the results can be unpredictable, particularly for the alignment of text.

Since the DXF format does not support solid fills, filled areas are exported as outlines only. For this reason, the DXF format is most appropriate for line drawings, such as floor plans and maps.

You can import two-dimensional DXF files into Flash. Flash does not support three-dimensional DXF files.

Although Flash doesn't support scaling in a DXF file, all imported DXF files produce 12-by-12-inch movies that you can scale with Modify > Transform > Scale. Also, Flash supports only ASCII DXF files. If your DXF files are binary, you must convert them to ASCII before importing them into Flash.

Converting bitmaps to vector graphics

The Trace Bitmap command converts a bitmap into a vector graphic with editable, discrete areas of color. Use this command to manipulate the image as a vector graphic, or to reduce file size.

If you convert a bitmap to a vector graphic, the vector graphic is no longer linked to the bitmap symbol in the Library window.

Note: If the imported bitmap contains complex shapes and many colors, the converted vector graphic can have a larger file size than the original bitmap. Try a variety of settings in the Trace Bitmap dialog box to find a balance between file size and image quality.

You can also break apart a bitmap to modify the image using Flash drawing and painting tools or to paint with the bitmap as a fill. See "Breaking apart a bitmap" on page 163.

To convert a bitmap to a vector graphic:

1 Select a bitmap in the current scene.

2 Choose Modify > Trace Bitmap.

3 Enter a Color Threshold value between 1 and 500.

When two pixels are compared, if the difference in the RGB color values is less than the color threshold, the two pixels are considered the same color. As you increase the threshold value, you decrease the number of colors.

4 For Minimum Area, enter a value between 1 and 1000 to set the number of surrounding pixels to consider when assigning a color to a pixel.

5 For Curve Fit, select an option from the pop-up menu to determine how smoothly outlines are drawn.

6 For Corner Threshold, select an option from the pop-up menu to determine whether sharp edges are retained or smoothed out.

To create a vector graphic that looks most like the original bitmap, enter the following values:

• Color Threshold: 10

• Minimum Area: 1 pixel

• Curve Fit: Pixels

• Corner Threshold: Many Corners

The results of using the Trace Bitmap command

Breaking apart a bitmap

Breaking apart a bitmap separates the pixels in the image into discrete areas that can be selected and modified separately. When you break apart a bitmap, you can modify the bitmap with the Flash drawing and painting tools. You can also paint with the bitmap as a fill.

Using the Lasso tool with the Magic Wand modifier, you can change the fill of selected areas of a bitmap that has been broken apart.

After you paint an area with a bitmap, you can use the Paint Bucket tool to rotate, skew, or scale the bitmap image. See "Using the Paint Bucket tool" on page 142.

To break apart a bitmap:

1 Select a bitmap in the current scene.

2 Choose Modify > Break Apart.

To paint with a bitmap's image:

1 Break apart the bitmap, as described above.

2 Select the Eyedropper tool and then click the bitmap.

   The Eyedropper tool sets the bitmap to be the current fill and changes the active tool to the Paint Bucket.

3 Paint with the Brush or Paint Bucket tool.

To change the fill of selected areas of a broken-apart bitmap:

1 Select a broken-apart bitmap in the scene.

 2 Select the Lasso tool and click the Magic Wand modifier.

3 Click the Magic Wand Settings modifier and set the following options:

- For Threshold, enter a value between 1 and 200 to define how closely the color of adjacent pixels must match to be included in the selection. A higher number includes a broader range of colors. If you enter 0, only pixels of the exact same color as the first pixel you click are selected.

- For Smoothing, select an option from the pop-up menu to define how much the edges of the bitmap will be smoothed.

4 Click the bitmap to select an area. Continue clicking to add to the selection.

5 Select a fill that you want to use to fill the selected areas in the bitmap. See "Specifying stroke and fill attributes" on page 136.

6 Select the Paint Bucket tool and click anywhere on the selected areas to add the new fill.

Editing bitmaps

If you have Fireworks 3 or later or another image-editing application installed on your system, you can launch the application from within Flash to edit an imported bitmap.

If you are editing a Fireworks PNG file imported as a flattened image, you can choose to edit the PNG source file for the bitmap, when available.

Note: You cannot edit bitmaps from Fireworks PNG files imported as editable objects in an external image editor.

To edit a bitmap with Fireworks 3 or later:

1 In the Library window, right-click (Windows) or Control-click (Macintosh) the bitmap's icon.

2 In the bitmap's context menu, select Edit with Fireworks 3.

3 In the Edit Image dialog box, specify whether the PNG source file or the bitmap file is to be opened.

4 Perform the desired modifications to the file in Fireworks.

5 Select File > Update.

   The file is automatically updated in Flash.

To edit a bitmap with another external editing application:

1 In the Library window, right-click (Windows) or Control-click (Macintosh) the bitmap's icon.

2 In the bitmap's context menu, select Edit With.

3 Choose an image-editing application to open the bitmap file, and click OK.

4 Perform the desired modifications to the file in the image-editing application.

5 In Flash, do one of the following:

• Select the bitmap's icon in the Library window and choose Update from the Library Options menu.

• Right-click (Windows) or Control-click (Macintosh) the bitmap's icon in the Library window and choose Update from the context menu.

   The file is automatically updated in Flash.

Setting bitmap properties

You can apply anti-aliasing to a bitmap to smooth the edges in the image. You can also select a compression option to reduce the bitmap file size and format the file for display on the Web.

To select bitmap properties, you use the Bitmap Properties dialog box.

Bitmap library item name

Bitmap preview

Bitmap size

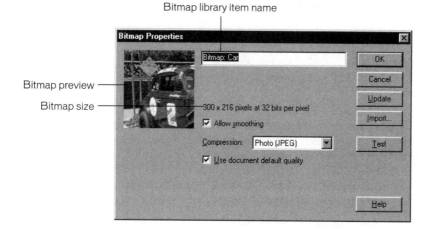

To set bitmap properties:

1 Select a bitmap in the Library window.

2 Do one of the following:

• Click the properties icon at the bottom of the Library window.

• Right-click (Windows) or Control-click (Macintosh) the bitmap's icon and choose Properties from the context menu.

• Choose Properties from the Options menu in the upper right corner of the Library window.

3 In the Bitmap Properties dialog box, select Allow Smoothing to smooth the edges of the bitmap with anti-aliasing.

4 For Compression, choose one of the following options:

• Choose Photo (JPEG) to compress the image in JPEG format. To use the default compression quality specified for the imported image, select Use Document Default Quality. To specify a new quality compression setting, deselect Use Document Default Quality and enter a value between 1 and 100 in the Quality text box. (A higher setting preserves greater image integrity but yields a smaller reduction in file size.)

• Choose Lossless (PNG/GIF) to compress the image with lossless compression, in which no data is discarded from the image.

Note: Use Photo compression for images with complex color or tonal variations, such as photographs or images with gradient fills. Use Lossless compression for images with simple shapes and relatively few colors.

5 Click Test to determine the results of the file compression. Compare the original file size to the compressed file size to determine if the selected compression setting is acceptable.

6 Click OK.

Note: JPEG Quality settings that you select in the Publish Settings dialog box do not specify a quality setting for imported JPEG files. You must specify a quality setting for imported JPEG files in the Bitmap Properties dialog box.

CHAPTER 6
Adding Sound

Flash offers a number of ways to use sounds. You can make sounds that play continuously, independent of the Timeline, or you can synchronize animation to a sound track. You can attach sounds to buttons to make them more interactive, and make sounds fade in and out for a more polished sound track.

You can use sounds in shared libraries, to link a sound from one library to multiple movies. You can also use sounds in Sound objects, to control sound playback with ActionScript.

There are two types of sounds in Flash: event sounds and stream sounds. An event sound must download completely before it begins playing, and it continues playing until explicitly stopped. Stream sounds begin playing as soon as enough data for the first few frames has been downloaded; stream sounds are synchronized to the Timeline for playing on a Web site.

You select compression options to control the quality and size of sounds in exported movies. You can select compression options for individual sounds with the Sound Properties dialog box, or define settings for all sounds in the movie in the Publish Settings dialog box.

For an interactive introduction to using sound in Flash, choose Help > Lessons > Sound.

Importing Sounds

You use the File > Import command to bring WAV (Windows only), AIFF (Macintosh only), or MP3 (either platform) sounds into Flash, just as you would import any other file type.

If you have QuickTime 4 or later installed on your system, you can import these additional sound file formats:

- Sound Designer II (Macintosh only)
- Sound Only QuickTime Movies (Windows or Macintosh)
- Sun AU (Windows or Macintosh)
- System 7 Sounds (Macintosh only)
- WAV (Windows or Macintosh)

Flash stores sounds in the library along with bitmaps and symbols. As with graphic symbols, you need only one copy of a sound file to use that sound in any number of ways in your movie. If you want to share sounds among Flash movies, you can include sounds in shared libraries. See "Using shared libraries" on page 95.

To use a sound in a shared library, you assign the sound file an identifier string in the Symbol Linkage Properties dialog box. The identifier can also be used to access the sound as an object in ActionScript. For information on objects in ActionScript, see the *ActionScript Reference Guide.*

Sounds can use considerable amounts of disk space and RAM. MP3 sound data, however, is compressed and smaller than WAV or AIFF sound data. Generally, when using WAV or AIFF files, it's best to use 16-bit 22 kHz mono sounds (stereo uses twice as much data as mono), but Flash can import either 8- or 16-bit sounds at sample rates of 11 kHz, 22 kHz, or 44 kHz. Flash can convert sounds to lower sample rates on export. See "Compressing sounds for export" on page 175.

Note: Sounds recorded in formats that are not multiples of 11 kHz (such as 8, 32, or 96 kHz) are resampled when imported into Flash.

If you want to add effects to sounds in Flash, it's best to import 16-bit sounds. If you have limited RAM, keep your sound clips short or work with 8-bit sounds instead of 16-bit sounds.

To import a sound:

1 Choose File > Import.

2 In the Import dialog box, locate and open the desired sound file.

   The imported sound is placed in the library for the current movie.

Note: You can also drag a sound from a common library into the library for the current movie. See "Working with common libraries" on page 94.

Adding sounds to a movie

To add sound to a movie, you assign a sound to a layer and set options in the Sound panel. It is recommended that you place each sound on a separate layer.

To add a sound to a movie:

1 Import the sound if it has not already been imported. See "Importing Sounds" on page 168.

2 Choose Insert > Layer to create a layer for the sound.

3 With the new sound layer selected, drag the sound from the library onto the Stage. The sound is added to the current layer.

You can place multiple sounds on one layer, or on layers containing other objects. However, it is recommended that each sound be placed on a separate layer. Each layer acts like a separate sound channel. The sounds on all layers are combined when you play back the movie.

4 Choose Window > Panels > Sound.

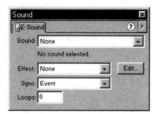

5 In the Sound panel, choose a sound file from the Sound pop-up menu.

6 Choose an effect option from the Effects pop-up menu:

• None applies no effects to the sound file. Choose this option to remove previously applied effects.

• Left Channel/Right Channel plays sound in the left or right channel only.

• Fade Left to Right/Fade Right to Left shifts the sound from one channel to the other.

• Fade In gradually increases the amplitude of a sound over its duration.

• Fade Out gradually decreases the amplitude of a sound over its duration.

• Custom lets you create your own In and Out points of sound using the Edit Envelope. See "Using the sound-editing controls" on page 172.

7 Choose a synchronization option from the Sync pop-up menu:

• Event synchronizes the sound to the occurrence of an event. An event sound plays when its starting keyframe is first displayed and plays in its entirety, independently of the Timeline, even if the movie stops. Event sounds are mixed when you play your published movie.

An example of an event sound is a sound that plays when a user clicks a button.

• Start is the same as Event, except that if the sound is already playing, a new instance of the sound is started.

• Stop silences the specified sound.

• Stream synchronizes the sound for playing on a Web site. Flash forces animation to keep pace with stream sounds. If Flash can't draw animation frames quickly enough, it skips frames. Unlike event sounds, stream sounds stop if the animation stops. Also, a stream sound can never play longer than the length of the frames it occupies. Stream sounds are mixed when you publish your movie.

An example of a stream sound is the voice of a character in an animation that plays in multiple frames.

Note: If you use an MP3 sound as a stream sound, you must recompress the sound for export. See "Compressing sounds for export" on page 175.

8 Enter a value for Loop to specify the number of times the sound should loop.

For continuous play, enter a number large enough to play the sound for an extended duration. For example, to loop a 15-second sound for 15 minutes, enter 60.

Note: Looping stream sounds is not recommended. If a stream sound is set to loop, frames are added to the movie and the file size is increased by the number of times the sound is looped.

Adding sounds to buttons

You can associate sounds with the different states of a button symbol. Because the sounds are stored with the symbol, they work for all instances of the symbol.

To add sound to a button:

1 Select the button in the library.

2 Choose Edit from the Library Options menu.

3 In the button's Timeline, add a layer for sound.

4 In the sound layer, create a regular or blank keyframe to correspond to the button state to which you want to add a sound.

   For example, to add a sound that plays when the button is clicked, create a keyframe in the frame labeled Down.

5 Click the keyframe you have just created.

6 Choose Window > Panels > Sound.

7 In the Sound panel, choose a sound file from the Sound pop-up menu.

8 Choose Event from the Synchronization pop-up menu.

   To associate a different sound with each of the button's keyframes, create a blank keyframe and add another sound file for each keyframe. You can also use the same sound file and apply a different sound effect for each button keyframe. See "Using the sound-editing controls" on page 172.

Using sounds with shared libraries or with Sound objects

You can link a sound from one library to multiple Flash movies by assigning linkage properties to the sound and including the sound in a shared library. For more information on using shared libraries, see "Using shared libraries" on page 95.

You can use the Sound object in ActionScript to add sounds to a movie and to control sounds in a movie. Controlling sounds includes adjusting the volume or the right and left balance while a sound is playing. See "Creating sound controls" in the interaction chapter of the *ActionScript Reference Guide*.

To use a sound in a shared library or a Sound action, you assign an identifier string to the sound in the Symbol Linkage dialog box.

To assign an identifier string to a sound:

1 Select the sound in the Library window.

2 Do one of the following:

• Choose Linkage from the Library Options menu.

• Right-click (Windows) or Control-click (Macintosh) the sound name in the Library window, and choose Linkage from the context menu.

3 Under Linkage in the Symbol Linkage Properties dialog box, select Export This Symbol.

4 Enter an identifier string in the text box, and then click OK.

Using the sound-editing controls

To define the starting point of a sound or to control the volume of the sound as it plays, you use the sound-editing controls in the Sound panel.

Flash can change the point at which a sound starts and stops playing. This is useful for making sound files smaller by removing unused sections.

To edit a sound file:

1   Add a sound to a frame (see "Adding sounds to a movie" on page 169), or select a frame already containing a sound.

2   Choose Window > Panels > Sound, and click Edit.

3   Do any of the following:

•   To change the start and end points of a sound, drag the Time In and Time Out controls in the Sound panel.

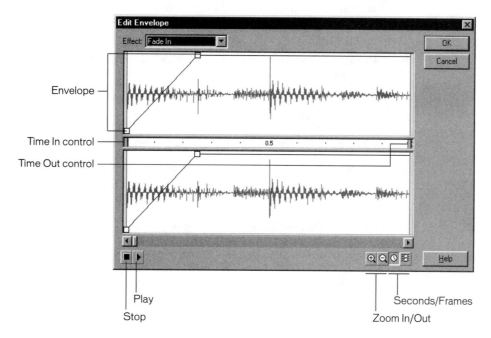

•   To change the sound envelope, drag the envelope handles to change levels at different points in the sound. Envelope lines show the volume of the sound as it plays. To create additional envelope handles (up to eight total), click the envelope lines. To remove an envelope handle, drag it out of the window.

•   To display more or less of the sound in the window, click the Zoom In/Out buttons.

•   To switch the time units between seconds and frames, click the Seconds and Frames buttons.

Starting and stopping sounds at keyframes

The most common sound-related task in Flash is starting and stopping sounds at keyframes in synchronization with animation.

To stop and start a sound at a keyframe:

1 Add a sound to a movie.

   To synchronize this sound with an event in the scene, choose a beginning keyframe that corresponds to the keyframe of the event in the scene. You can choose any of the synchronization options. See "Adding sounds to a movie" on page 169.

2 Create a keyframe in the sound layer's Timeline at the frame where you want the sound to end.

   A representation of the sound file appears in the Timeline.

3 Choose Window > Panels > Sound.

4 Choose the same sound from the Sound pop-up menu.

5 Choose Stop from the Synchronization pop-up menu.

   When you play the movie, the sound stops playing when it reaches the ending keyframe.

To play back the sound, simply move the playhead.

Compressing sounds for export

To choose sound compression options, you use the options in the Export Settings area of the Sound Properties dialog box. The options available depend on the compression method you select. You can also use the Sound Properties dialog box to update sounds that you have modified in an external sound editor, or to test the sound.

The sampling rate and degree of compression make a significant difference in the quality and size of sounds in exported movies. The more you compress a sound and the lower the sampling rate, the smaller the size and the lower the quality. You should experiment to find the optimal balance between sound quality and file size.

MP3 sound files are already compressed when imported. However, you can recompress MP3 files for export if needed. For example, if the MP3 file is to be used as a stream sound, you must recompress the file, because stream sounds must be compressed for export.

If there are no export settings defined for a sound, Flash exports the sound using the sound settings in the Publish Settings dialog box. You can override the export settings specified in the Sound Properties dialog box by selecting Override Sound Settings in the Publish Settings dialog box. This option is useful if you want to create a larger high-fidelity audio movie for local use, and a smaller low-fidelity version for the Web. (See "Publishing a Flash Player movie" on page 322.)

Note: In Windows, you can also export all the sounds from a movie as a WAV file using File > Export Movie. See "Exporting movies and images" on page 339.

To set export properties for an individual sound:

1 Do one of the following:

- Double-click the sound's icon in the Library window.

- Right-click (Windows) or Control-click (Macintosh) a sound file in the Library window and choose Properties from the context menu.

- Select a sound in the Library window and choose Properties from the Library Options menu.

- Select a sound in the Library window and click the properties icon at the bottom of the Library window.

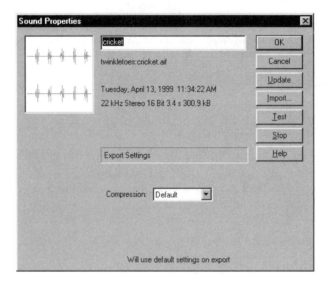

2 If the sound file has been edited externally, click Update.

3 For Compression, choose Default, ADPCM, MP3, or Raw. To select options for the compression format you choose, see the section below corresponding to the selected format.

4 Set export settings.

5 Click Test to play and stop the sound, and click Stop to stop the sound.

6 Adjust export settings if necessary until the desired sound quality is achieved.

7 Click OK.

The Default compression option

The Default compression option uses the default compression settings in the Publish Settings dialog box when you export your movie. If you select Default, no additional export settings are available.

Using the ADPCM compression option

The ADPCM compression option sets compression for 8-bit or 16-bit sound data. Use the ADPCM setting when you are exporting short event sounds such as button clicks.

To use ADPCM compression:

1   In the Sound Properties dialog box, choose ADPCM from the Compression menu.

2   For Preprocessing, select Convert Stereo to Mono to convert mixed stereo sounds to mono (monaural). (Mono sounds are unaffected by this option.)

3   For Sample Rate, select an option to control sound fidelity and file size. Lower rates decrease file size but can also degrade sound quality. Rate options are as follows:

- 5 kHz is barely acceptable for speech.

- 11 kHz is the lowest recommended quality for a short segment of music and is one-quarter of the standard CD rate.

- 22 kHz is a popular choice for Web playback and is half the standard CD rate.

- 44 kHz is the standard CD audio rate.

Note: Flash cannot increase the kHz rate of an imported sound above the rate at which it was imported.

Using the MP3 compression option

The MP3 compression option lets you export sounds with MP3 compression. Use MP3 when you are exporting longer stream sounds such as music sound tracks.

To use MP3 compression:

1 In the Sound Properties dialog box, choose MP3 from the Compression menu.

2 For Bit Rate, select an option to determine the maximum bit rate of the sound produced by the MP3 encoder. Flash supports 8 kbps through 160 kbps CBR (constant bit rate). When you are exporting music, set the bit rate to 16 Kbps or higher for the best results.

3 For Preprocessing, select Convert Stereo to Mono to convert mixed stereo sounds to mono (monaural). (Mono sounds are unaffected by this option.)

Note: The Preprocessing option is available only if you select a bit rate of 20 Kbps or higher.

4 For Quality, select an option to determine the compression speed and sound quality:

• Fast yields faster compression but lower sound quality.

• Medium yields somewhat slower compression but higher sound quality.

• Slow yields the slowest compression and the highest sound quality.

Using the Raw compression option

The Raw compression option exports sounds with no sound compression.

To use raw compression:

1 In the Sound Properties dialog box, choose Raw from the Compression menu.

2 For Preprocessing, select Convert Stereo to Mono to convert mixed stereo sounds to mono (monaural). (Mono sounds are unaffected by this option.)

3 For Sample Rate, select an option to control sound fidelity and file size. Lower rates decrease file size but can also degrade sound quality. Rate options are as follows:

• 5 kHz is barely acceptable for speech.

• 11 kHz is the lowest recommended quality for a short segment of music and is one-quarter of the standard CD rate.

• 22 kHz is a popular choice for Web playback and is half the standard CD rate.

• 44 kHz is the standard CD audio rate.

Note: Flash cannot increase the kHz rate of an imported sound above the rate at which it was imported.

Guidelines for exporting sound in Flash movies

Aside from sampling rate and compression, there are several ways to use sound efficiently in a movie and keep file size down:

- Set the in and out points to prevent silent areas from being stored in the Shockwave Flash file and to reduce the size of the sound.

- Get more out of the same sounds by applying different effects for sounds (such as volume envelopes, looping, and in/out points) at different keyframes. You can get a number of sound effects using only one sound file.

- Use looping to extract the common part of the sound and play it repeatedly. Loop short sounds for background music.

- Do not set streaming sound to loop.

Guidelines for exporting sound in QuickTime movies

Movies that you export as QuickTime files use sound differently than Shockwave Flash movies do. Guidelines for exporting sound with QuickTime movies include the following:

- Use as many sounds and channels as you want without worrying about file size. The sounds are combined into a single sound track when you export as a QuickTime file. The number of sounds you use has no effect on the final file size.

- Use stream synchronization to keep the animation synchronized to your sound track when you preview your animation in the editor. If your computer is not fast enough to draw the animation frames so that they keep up with your sound track, Flash skips frames.

CHAPTER 7
Working with Objects

In Flash, objects are items on the Stage. Flash lets you move, copy, delete, transform, stack, align, and group objects. You can also link an object to a URL. Note that modifying lines and shapes can alter other lines and shapes on the same layer. See Chapter 3, "Drawing."

Note: The term *object* is used in the ActionScript programming language with a different meaning. Be careful not to confuse the two uses of the term. Refer to the *ActionScript Reference Guide* for more on objects in the programming language.

Selecting objects

To modify an object, you must first select it. Flash provides a variety of methods for making selections, including the Arrow tool, the Lasso tool, and keyboard commands. You can group individual objects to manipulate them as a single object. See "Grouping objects" on page 186.

Flash highlights objects that have been selected. Strokes are highlighted with a colored line. Fills are highlighted with a dot pattern. Selected groups are highlighted with bounding boxes.

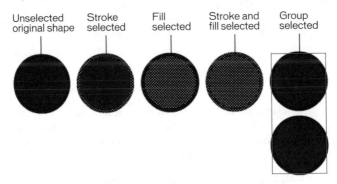

Unselected original shape   Stroke selected   Fill selected   Stroke and fill selected   Group selected

The stroke and fill are highlighted with the color used for the outline of the layer that contains the selected object. You can change the layer outline color in the Layer Properties dialog box. See "Viewing layers" on page 202.

You can choose to select only strokes or only fills of an object. You can hide selection highlighting in order to edit objects without viewing highlighting.

You might want to prevent a group or symbol from being selected and accidentally changed. To do this, you can lock the group or symbol.

Selected bitmaps and symbols are highlighted with a dot pattern. See Chapter 5, "Using Imported Artwork."

Using the Arrow tool

The Arrow tool allows you to select entire objects by clicking an object or dragging to enclose the object within a rectangular selection marquee.

Note: To select the Arrow tool you can also press the V key. To temporarily switch to the Arrow tool when another tool is active, hold down the Control key (Windows) or Command key (Macintosh).

To select a stroke, fill, group, instance, or text block:

Select the Arrow tool and click the object.

To select connected lines:

Select the Arrow tool and double-click one of the lines.

To select a filled shape and its stroked outline:

Select the Arrow tool and double-click the fill.

To select objects within a rectangular area:

Select the Arrow tool and drag a marquee around the object or objects that you want to select. Instances, groups, and type blocks must be completely enclosed to be selected.

Modifying selections

You can add to selections, select or deselect everything on every layer in a scene, select everything between keyframes, or lock and unlock selected symbols or groups.

To add to a selection:

Hold down the Shift key while making additional selections.

Note: To disable the Shift-select option, deselect the option in Flash General Preferences. See "Flash preferences" on page 111.

To select everything on every layer of a scene:

Choose Edit > Select All, or press Control+A (Windows) or Command+A (Macintosh). Select All doesn't select objects on locked or hidden layers, or layers not on the current timeline.

To deselect everything on every layer:

Choose Edit > Deselect All, or press Control+Shift+A (Windows) or Command+Shift+A (Macintosh).

To select everything on one layer between keyframes:

Click a frame in the Timeline. For more information, see "Using the Timeline" on page 82.

To lock a group or symbol:

Select the group or symbol and choose Modify > Arrange > Lock.

Choose Modify > Arrange > Unlock All to unlock all locked groups and symbols.

Using the Lasso tool

To select objects by drawing either a freehand or a straight-edged selection area, you can use the Lasso tool and its Polygon Mode modifier. When using the Lasso tool, you can switch between the freeform and straight-edged selection modes.

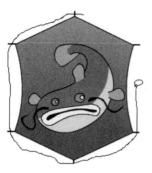

To select objects by drawing a freehand selection area:

 Select the Lasso tool and drag around the area. End the loop approximately where you started, or let Flash automatically close the loop with a straight line.

To select objects by drawing a straight-edged selection area:

1 Select the Lasso tool and select the Polygon Mode modifier in the Options section of the toolbox.

2 Click to set the starting point.

3 Position the pointer where you want the first line to end, and click. Continue setting end points for additional line segments.

4 To close the selection area, double-click.

To select objects by drawing both freehand and straight-edged selection areas:

1 Select the Lasso tool and deselect the Polygon Mode modifier.

2 To draw a freehand segment, drag on the Stage.

3 To draw a straight-edged segment, hold down Alt (Windows) or Option (Macintosh) and click to set start and end points. You can continue switching between drawing freehand and straight-edged segments.

4 To close the selection area, do one of the following:

• If you are drawing a freehand segment, release the mouse button.

• If you are drawing a straight-edged segment, double-click.

Hiding selection highlighting

You can hide selection highlights in order to edit objects without viewing their highlighting. Hiding highlights enables you to see how artwork will appear in its final state while you are selecting and editing objects.

To hide selection highlighting:

Choose View > Hide Edges. Choose the command again to deselect the feature.

Grouping objects

To manipulate elements as a single object, you need to group them. For example, after creating a drawing such as a tree or flower, you might group the elements of the drawing so that you can easily select and move the drawing as a whole.

You can edit groups without ungrouping them. You can also select an individual object in a group for editing, without ungrouping the objects.

To create a group:

1 Select the objects on the Stage that you want to group.

   You can select shapes, other groups, symbols, text, and so on.

2 Choose Modify > Group, or press Control+G (Windows) or Command+G (Macintosh).

To ungroup objects:

Choose Modify > Ungroup.

To edit a group or an object within a group:

1 With the group selected, choose Edit > Edit Selected, or double-click the group with the Arrow tool.

   Everything on the page that is not part of the group is dimmed, indicating it is inaccessible.

2 Edit any element within the group.

3 Choose Edit > Edit All, or double-click a blank spot on the Stage with the Arrow tool.

   Flash restores the group to its status as a single entity, and you can work with other elements on the Stage.

Moving, copying, and deleting objects

You can move objects by dragging them on the Stage, cutting and pasting them, using the Arrow keys, or using the Object panel to specify an exact location for them. You can also move objects between Flash and other applications using the Clipboard. You can copy objects by dragging or pasting them, or while transforming them.

When moving an object with the Arrow tool, you can use the Snap modifier for the Arrow tool to quickly align the object with points on other objects.

Moving objects

To move an object, you can drag the object, use the Arrow keys, or use the Info panel.

To move objects or copies of objects by dragging:

1 Select an object or multiple objects.

2 Select the Arrow tool, position the pointer over the object, and drag to the new position. To copy the object and move the copy, Alt-drag (Windows) or Option-drag (Macintosh). To constrain movement of the object to multiples of 45°, Shift-drag.

To move objects using the arrow keys:

1 Select an object or multiple objects.

2 Press the arrow key for the direction in which you want the object to move by 1 pixel at a time. Press Shift+arrow key to move the selection by 8 pixels at a time.

To move objects using the Info panel:

1 Select an object or multiple objects.

2 Choose Window > Panels> Info.

3 In the Info panel, enter values for the location of the top left corner of the selection. The units are relative to the top left corner of the Stage.

Note: The Info panel uses the units specified for the Ruler Units option in the Movie Properties dialog box. To change the units, see "Creating a new movie and setting its properties" on page 74.

Moving and copying objects by pasting

When you need to move or copy objects between layers, scenes, or other Flash files, you should use the pasting technique. You can paste an object in the center of the Stage or in a position relative to its original position.

To move or copy objects by pasting:

1 Select an object or multiple objects.

2 Choose Edit > Cut or Edit > Copy.

3 Select another layer, scene, or file and do one of the following:

• Choose Edit > Paste to paste the selection in the center of the Stage.

• Choose Edit > Paste in Place to paste the selection in the same position relative to the Stage.

About copying artwork with the Clipboard

Elements copied to the Clipboard are anti-aliased, so they look as good in other applications as they do in Flash. This is particularly useful for frames that include a bitmap image, gradients, transparency, or a mask layer.

Graphics pasted from other movies or programs are placed in the current frame of the current layer. How a graphic element is pasted into a Flash scene depends on the type of element it is, its source, and the preferences you have set:

• Text from a text editor becomes a single text object.

• Vector-based graphics from any drawing program become a group that can be ungrouped and edited like any other Flash element.

• Bitmaps become a single grouped object just like imported bitmaps. You can break apart pasted bitmaps or convert pasted bitmaps to vector graphics.

   For information on converting bitmaps to vector graphics, see "Converting bitmaps to vector graphics" on page 161.

Note: Before pasting graphics from FreeHand into Flash, set your FreeHand export preferences to convert colors to CMYK and RGB for Clipboard formats.

Copying transformed objects

To create a scaled, rotated, or skewed copy of an object, you can use the Transform panel.

To create a transformed copy of an object:

1 Select an object.

2 Choose Window > Panels > Transform.

3 Enter scale, rotation, or skew values. See "Scaling objects" on page 191, "Rotating objects" on page 192, and "Skewing objects" on page 194.

4 Click the Create Copy button in the Transform panel (the left button in the bottom right corner of the panel).

Deleting objects

Deleting an object removes it from the file. Deleting an instance on the Stage does not delete the symbol from the library.

To delete objects:

1 Select an object or multiple objects.

2 Do one of the following:

• Press Delete or Backspace.

• Choose Edit > Clear.

• Choose Edit > Cut.

• Right-click (Windows) or Control-click (Macintosh) the object and select Cut from the context menu.

Stacking objects

Within a layer, Flash stacks objects based on the order in which they were created, placing the most recently created object on the top of the stack. The stacking order of objects determines how they appear when they are overlapping.

Drawn lines and shapes always appear below groups and symbols on the stack. To move them up the stack, you must group them or make them into symbols. You can change the stacking order of objects at any time.

Note that layers also affect the stacking order. Everything on Layer 2 appears on top of everything on Layer 1, and so on. To change the order of layers, drag the layer name in the Timeline to a new position. See Chapter 8, "Using Layers."

To change the stacking order of an object:

1 Select the object.

2 Use one of the following commands:

• Choose Modify > Arrange > Bring to Front or Send to Back to move the object or group to the top or bottom of the stacking order.

• Choose Modify > Arrange > Bring Forward or Send Backward to move the object or group up or down one position in the stacking order.

If more than one group is selected, the groups move in front of or behind all unselected groups, while maintaining their order relative to each other.

Scaling objects

Scaling an object enlarges or reduces the object horizontally, vertically, or both. You can scale an object by dragging or by entering values in the Transform panel. Instances, groups, and type blocks are scaled in relation to their registration point. See "Moving an object's registration point" on page 198.

To scale an object by dragging:

1 Select the object.

 2 Select the Arrow tool and click the Scale modifier in the Options section of the toolbox, or choose Modify > Transform > Scale.

3 Do one of the following:

• To scale the object both horizontally and vertically, drag one of the corner handles. Proportions are maintained as you scale.

• To scale the object either horizontally or vertically, drag a center handle.

4 Click a blank area on the Stage or choose Modify > Transform > Scale to hide the scale handles.

Note: When you increase the size of a number of items, those near the edges of the bounding box might be moved out of the Stage. If this occurs, choose View > Work Area to see the elements that are beyond the edges of the Stage.

To scale an object with the Transform panel:

1 Select the object.

2 Choose Window > Panels > Transform.

3 Enter a scale value between 1 and 1000 for vertical, horizontal, or both.

4 Select Constrain to maintain proportions.

5 Press Enter (Windows) or Return (Macintosh).

Rotating objects

Rotating an object turns it around its registration point. By default, the registration point is at the center of the object, but you can move it. See "Moving an object's registration point" on page 198. You can rotate an object by using the Rotate commands, by dragging, or by specifying an angle in the Transform panel.

Original, rotated right, and rotated left, respectively

To rotate an object by dragging:

1 Select the object.

2 Do one of the following:

• Select the Arrow tool and click the Rotate modifier in the Options section of the toolbox.

• Choose Modify > Transform > Rotate.

3 Drag one of the corner handles.

4 Click a blank area on the Stage or choose Modify > Transform > Rotate to hide the rotation handles.

To rotate an object by 90°:

1 Select the object.

2 Choose Modify > Transform > Rotate 90° CW to rotate clockwise, or Rotate 90° CCW to rotate counterclockwise.

To rotate an object using the Transform panel:

1 Select the object.

2 Choose Window > Panels > Transform.

3 Click Rotate.

4 Enter a rotation angle.

5 Press Enter (Windows) or Return (Macintosh) to apply the rotation.

To rotate and scale an object simultaneously:

1 Select the object.

2 Choose Modify > Transform > Scale and Rotate.

3 Enter values for Scale and Rotation.

4 Click OK.

Flipping objects

You can flip objects across their vertical or horizontal axis without moving their relative position on the Stage.

Original, flipped horizontally, and flipped vertically, respectively

To flip an object:

1 Select the object.

2 Choose Modify > Transform > Flip Vertical or Flip Horizontal.

Skewing objects

Skewing an object transforms it by slanting it along one or both axes. You can skew an object by dragging or by entering a value in the Transform panel.

To skew an object by dragging:

1 Select the object.

2 Do one of the following:

• Select the Arrow tool and click the Rotate modifier in the Options section of the toolbox.

• Choose Modify > Transform > Rotate.

3 Drag a center handle.

4 Click a blank area on the Stage or choose Modify > Transform > Rotate to hide the rotation handles.

To skew an object using the Transform panel:

1 Select the object.

2 Choose Window > Panels> Transform.

3 Click Skew.

4 Enter angles for the horizontal and vertical values.

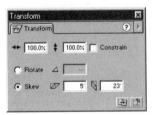

Restoring transformed objects

When you scale, rotate, and skew instances, groups, and type with the Transform panel, Flash saves the original size and rotation values with the object. Thus, you can remove the last transformation applied and restore the original values.

You can also undo a transformation performed in the Transform panel by clicking the Undo button in the panel.

To restore a transformed object to its original state:

1   Select the transformed object.

2   Choose Modify > Transform > Remove Transform.

To undo a transformation performed in the Transform panel:

1   With the transformed object still selected, click the Undo button in the Transform panel (the right button at the bottom right corner of the panel).

Aligning objects

The Align panel enables you to align selected objects along the horizontal or vertical axis. You can align objects vertically along the right edge, center, or left edge of the selected objects, or horizontally along the top edge, center, or bottom edge of the selected objects. Edges are determined by the bounding boxes enclosing each selected object.

Using the Align panel, you can distribute selected objects so that their centers or edges are evenly spaced. You can resize selected objects so that the horizontal or vertical dimensions of all objects match those of the largest selected object. You can also align selected objects to the Stage. You can apply one or more Align options to selected objects.

Original

Objects aligned to the top edge of the uppermost object.

To align objects:

1   Select the objects to align.

2   Choose Window > Panels > Align.

3   In the Align Panel, select To Stage to apply alignment modifications relative to stage dimensions.

4   Select alignment buttons to modify the selected objects:

•   For Align, select Align Left, Align Horizontal Center, Align Right, Align Top, Align Vertical Center, or Align Bottom.

•   For Distribute, select Distribute Top, Distribute Horizontal Center, Distribute Bottom, Distribute Left, Distribute Vertical Center, or Distribute Right.

•   For Match Size, select Match Width, Match Height, or Match Width and Height.

•   For Space, select Space Horizontally or Space Vertically.

Moving an object's registration point

All groups, instances, type blocks, and bitmaps have a registration point that Flash uses for positioning and transformations. By default, this point is located at the center of the object. By moving an object's registration point, you can position and transform the object relative to, for example, the object's lower left corner. Lines and shapes do not have registration points and are positioned and transformed relative to their upper left corner.

Registration point moved

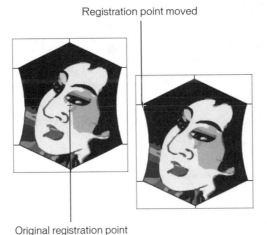

Original registration point

To edit the registration point of an instance, you'll probably have better results if you edit the symbol, and then move it in symbol-editing mode so that the registration point appears where you'd like it. See "Editing symbols" on page 238.

To edit the registration point of a group, instance, type block, or bitmap:

1 Select the object.

2 Choose Modify > Transform > Edit Center.

   A cross hair representing the center point is highlighted.

3 Drag the highlighted cross hair to a new location.

4 Click a blank area on the Stage or choose Modify > Transform > Edit Center to hide the cross hair.

Breaking apart groups and objects

To separate groups, text blocks, instances, and bitmaps into ungrouped editable elements, you use the Break Apart command. Breaking apart significantly reduces the file size of imported graphics.

Breaking apart is not entirely reversible, and it affects objects as follows:

- It severs a symbol instance's link to its master symbol.

- It discards all but the current frame in an animated symbol.

- It converts a bitmap to a fill.

- It converts text characters to outlines.

The Break Apart command should not be confused with the Ungroup command. The Ungroup command separates grouped objects into discrete components, returning grouped elements to the state they were in prior to grouping. It does not break apart bitmaps, instances, or type, or convert type to outlines.

To break apart groups or objects:

1 Select a group, text block, bitmap, or symbol that you want to break apart.

2 Choose Modify > Break Apart.

Note: Breaking apart animated symbols, or groups within an interpolated animation, is not recommended and might have unpredictable results. Breaking apart complex symbols and large blocks of text can take a long time. You might need to increase the application's memory allocation to properly break apart complex objects.

CHAPTER 8
Using Layers

Layers are like transparent sheets of acetate stacked on top of each other. When you create a new Flash movie, it contains one layer. You can add more layers to organize the artwork, animation, and other elements in your movie. You can draw and edit objects on one layer without affecting objects on another layer. Where there is nothing on a layer, you can see through it to the layers below.

The number of layers you can create is limited only by your computer's memory, and layers do not increase the file size of your published movie. You can hide layers, lock layers, or display layer contents as outlines. You can also change the order of layers.

In addition, you can use special guide layers to make drawing and editing easier, and mask layers to help you create sophisticated effects.

It's a good idea to use separate layers for sound files, actions, frame labels, and frame comments. This helps you find these items quickly when you need to edit them.

For an interactive introduction to layers, choose Help > Lessons > Layers.

Creating layers

When you create a new layer, it appears above the selected layer. A newly added layer becomes the active layer.

To create a layer, do one of the following:

 • Click the Add Layer button at the bottom of the Timeline.

• Choose Insert > Layer.

• Right-click (Windows) or Control-click (Macintosh) on a layer name in the Timeline and choose Insert Layer from the context menu.

Viewing layers

As you work, you may want to show or hide layers. A red X next to a layer's name indicates that the layer is hidden. Hidden layers are preserved when a movie is published. However, you cannot edit the hidden layers in the SWF file if you open the SWF file in Flash.

To help you distinguish which layer objects belong to, you can display all objects on a layer as colored outlines. You can change the outline color used by each layer.

You can change the height of layers in the Timeline in order to display more information (such as sound waveforms) in the Timeline. You can also change the number of layers displayed in the Timeline.

The layer containing the logo has red outlines.

To show or hide a layer, do one of the following:

- Click in the Eye column to the right of the layer's name to hide that layer. Click in it again to show the layer.

- Click the eye icon to hide all the layers. Click it again to show all layers.

- Drag through the Eye column to show or hide multiple layers.

- Alt-click (Windows) or Option-click (Macintosh) in the Eye column to the right of a layer's name to hide all other layers. Alt-click or Option-click it again to show all layers.

To view the content of a layer as outlines, do one of the following:

- Click in the Outline column to the right of the layer's name to display all objects on that layer as outlines. Click in it again to turn off outline display.

- Click the outline icon to display objects on all layers as outlines. Click it again to turn off outline display on all layers.

- Alt-click (Windows) or Option-click (Macintosh) in the Outline column to the right of a layer's name to display objects on all other layers as outlines. Alt-click or Option-click in it again to turn off outline display for all layers.

To change a layer's outline color:

1 Do one of the following:

• Double-click the layer's icon (the icon to the left of the layer name) in the Timeline.

• Right-click(Windows) or Control-click (Macintosh) the layer name and choose Properties from the context menu.

• Select the layer in the Timeline and choose Modify > Layer.

2 In the Layer Properties dialog box, click the Outline Color color box and select a new color, enter the hexadecimal value for a color, or click the Color Picker button and choose a color.

3 Click OK.

To change layer height in the Timeline:

1 Do one of the following:

• Double-click the layer's icon (the icon to the left of the layer name) in the Timeline.

• Right-click(Windows) or Control-click (Macintosh) the layer name and choose Properties from the context menu.

• Select the layer in the Timeline and choose Modify > Layer.

2 In the Layer Properties dialog box, choose an option for Layer Height and click OK.

To change the number of layers displayed in the Timeline:

Drag the bar that separates the Timeline from the Stage area.

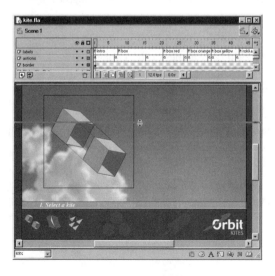

Editing layers

To draw, paint, or otherwise modify a layer, you select the layer to make it active. A pencil icon next to a layer's name indicates that the layer is active. Only one layer can be active at one time (although more than one layer can be selected at one time). You can rename, copy, and delete layers. You can lock layers to prevent them from being edited, and you can change the order of layers.

By default, new layers are named by the order in which they are created: Layer 1, Layer 2, and so on. You can rename layers to better reflect their contents.

You can hide layers or display layer contents as outlines while editing other layers, to keep the work area uncluttered. See "Viewing layers" on page 202.

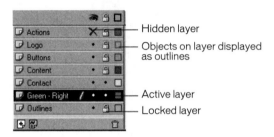

Hidden layer
Objects on layer displayed as outlines
Active layer
Locked layer

To select a layer, do one of the following:

- Click the layer's name in the Timeline.

- Click a frame in the Timeline of the layer you want to select.

- Select an object on the Stage that is located on the layer you want to select.

To select two or more layers, do one of the following:

- To select contiguous layers, Shift-click layer names in the Timeline.

- To select discontiguous layers, Control-click (Windows) or Command-click (Macintosh) layer names in the Timeline.

To rename a layer, do one of the following:

- Double-click the layer name and enter a new name.

- Right-click (Windows) or Control-click (Macintosh) the layer name and choose Properties from the context menu. Enter the new name in the Name text box and click OK.

- Select the layer in the Timeline and choose Modify > Layer. In the Layer Properties dialog box, enter the new name in the Name text box and click OK.

To copy a layer:

1 Click the layer name to select the entire layer.

2 Choose Edit > Copy Frames.

3 Click the Add Layer button to create a new layer.

4 Click the new layer and choose Edit > Paste Frames.

To delete a layer:

1 Select the layer.

2 Do one of the following:

• Click the Delete Layer button in the Timeline.

• Drag the layer to the Delete Layer button.

• Right-click (Windows) or Control-click (Macintosh) the layer name and choose Delete Layer from the context menu.

To lock or unlock one or more layers, do one of the following:

• Click in the Lock column to the right of a layer's name to lock that layer. Click in the Lock column again to unlock the layer.

• Click the padlock icon to lock all layers. Click it again to unlock all layers.

• Drag through the Lock column to lock or unlock multiple layers.

• Alt-click (Windows) or Option-click (Macintosh) in the Lock column to the right of a layer's name to lock all other layers. Alt-click or Option-click in the Lock column again to unlock all layers.

To change the order of layers:

Drag one or more layers in the Timeline.

Using guide layers

For help when drawing, you can use guide layers. You can make any layer a guide layer. Guide layers are indicated by a guide icon to the left of the layer name. Guide layers do not appear in a published Flash Player movie.

Guide layer ——

You can also create a motion guide layer to control the movement of objects in a motion tweened animation. See "Tweening motion along a path" on page 258.

Note: Dragging a normal layer onto a guide layer converts the guide layer to a motion guide layer. To prevent accidentally converting a guide layer, place all guide layers at the bottom of the layer order.

To designate a layer as a guide layer:

Select the layer and right-click (Windows) or Control-click (Macintosh), then choose Guide from the context menu. Choose Guide again to revert the layer to a normal layer.

Using mask layers

For spotlight effects and transitions, you can use a mask layer to create a hole through which the contents of one or more underlying layers are visible. You can group multiple layers together under a single mask layer to create sophisticated effects. You can also use any type of animation, except motion paths, to make the mask move. You cannot mask layers inside of buttons.

To create a mask layer, you place a filled shape on the layer. The mask layer reveals the area of linked, underlying layers that lie beneath the filled shape, and it conceals all other areas. Mask layers can contain only a single shape, instance, or type object. (Flash mask layers provide similar functionality to the Paste Inside command in FreeHand.)

To create a mask layer:

1   Select or create a layer containing the content that will be visible through the holes in the mask.

2   With the layer selected, choose Insert > Layer to create a new layer above it.

A mask layer always masks the layer immediately below it, so be sure to create the mask layer in the proper place.

3   Draw a filled shape, place type, or create an instance of a symbol on the mask layer. Flash ignores bitmaps, gradients, transparency, colors, and line styles in a mask layer. Any filled area will be completely transparent in the mask; any nonfilled area will be opaque.

4   Right-click (Windows) or Control-click (Macintosh) the mask layer's name in the Timeline and choose Mask from the context menu.

The layer is converted to a mask layer, indicated by a down arrow icon. The layer immediately below it is linked to the mask layer, and its contents show through the filled area on the mask. The masked layer name is indented, and its icon changes to a right-pointing arrow.

To display the mask effect in Flash, lock the mask layer and the masked layer.

A mask layer; the filled shape that will be transparent in the mask; the masked layer; and the final mask effect

To mask additional layers after creating a mask layer, do one of the following:

• Drag an existing layer directly below the mask layer.

• Create a new layer anywhere below the mask layer.

• Choose Modify > Layer and select Masked in the Layer Properties dialog box.

To unlink layers from a mask layer:

1 Select the layer you want to unlink.

2 Do one of the following:

• Drag the layer above the mask layer.

• Choose Modify > Layer and select Normal.

To toggle a layer between being masked and unmasked:

Alt-click (Windows) or Option-click (Macintosh) the layer.

CHAPTER 9
Using Type

If you use type in your Flash movies, you can set its size, typeface, style, spacing, color, and alignment. You can transform type like an object—rotating, scaling, skewing, and flipping it—and still edit its characters. Your movies can include text boxes for user input or for displaying text that can update dynamically. And you can link text blocks to URLs.

You can also break type apart and reshape its characters. For additional text-handling capabilities, you can manipulate text in FreeHand and import the FreeHand file into Flash, or export the file from FreeHand as a SWF file.

For an interactive introduction to creating type in Flash, choose Help > Lessons > Type.

Flash movies can use Type 1 PostScript fonts, TrueType, and bitmap fonts (Macintosh only). To use PostScript fonts, you must have Adobe Type Manager (ATM) installed on your system (except for systems using Windows 2000, which does not require ATM). See TechNote #4105 on the Macromedia Flash Support Site, http://www.macromedia.com/support/flash/.

Note: If you experience problems when using PostScript fonts in Flash on Windows NT, you may be experiencing incompatibility issues between ATM and Windows NT. Please consult with the technical support services for ATM and Windows NT if problems occur.

When you work with Flash FLA files, Flash substitutes fonts in the movie with other fonts installed on your system when necessary. Flash also allows you to create a symbol from a font so that you can export the font as part of a shared library and use it in other Flash movies.

You can spell-check text by copying text to the Clipboard using the Movie Explorer and pasting the text into an external text editor. See "Using the Movie Explorer" on page 98.

About embedded fonts and device fonts

When you use a font installed on your system in a Flash movie, Flash embeds the font information in the Flash SWF file, ensuring that the font displays properly in the Flash Player. Not all fonts displayed in Flash can be exported with a movie. To verify that a font can be exported, use the View > Antialias Text command to preview the text; jagged type indicates that Flash does not recognize that font's outline and will not export the text.

As an alternative to embedding font information, you can use special fonts in Flash called device fonts. Device fonts are not embedded in the Flash SWF file. Instead, the Flash Player uses whatever font on the local computer most closely resembles the device font. Because device font information is not embedded, using device fonts yields a somewhat smaller Flash movie file size. In addition, device fonts can be sharper and more legible than embedded fonts at small type sizes (below 10 points). However, because device fonts are not embedded, if users do not have a font installed on their system that corresponds to the device font, type may look different than expected on a user's system.

Flash includes three device fonts, named _sans (similar to Helvetica or Arial), _serif (similar to Times Roman), and _typewriter (similar to Courier). To specify a font as a device font, you select one of the Flash device fonts in the Character panel, or select Use Device Fonts in the Text Options panel. You can specify text set in a device font to be selectable, so that users can copy and paste text that appears in your movie. See "Using device fonts" on page 216.

You can use device fonts for static text (text that you create when authoring a movie and that does not change when the movie is displayed) or dynamic text (text that updates periodically through input from a file server, such as sports scores or weather data). For information on dynamic text, see "Creating text boxes for user input or dynamically updating text" on page 218.

Creating text

To place text blocks on the Stage, you use the Text tool. You can place type on a single line that expands as you type or in a fixed-width block that wraps words automatically. Flash displays a round handle at the upper right corner of text blocks that extend, and a square handle for text blocks with a defined width.

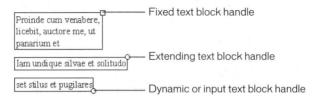

Fixed text block handle

Extending text block handle

Dynamic or input text block handle

Flash displays a square handle at the bottom right corner of editable text boxes, indicating that you can size the text box vertically and horizontally according to the amount of text to be entered.

To create text:

1 Select the Text tool.

2 Choose Window > Panels > Character and Window > Panels > Paragraph to view the Character and Paragraph panels, and select type attributes as described in the following section.

3 Do one of the following:

• To create a text block that widens as you type, click where you want the type to start.

• To create a text block with a fixed width, position the pointer where you want the text to start and drag to the desired width.

Note: If you create a text block that extends past the right or bottom edge of the Stage as you type, the text isn't lost. To make the handle accessible again, add line breaks, move the text block, or choose View > Work Area.

To change the dimensions of a text block:

Drag its resize handle.

To switch a text block between fixed-width and extending:

Double-click the resize handle.

Setting type attributes

You can set the font and paragraph attributes of type. A font is an assortment of alphanumeric characters in a particular typeface design. Font attributes include font family, type size, style, color, tracking, auto kerning, and baseline shift. (You can use embedded fonts or device fonts. See "About embedded fonts and device fonts" on page 210.) Paragraph attributes include alignment, margins, indents, and line spacing.

To change font and paragraph attributes, you use the Character panel and the Paragraph panel. To direct Flash to use device fonts rather than embedding font information, you use the Text Options panel.

When creating new type, Flash uses the current type attributes. To change the font or paragraph attributes of existing type, you must first select the type.

To use the Character panel:

Choose Window > Panels > Character.

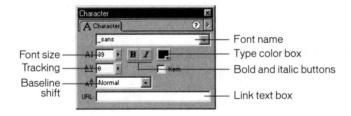

To use the Paragraph panel:

Choose Window > Panels > Paragraph.

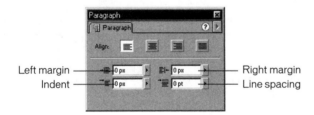

Choosing a font, type size, style, and color

You can set the font, type size, style, and color for selected type using the Character panel.

When setting the color of type, you can use only solid colors, not gradients. To apply a gradient to type, you must convert the type to its component lines and fills. See "Reshaping type" on page 223.

To choose a font, type size, style, and color with the Character panel:

1 If the Character panel is not already displayed, choose Window > Panels > Character.

2 Click the triangle next to the Font text box and select a font from the list, or enter a font name.

   Note: The fonts _sans, _serif, and _typewriter are device fonts. Font information for these fonts is not embedded in the Flash SWF file. See "About embedded fonts and device fonts" on page 210.

3 Click the triangle next to the Font Size value and drag the slider to select a value, or enter a font size value.

   Type size is set in points, regardless of the current ruler units.

4 To apply bold or italic style, click the Bold button or the Italic button.

5 To choose a fill color for type, click the color box and do one of the following:

• Choose a color swatch from the palette.

• Type a color's hexadecimal value in the text box.

• Click the Color Picker button and choose a color from the Color Picker.

   For more information on selecting colors, see Chapter 4, "Working with Color."

Setting tracking, kerning, and baseline shift

Tracking inserts a uniform amount of space between characters. You use tracking to adjust the spacing of selected characters or entire blocks of type.

Kerning controls the spacing between pairs of characters. Many fonts have built-in kerning information. For example, the spacing between an *A* and a *V* is often less than the spacing between an *A* and a *D*. To use a font's built-in kerning information to space characters, you use the Kern option.

Baseline shift controls where type appears in relation to its baseline.

Tracking, auto kerning, and baseline shift options are located in the Character panel.

To set tracking, kerning, and baseline shift:

1 If the Character panel is not displayed, choose Window > Panels > Character.

2 In the Character panel, set the following options:

• To specify tracking, click the triangle next to the Tracking value and drag the slider to select a value, or enter a value in the text box.

• To use a font's built-in kerning information, select Kern.

• To specify baseline shift, click the triangle next to the Baseline Shift option and select a position from the menu: Normal places type on the baseline, Superscript places type above the baseline, and Subscript places type below the baseline.

Setting alignment, margins, indents, and line spacing

Alignment determines the position of each line of type in a paragraph relative to the left and right edges of the text block. Type can be aligned to the left or right edge of the text block, centered within the text block, or aligned to both edges of the text block (full justification).

Margins determine the amount of space between the border of a text block and a paragraph of text. Indents determine the distance between the margin of a paragraph and the beginning of the first line. Line spacing determines the distance between adjacent lines in a paragraph.

To specify alignment, margins, indents, and line spacing, you use the Paragraph panel.

To set alignment, margins, indents, and line spacing:

1 If the Paragraph panel is not already displayed, choose Window > Panels > Paragraph.

2 In the Paragraph panel, set the following options:

• To set alignment, click the Left, Center, Right, or Full Justification button.

• To set left or right margins, click the triangle next to the Left Margin or Right Margin value and drag the slider to select a value, or enter a value in the numeric field.

• To specify indents, click the triangle next to the Indent value and drag the slider to select a value, or enter a value in the numeric field.

• To specify line spacing, click the triangle next to the Line Spacing value and drag the slider to select a value, or enter a value in the numeric field.

Using device fonts

Using the Text Options panel, you can specify that the Flash Player use device fonts to display certain text blocks, so that Flash does not embed the font for that text. This can decrease the file size of the movie and increase legibility at small type sizes.

You can specify that text set in device fonts be selectable by users viewing your movie.

To specify that text be displayed using a device font:

1 Use the Text tool to select text blocks on the Stage that you want to be displayed in the Flash Player using a device font.

2 Choose Window > Panels > Text Options.

3 Choose Static Text from the pop-up menu.

4 Select Use Device Fonts.

To make type selectable by a user:

1 Select the type that you want to make selectable by a user.

2 Choose Window > Panels > Text Options.

3 Choose Static Text from the pop-up menu.

4 If the type is not already specified as using a device font, select Use Device Fonts.

5 Click Selectable.

Creating font symbols

To use a font as a shared library item, you can create a font symbol in the Library window. This enables you to link to the font and use it in a Flash movie without having to embed the font in the movie. (See "Using shared libraries" on page 95.)

To use the font symbol in a shared library, you assign the symbol an identifier string. The identifier can also be used to access the symbol as an object in ActionScript. For information on objects in ActionScript, see the *ActionScript Reference Guide.*

To create a font symbol:

1 Open the library to which you want to add a font symbol.

2 Choose New Font from the Options menu in the upper right corner of the Library window.

3 In the Font Symbol Properties dialog box, enter a name for the font symbol in the Name text box.

4 Select a font from the Font menu or enter the name of a font in the Font text box.

5 If desired, select Bold or Italic to apply the selected style to the font.

6 Click OK.

To assign an identifier string to a font symbol:

1 Select the font symbol in the Library window.

2 Do one of the following:

• Choose Linkage from the Options menu in the upper right corner of the Library window.

• Right-click (Windows) or Control-click (Macintosh) the font symbol name in the Library window, and choose Linkage from the context menu.

3 Under Linkage in the Symbol Linkage Properties dialog box, select Export This Symbol.

4 Enter an identifier string in the text box, and then click OK.

Creating text boxes for user input or dynamically updating text

Input text boxes enable users to input text in forms or surveys. Dynamic text boxes display dynamically updating text, such as sport scores, stock quotes, or weather reports. You create both kinds of these editable text boxes using the Text Options panel. You choose options to determine the appearance of input or dynamic text in a Flash movie. You can preserve rich text formatting as HTML formatting. See "About preserving rich text formatting" on page 219.

When you create a text box, you assign a variable to it. A variable is a fixed name for a value that changes. The text box is like a window that displays the value for the variable. You can use actions to pass the variable to other parts of the movie, to a server-side application for storing in a database, and so on. You can also replace the value of a variable by reading it from a server-side application or by loading it from another part of the movie. For more information on using variables, see the *ActionScript Reference Guide*.

To create an editable text box:

1 Do one of the following to create or select a text block:

• Select the Text tool and drag to create a text block of the desired width and height.

• Click inside an existing text block.

2 Choose Window > Panels > Text Options.

3 Choose an option from the Text Type pop-up menu:

• Choose Dynamic Text to create a text box that displays dynamically updating text.

• Choose Input Text to create a text box in which users can input text.

About preserving rich text formatting

Flash enables you to preserve rich text formatting in editable text boxes. You can select the HTML formatting option for dynamic or input text boxes in the Text Options panel. With the HTML option selected, basic text formatting (including font name, style, color, and size) and hyperlinks in the text box are preserved by automatically applying the corresponding HTML tags to the specified text box. The following HTML tags are supported in editable text boxes:

- <A>
- <B>
- <FONT COLOR>
- <FONT FACE>
- <FONT SIZE>
- <I>
- <P>
- <U>

You can also apply HTML tags to text boxes in the Actions panel, as part of the variable value for a text box. When you select the HTML formatting option in the Text Options panel, supported HTML tags that you applied in the Actions panel are preserved when you export the movie's SWF file.

Setting dynamic text options

You can specify options for dynamic text to control the way it appears in the Flash movie.

To set options for dynamic text:

1 If the Text Options panel isn't already displayed, choose Window > Panels > Text Options.

2 Choose Dynamic Text from the Text Type pop-up menu.

3 Set any of the following options:

• From the Line Display pop-up menu, choose Multiline to display the text in multiple lines, or Single Line to display the text as one line.

• Select HTML to preserve rich text formatting, such as font, font style, hyperlink, paragraph, and other text parameters, with the appropriate HTML tags.

• Select Draw Border and Background to display a border and background for the text box.

• If you selected Multiline above, select Word Wrap to automatically break lines at the end of the text box.

• Select Selectable (selected by default) to enable users to select dynamic text. Deselect this option to prevent users from selecting text in the dynamic text box.

• For Variable, enter the variable name for the text box.

• For Embed Fonts, choose one or more buttons to specify which characters from the font set used in the dynamic text will be embedded. Select the Full Font button (the far left button) to embed the full character set for the font.

Setting input text options

You can specify options for input text to control the way it appears in the Flash movie.

To specify options for input text:

1 If the Text Options panel isn't already displayed, choose Window > Panels > Text Options.

2 Choose Input Text from the Text Type pop-up menu.

3 Set any of the following options:

• From the Line Display pop-up menu, choose Multiline to display the text in multiple lines, Single Line to display the text as one line, or Password to display the text as asterisks to preserve password security.

Note: Selecting the Password option affects only the display of the text entered by the user. To create password functionality, see the *ActionScript Reference Guide.*

• Select HTML to preserve rich text formatting, such as font, font style, hyperlink, paragraph, and other text parameters, with the appropriate HTML tags.

• Select Draw Border and Background to display a border and background for the text box.

• If you selected Multiline above, select Word Wrap to automatically break lines at the end of the text box.

• For Variable, enter the variable name for the text box.

• For Maximum Characters, enter the maximum number of characters that the user can enter in the input text box.

• For Embed Fonts, choose one or more buttons to specify which characters from the font set used in the dynamic text will be embedded. Select the Full Font button (the far left button) to embed the full character set for the font.

Editing text

You can use most common word-processing techniques to edit text in Flash. You can use the Cut, Copy, and Paste commands to move type within a Flash file as well as between Flash and other applications.

To spell-check text, you can copy text to the Clipboard using the Movie Explorer, and paste the text into an external text editor. See "Using the Movie Explorer" on page 98.

Selecting text

When editing text or changing type attributes, you must first select the characters you want to change.

To select characters within a text block:

1 Select the Text tool.

2 Do one of the following:

- Drag to select characters.

- Double-click to select a word.

- Click to specify the beginning of the selection and Shift-click to specify the end of the selection.

- Press Ctrl+A (Windows) or Command+A (Macintosh) to select all the characters in the block.

To select text blocks:

Select the Arrow tool and click a text block. Shift-click to select multiple text blocks.

About transforming type

You can transform text blocks in the same ways you can other objects. You can scale, rotate, skew, and flip text blocks to create interesting effects. When you scale a text block as an object, increases or decreases in point size are not reflected in the Character panel.

The text in a transformed text block can still be edited, although severe transformations may make it difficult to read.

For more information about transforming text blocks, see Chapter 7, "Working with Objects."

Reshaping type

To reshape, erase, and otherwise manipulate type, you convert it to its component lines and fills. As with any other shape, you can individually group these converted characters, or change them to symbols and animate them. Once you've converted type to lines and fills, you can no longer edit them as text.

You can convert only entire text blocks to shapes, not characters within a text block.

To convert type to its component lines and fills:

1 Select the Arrow tool and click a text block.

2 Choose Modify > Break Apart. The characters in the selected text are converted to shapes on the Stage.

Note: Break Apart applies only to outline fonts such as TrueType fonts. Bitmap fonts disappear from the screen when you break them apart. PostScript fonts can be broken apart only on Macintosh systems running Adobe Type Manager (ATM).

Linking text blocks to URLs

You can link text blocks to URLs to allow users to jump to other files by clicking the text.

To link a text block to a URL:

1 Use the Arrow tool to select the text block on the Stage.

2 If the Character panel is not already displayed, choose Window > Panels > Character.

3 For Link, enter the URL to which you want to link the text block.

CHAPTER 10
Using Symbols and Instances

A *symbol* is a graphic, button, or movie clip that you create once and then can reuse throughout your movie or in other movies. Any symbol you create automatically becomes part of the library. An *instance* is a copy of a symbol located on the Stage or nested inside another symbol. An instance can be very different from its symbol in color, size, and function. Editing the symbol updates all of its instances. But editing an instance of a symbol updates only that instance.

Note: You can also create font symbols in Flash. See "Creating font symbols" on page 217.

Using symbols in your movies dramatically reduces file size; saving several instances of a symbol requires less storage space than saving a complete description of the element for each occurrence. For example, you can reduce the file size of your movies if you convert static graphics such as background images into symbols that you then reuse. Using symbols can also speed movie playback, because a symbol needs to be downloaded to a browser only once.

Using symbols also enables you to share images and other elements, such as movie clips or sounds, among Flash movies. You can include symbols in a shared library, and link to items in the shared library from any of your Flash movies, without importing the items into the movies. See "Using shared libraries" on page 95.

For an interactive introduction to using symbols and instances, choose Help > Lessons > Symbols.

Options menu

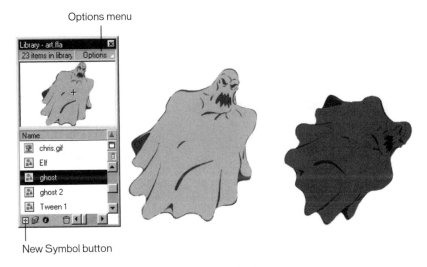

New Symbol button

A symbol in the library and two instances on the Stage

Types of symbol behavior

Each symbol has a unique Timeline and Stage, complete with layers. When you create a symbol, you choose how the symbol will behave, depending on how you want to use it in the movie.

- Use graphic symbols for static images and to create reusable pieces of animation that are tied to the Timeline of the main movie. Graphic symbols operate in sync with the Timeline of the main movie. Interactive controls and sounds won't work in a graphic symbol's animation sequence.

- Use button symbols to create interactive buttons in the movie that respond to mouse clicks or rollovers or other actions. You define the graphics associated with various button states, and then assign actions to a button instance. See "Assigning actions to objects" on page 277.

- Use movie clip symbols to create reusable pieces of animation. Movie clips have their own multiframe Timeline that plays independent of the main movie's Timeline—think of them as mini-movies inside a main movie that can contain interactive controls, sounds, and even other movie clip instances. You can also place movie clip instances inside the Timeline of a button symbol to create animated buttons.

  You can assign clip parameters (variables with values) to a movie clip to create a "smart" clip. You can also add clip actions and script the smart clip to create interface elements—such as radio buttons, pop-up menus, or tooltips—that respond to mouse clicks and other events. For more information, see the *ActionScript Reference Guide*.

Note: Interactivity and animation in movie clip symbols do not work when you play a movie in the Flash authoring environment. To see movie clip animation and interactivity, choose Control > Test Movie or Control > Test Scene. See "Previewing and testing movies" on page 74.

Creating symbols

You can create a symbol from selected objects on the Stage, or you can create an empty symbol and make or import the content in symbol-editing mode. Symbols can have all the functionality that you can create with Flash, including animation.

By using symbols that contain animation, you can create movies with a lot of movement while minimizing file size. Consider creating animation in a symbol when there is a repetitive or cyclic action—the up-and-down motion of a bird's wings, for example.

To create a new symbol with selected elements:

1   Select an element or several elements on the Stage and choose Insert > Convert to Symbol.

2   In the Symbol Properties dialog box, type the name of the symbol and choose the behavior—Graphic, Button, or Movie Clip. See "Types of symbol behavior" on page 227.

3   Click OK.

   Flash adds the symbol to the library. The selection on the Stage becomes an instance of the symbol. You can no longer edit the object directly on the Stage—you must open it in symbol-editing mode; see "Editing symbols" on page 238.

To create a new empty symbol:

1 Make sure that nothing is selected on the Stage and do one of the following:

• Choose Insert > New Symbol.

• Click the New Symbol button at the bottom left of the Library window.

• Choose New Symbol from the Library Options menu in the upper right corner of the Library window.

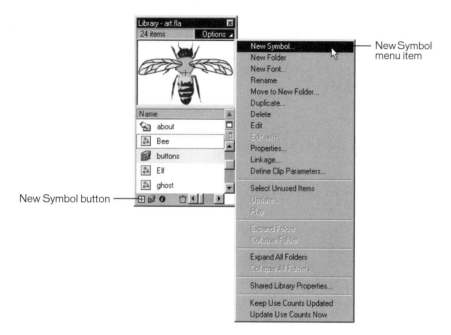

2 In the Symbol Properties dialog box, type the name of the symbol and choose the behavior—Graphic, Button, or Movie Clip. See "Types of symbol behavior" on page 227.

3 Click OK.

Flash adds the symbol to the library and switches to symbol-editing mode. In symbol-editing mode, the name of the symbol appears above the top left corner of the window, above the Timeline, and a cross hair indicates the symbol's registration point.

4 To create the symbol content, use the Timeline, draw with the drawing tools, import media, or create instances of other symbols.

5 When you have finished creating the symbol content, do one of the following to return to movie-editing mode:

- Choose Edit > Edit Movie.

- Click the Scene button in the upper left corner of the document window.

- Click the Edit Scene button in the upper right corner of the document window and choose a scene from the menu.

Converting animation on the Stage into a movie clip

If you've created an animated sequence on the Stage and want to reuse it elsewhere in the movie, or if you want to manipulate it as an instance, you can select it and save it as a movie clip symbol.

To convert animation on the Stage into a movie clip:

1   On the main Timeline, select every frame in every layer of the animation on the Stage that you want to use.

2   Do one of the following to copy the frames:

•   Right-click (Windows) or Control-click (Macintosh) any selected frame and choose Copy Frames from the context menu.

•   Choose Edit > Copy Frames.

3   Deselect your selection and make sure nothing on the Stage is selected. Choose Insert > New Symbol.

4   In the Symbol Properties dialog box, name the symbol. For Behavior, choose Movie Clip, then click OK.

Flash opens a new symbol for editing in symbol-editing mode.

5   On the Timeline, click Frame 1 on Layer 1, and choose Edit > Paste Frames.

This pastes the frames you copied from the main Timeline to the Timeline of this movie clip symbol. Any animation, buttons, or interactivity from the frames you copied now becomes an independent animation (a movie clip symbol) that you can reuse throughout your movie.

6   Do one of the following to exit symbol-editing mode:

•   Choose Edit > Edit Movie.

•   Click the Scene button in the upper left corner of the document window.

•   Click the Edit Scene button in the upper right corner of the document window and choose a scene from the menu.

7   Delete the animation from the main movie Timeline by selecting every frame in every layer of the animation and choosing Insert > Remove Frame.

Duplicating symbols

Duplicating a symbol lets you use an existing symbol as a starting point for creating a new symbol.

To duplicate a symbol:

1 Select a symbol in the Library window.

2 Do one of the following to duplicate the symbol:

• Right-click (Windows) or Control-click (Macintosh) and choose Duplicate from the context menu.

• Choose Duplicate from the Library Options menu.

Creating instances

Once you've created a symbol, you can create instances of that symbol wherever you like throughout the movie, including inside other symbols.

To create a new instance of a symbol:

1 Select a layer in the Timeline.

Flash can place instances only in keyframes, always on the current layer. If you don't select a keyframe, the instance will be added to the first keyframe to the left of the current frame.

2 Choose Window > Library to open the library.

3 Drag the symbol from the library to the Stage.

4 If you created an instance of a graphic symbol, choose Insert > Frame to add the number of frames that will contain the graphic symbol.

After creating an instance of a symbol, use the Instance panel (Windows > Panels > Instance) to specify color effects, assign actions, set the graphic display mode, or change the behavior of the instance. The behavior of the instance is the same as the symbol behavior, unless you specify otherwise. Any changes you make affect only the instance and not the symbol. See "Changing the color and transparency of an instance" on page 241.

Creating buttons

Buttons are actually four-frame interactive movie clips. When you select the button behavior for a symbol, Flash creates a Timeline with four frames. The first three frames display the button's three possible states; the fourth frame defines the active area of the button. The Timeline doesn't actually play; it simply reacts to pointer movement and actions by jumping to the appropriate frame.

To make a button interactive in a movie, you place an instance of the button symbol on the Stage and assign actions to the instance. The actions must be assigned to the instance of the button in the movie, not to frames in the button's Timeline.

Each frame in the Timeline of a button symbol has a specific function:

- The first frame is the Up state, representing the button whenever the pointer is not over the button.

- The second frame is the Over state, representing the button's appearance when the pointer is over it.

- The third frame is the Down state, representing the button's appearance as it is clicked.

- The fourth frame is the Hit state, defining the area that will respond to the mouse click. This area is invisible in the movie.

Typical contents of the Up, Over, and Down and Hit frames (combined in the third frame)

For an interactive lesson on creating buttons in Flash, choose Help > Lessons > Buttons.

To create a button:

1 Choose Edit > Deselect All to ensure that nothing is selected on the Stage.

2 Choose Insert > New Symbol, or press Control+F8 (Windows) or Command+F8 (Macintosh).

To create the button, you convert the button frames to keyframes.

3 In the Symbol Properties dialog box, enter a name for the new button symbol, and for Behavior choose Button.

Flash switches to symbol-editing mode. The Timeline header changes to display four consecutive frames labeled Up, Over, Down, and Hit. The first frame, Up, is a blank keyframe.

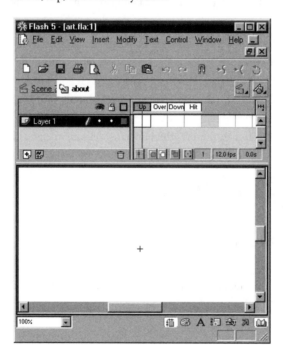

4 To create the Up state button image, use the drawing tools, import a graphic, or place an instance of another symbol on the Stage.

You can use a graphic or movie clip symbol in a button, but you cannot use another button in a button. Use a movie clip symbol if you want the button to be animated.

5 Click the second frame, labeled Over, and choose Insert > Keyframe.

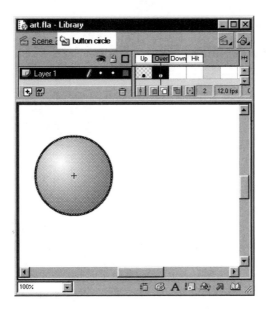

Flash inserts a keyframe that duplicates the contents of the Up frame.

6 Change the button image for the Over state.

7 Repeat steps 5 and 6 for the Down frame and the Hit frame.

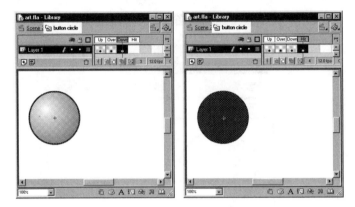

The Hit frame is not visible on the Stage, but it defines the area of the button that responds when clicked. Make sure that the graphic for the Hit frame is a solid area large enough to encompass all the graphic elements of the Up, Down, and Over frames. It can also be larger than the visible button. If you do not specify a Hit frame, the image for the Up state is used as the Hit frame.

You can create a disjoint rollover by placing the Hit frame in a different location than the other button frames.

8 To assign a sound to a state of the button, select that state's frame in the Timeline, choose Modify > Frame to display the Frame panel, and then click the Sound tab in the Frame panel. See "Adding sounds to buttons" on page 171.

9 When you've finished, choose Edit > Edit Movie. Drag the button symbol out of the Library window to create an instance of it in the movie.

Enabling, editing, and testing buttons

By default, Flash keeps buttons disabled as you create them, to make it easier to select and work with them. When a button is disabled, clicking the button selects it. When a button is enabled, it responds to the mouse events that you've specified as if the movie were playing. You can still select enabled buttons, however. In general, it is best to disable buttons as you work, and enable buttons to quickly test their behavior.

To enable and disable buttons:

Choose Control > Enable Simple Buttons. A check mark appears next to the command to indicate buttons are enabled. Choose the command again to disable buttons.

Any buttons on the Stage now respond. As you move the pointer over a button, Flash displays the Over frame; when you click within the button's active area, Flash displays the Down frame.

To select an enabled button:

Use the Arrow tool to drag a selection rectangle around the button.

To move or edit an enabled button:

1 Select the button, as described above.

2 Do one of the following:

• Use the arrow keys to move the button.

• Choose Window > Panels > Instance to edit the button, or Alt-double-click (Windows) or Option-double-click the button (Macintosh).

To test a button, do one of the following:

• Choose Control > Enable Simple Buttons. Move the pointer over the enabled button to test it.

• Select the button in the Library window and click the Play button in the Library preview window.

   Movie clips in buttons are not visible in the Flash authoring environment. See "Previewing and testing movies" on page 74.

• Choose Control > Test Scene or Control > Test Movie.

Editing symbols

When you edit a symbol, Flash updates all the instances of that symbol in the movie. You can edit the symbol in context with the other objects on the Stage using the Edit in Place command. Other objects are dimmed to distinguish them from the symbol you are editing.

You can also edit a symbol in a separate window, using the Edit in New Window command or the symbol-editing mode. Editing a symbol in a separate window lets you see both the symbol and the main Timeline at the same time.

In symbol-editing mode, the window changes from the Stage view to a view of only the symbol; a cross hair indicates the symbol's registration point. In addition, the Instance panel is dimmed, and the name of the symbol appears above the top left corner of the window, above the Timeline.

To edit a symbol in place, do one of the following:

- Double-click the instance on the Stage.

- Select an instance of the symbol on the Stage and right-click (Windows) or Control-click (Macintosh), and choose Edit in Place from the context menu.

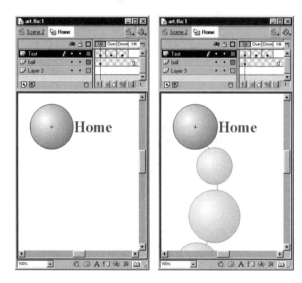

To edit a symbol in a new window:

- Select an instance of the symbol on the Stage and right-click (Windows) or Control-click (Macintosh), and choose Edit in New Window from the context menu.

- Double-click a symbol's icon in the Library window.

To edit a symbol in symbol-editing mode, do one of the following:

- Select an instance of the symbol on the Stage and click the Edit Symbol button at the bottom of the Instance panel.

- Select an instance of the symbol on the Stage; choose Edit > Edit Symbols, or right-click (Windows) or Control-click (Macintosh) and choose Edit from the context menu.

- Double-click the symbol in the Library window or in the Library preview window; then choose Edit from the Library Options menu, or right-click (Windows) or Control-click (Macintosh) and choose Edit from the context menu.

The symbol attached to the instance opens in symbol-editing mode. You can now edit the symbol. All instances of the symbol throughout the movie are updated to reflect your edits.

While editing a symbol, you can use any of the drawing tools, import media, or create instances of other symbols.

To exit symbol-editing mode and return to editing the movie, do one of the following:

- Choose Edit > Edit Movie.

- Click the scene name in the upper left corner of the document window.

- Click the Edit Scene button in the upper right corner of the document window and choose a scene from the menu.

Return to scene — 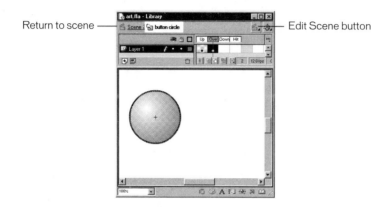 — Edit Scene button

Changing instance properties

Each instance has its own properties that are separate from the symbol. You can change the tint, transparency, and brightness of an instance; redefine how the instance behaves (for example, change a graphic to a movie clip); and set how animation plays inside a graphic instance. You can also skew, rotate, or scale an instance without affecting the symbol.

In addition, you can name a movie clip instance so that you can use it in ActionScript.

To edit instance properties, you use the Instance panel (Windows > Panels > Instance) and the Effect panel (Windows > Panels > Effect).

The properties of an instance are saved with it. If you edit a symbol or relink an instance to a different symbol, any instance properties you've changed still apply to the instance.

Original symbol and two modified instances

Changing the color and transparency of an instance

Each instance of a symbol can have its own color effect. To set color and transparency options for instances, you use the Effect panel, which is docked with the Instance panel. Settings on the Effect panel also affect bitmaps placed within symbols.

Symbol instances, each with its own color effect

When you change the color and transparency for an instance in a specific frame, Flash makes the change as soon as it displays that frame. To make gradual color changes, you must tween the color change. When tweening color, you enter different effect settings in starting and ending keyframes of an instance, and then tween the settings to make the instance's colors shift over time. See "Tweening instances, groups, and type" on page 254.

Note: If you apply a color effect to a movie clip that includes multiple frames, Flash applies the effect to every frame in the movie clip.

To change the color and transparency of an instance:

1 Select the instance on the Stage and choose Window > Panels > Effect.

You can also Alt-double-click (Windows) or Option-double-click (Macintosh) the instance on the Stage to bring the Instance panel forward, and then click the Effect tab.

2 Choose one of the following options in the Effect panel:

- Brightness adjusts the relative lightness or darkness of the image, measured on a scale from black (–100%) to white (100%).

- Tint colors the instance with the same hue. Use the Tint slider at the top of the panel to set the tint percentage, from transparent (1%) to completely saturated (100%). To select a color, enter red, green, and blue values in the respective text boxes or drag the component sliders; or use the Color Picker.

- Alpha adjusts the transparency of the instance.

- Advanced separately adjusts the red, green, blue, and transparency values of an instance. This is most useful when you want to create and animate subtle color effects on objects such as bitmaps. The controls on the left let you reduce the color or transparency values by a specified percentage. The controls on the right let you reduce or increase the color or transparency values by a constant value.

The current red, green, blue, and alpha values are multiplied by the percentage values, and then added to the constant values in the right column, producing the new color values. For example, if the current red value is 100, setting the left slider to 50% and the right slider to 100 produces a new red value of 150 ((100 x .5) + 100 = 150).

Any changes you make update automatically on the Stage.

You can also change color using the ActionScript Color object. For more information, see the *ActionScript Reference Guide.*

Replacing an instance with another symbol

Assigning a different symbol to an instance displays a different instance on the Stage while leaving all the original instance properties (such as color effects and button actions) intact.

For example, say you're creating a cartoon with a Rat symbol for your character, but decide to change the character to Cat. You could switch the Cat for the Rat symbol and have the updated character appear in roughly the same location in all of your frames.

To assign a different symbol to an instance:

1 Select the instance on the Stage and choose Window > Panels > Instance; or Alt-double-click (Windows) or Option-double-click (Macintosh) the instance on the Stage to bring the Instance panel forward.

2 Click the Swap Symbol button at the bottom of the Instance panel.

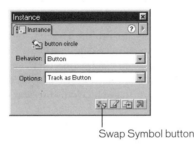

Swap Symbol button

3 In the Swap Symbol dialog box, select a symbol that will replace the one currently assigned to the instance. To duplicate a selected symbol, click the Duplicate Symbol button at the bottom of the dialog box.

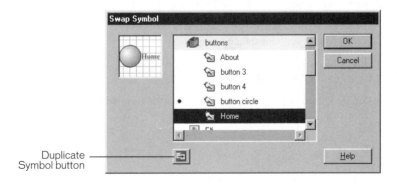

Duplicate Symbol button

Duplicating lets you base a new symbol on an existing one in the library and minimizes copying if you're making several symbols that differ just slightly.

Changing an instance's type

You can change an instance's type to redefine its behavior in the movie. For example, if a graphic instance contains animation that you want to play independently of the main movie's Timeline, you could redefine the graphic instance as a movie clip instance.

To change an instance's type:

1 Select the instance on the Stage and choose Window > Panels > Instance; or Alt-double-click (Windows) or Option-double-click (Macintosh) the instance on the Stage to bring the Instance panel forward.

2 For Behavior, choose Graphic, Button, or Movie Clip.

Setting the animation for graphic instances

You can determine how animation sequences inside a graphic instance play during the movie by setting options in the Instance panel.

An animated graphic symbol is tied to the Timeline of the movie in which the symbol is placed. In contrast, a movie clip symbol has its own independent Timeline. Animated graphic symbols, because they use the same Timeline as the main movie, display their animation in movie-editing mode. Movie clip symbols appear as static objects on the Stage and do not appear as animations in the Flash editing environment.

To set the animation of a graphic instance:

1 Select a graphic instance on the Stage and choose Window > Panels > Instance; or Alt-double-click (Windows) or Option-double-click (Macintosh) the instance on the Stage to bring the Instance panel forward.

2 Choose an animation option from the pop-up menu below the instance type:

- Loop loops all the animation sequences contained in the current instance for as many frames as the instance occupies.

- Play Once plays the animation sequence beginning from the frame you specify to the end of the animation and then stops.

- Single Frame displays one frame of the animation sequence. Specify which frame to display.

Breaking apart instances

To break the link between an instance and a symbol and make the instance into a collection of ungrouped shapes and lines, you break apart the instance. This is useful for changing the instance substantially without affecting any other instance. If you modify the source symbol after breaking apart the instance, the instance is not updated with the changes.

To break apart an instance of a symbol:

1 Select the instance on the Stage.

2 Choose Modify > Break Apart.

   This breaks the instance into its component graphic elements.

3 Use the painting and drawing tools to modify these elements as desired.

Getting information about instances on the Stage

As you create a movie, it can be difficult to identify a particular instance of a symbol on the Stage, particularly if you are working with multiple instances of the same symbol. You can identify instances using the Instance panel, Info panel, or Movie Explorer.

All panels display the selected instance's name and icons that indicate its type—graphic, button, or movie clip. In addition, you can view the following information:

- In the Instance panel, you can view the instance's behavior and settings—for graphics, the loop mode and the length of the symbol in frames; for buttons, the tracking option; and for movie clips, the length of the movie clip.

- In the Info panel, you can view the location and size of a selected instance.

- In the Movie Explorer, you can view the contents of the current movie, including instances and symbols. See "Using the Movie Explorer" on page 98.

In addition, in the Actions panel, you can view any actions assigned to a graphic, button, or movie clip.

To get information about an instance on the Stage:

1 Select the instance on the Stage.

2 Display the panel you want to use:

- To display the Instance panel, choose Window > Panels > Instance or Alt-double-click (Windows) or Option-double-click (Macintosh) the selected instance.

- To display the Info panel, choose Window > Panels > Info.

- To display the Actions panel, choose Window > Actions.

- To display the Movie Explorer, choose Window > Movie Explorer.

  For more information on the Movie Explorer, see "Using the Movie Explorer" on page 98.

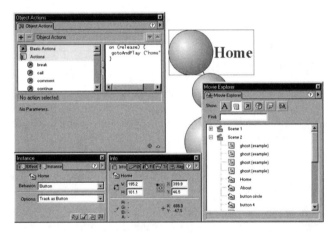

A selected button instance and information displayed in the Instance panel, Info panel, Movie Explorer, and Actions panel

To view the symbol definition for the selected symbol in the Movie Explorer:

1 Click the Show Buttons, Movie Clips, and Graphics button at the top of the Movie Explorer.

2 Right-click (Windows) or Control-click (Macintosh) and choose Show Symbol Instances and Go to Symbol Definition from the context menu; or choose these options from the pop-up menu in the upper right corner of the Movie Explorer.

To jump to the scene containing instances of a selected symbol:

1 Display the symbol definitions as described in the previous procedure.

2 Right-click (Windows) or Control-click (Macintosh) and choose Show Movie Elements and Select Symbol Instances from the context menu; or choose these options from the pop-up menu in the upper right corner of the Movie Explorer.

CHAPTER 11
Creating Animation

11

You create animation by changing the content of successive frames. You can make an object move across the Stage, increase or decrease its size, rotate, change color, fade in or out, or change shape. Changes can occur independently of, or in concert with, other changes. For example, you can make an object rotate and fade in as it moves across the Stage.

There are two methods for creating an animation sequence in Flash: frame-by-frame animation and tweened animation. In frame-by-frame animation you create the image in every frame. In tweened animation, you create starting and ending frames and let Flash create the frames in between. Flash varies the object's size, rotation, color, or other attributes evenly between the starting and ending frames to create the appearance of movement.

Tweened animation is an effective way to create movement and changes over time while minimizing file size. In tweened animation, Flash stores only the values for the changes between frames. In frame-by-frame animation, Flash stores the values for each complete frame.

For an interactive introduction to animation, choose Help > Lessons > Animation.

Note: You can also create animation by using the Set Property action. See *the ActionScript Reference Guide* .

Creating keyframes

A keyframe is a frame where you define changes in the animation. When you create frame-by-frame animation, every frame is a keyframe. In keyframe (tweened) animation, you define keyframes at important points in the animation and let Flash create the content of frames in between. Flash displays the interpolated frames of a tweened animation as light blue or green with an arrow drawn between keyframes. Flash redraws shapes in each keyframe. You should create keyframes only at those points in the artwork where something changes.

Keyframes are indicated in the Timeline: a keyframe with content on it is represented by a solid circle, and an empty keyframe is represented by a vertical line before the frame. Subsequent frames that you add to the same layer will have the same content as the keyframe.

To create a keyframe, do one of the following:

• Select a frame in the Timeline and choose Insert > Keyframe.

• Right-click (Windows) or Control-click (Macintosh) a frame in the Timeline and choose Insert Keyframe.

Representations of animations in the Timeline

Flash distinguishes tweened animation from frame-by-frame animation in the Timeline as follows:

- Motion-tweened keyframes are indicated by a black dot and intermediate tweened frames have a black arrow with a light blue background.

- Shape-tweened keyframes are indicated by a black dot and intermediate frames have a black arrow with a light green background.

- A dashed line indicates that the final keyframe is missing.

- A single keyframe is indicated by a black dot. Light-gray frames after a single keyframe contain the same content with no changes and have a black line with a hollow rectangle at the last frame of the span.

- A small *a* indicates that the frame has been assigned a frame action with the Actions panel.

- A red flag indicates that the frame contains a label or comment.

About layers in animation

Each scene in a Flash movie can consist of any number of layers. As you animate, you use layers to organize the components of an animation sequence and to separate animated objects so they don't erase, connect, or segment each other. If you want Flash to tween the movement of several groups or symbols at once, each must be on a separate layer. Typically, the background layer contains static artwork. Additional layers contain one separate animated object each.

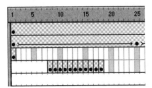

Layers appear as rows in the Timeline.

When a movie has several layers, tracking and editing the objects on one or two of them can be difficult. This task is easier if you work with the content one layer at a time. See Chapter 8, "Using Layers."

About frame rates

A frame rate that's too slow makes the animation appear to stop and start; a frame rate that's too fast blurs the details of the animation. A frame rate of 12 frames per second (fps) usually gives the best results on the Web. QuickTime and AVI movies generally have a frame rate of 12 fps, while the standard motion-picture rate is 24 fps.

The complexity of the animation and the speed of the computer on which the animation is being played affect the smoothness of the playback. Test your animations on a variety of machines to determine optimum frame rates.

Because you specify only one frame rate for the entire Flash movie, it is a good idea to set this rate before you begin creating animation. See "Creating a new movie and setting its properties" on page 74.

Extending still images

When you create a background for animation, it's often necessary to make a still image span several frames. Adding new frames (not keyframes) to a layer extends the contents of the last keyframe in all the new frames.

To extend a still image through multiple frames:

1 Create an image in the first keyframe of the sequence.

2 Select a frame to the right, at the end of the span that you want to add.

3 Choose Insert > Frame.

To use a shortcut to extend still images:

1 Create an image in the first keyframe.

2 Alt-drag the keyframe to the right. This creates a new span, but without a new keyframe at the end point.

About tweened animation

Flash can create two types of tweened animation. In *motion tweening*, you define properties such as position, size, and rotation for an instance, group, or text block at one point in time, and then you change those properties at another point in time. In *shape tweening*, you draw a shape at one point in time, and then you change that shape or draw another shape at another point in time. Flash interpolates the values or shapes for the frames in between, creating the animation.

Tweening instances, groups, and type

To tween the changes in properties of instances, groups, and type, you use motion tweening. Flash can tween position, size, rotation, and skew of instances, groups, and type. Additionally, Flash can tween the color of instances and type, creating gradual color shifts or making an instance fade in or out. To tween the color of groups or type, you must make them into symbols. See "Creating symbols" on page 228.

If you change the number of frames between the two keyframes, or move the group or symbol in either keyframe, Flash automatically tweens the frames again.

You can create a motion tween using one of two methods:

- Create the starting and ending keyframes for the animation and use the Motion Tweening option in the Frame Properties panel.

- Create the first keyframe for the animation, and then choose Insert > Create Motion Tween and move the object to the new location on the Stage. Flash automatically creates the ending keyframe.

When tweening position, you can make the object move along a nonlinear path. See "Tweening motion along a path" on page 258.

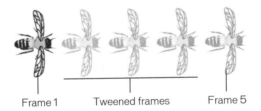

Frame 1   Tweened frames   Frame 5

The bee's second, third, and fourth frames result from tweening the first and last keyframes.

To create a motion tween using the Motion Tweening option:

1 Click a layer name to make it the current layer, and select an empty keyframe in the layer where you want the animation to start.

2 Create an instance, group, or text block on the Stage, or drag an instance of a symbol from the Library window.

   To motion tween an object you have drawn, you must convert it to a symbol.

3 Create a second keyframe where you want the animation to end.

4 Do one of the following to modify the instance, group, or text block in the ending frame:

- Move the item to a new position.

- Modify the item's size, rotation, or skew.

- Modify the item's color (instance or text block only).

   To tween the color of elements other than instances or text blocks, use shape tweening. See "Tweening shapes" on page 260.

5 Choose Window > Panels > Frame.

6 For Tweening, select Motion.

7 If you modified the size of the item in step 4, select Scale to tween the size of the selected item.

8 Click and drag the arrow next to the Easing value or enter a value to adjust the rate of change between tweened frames:

- To begin the motion tween slowly and accelerate the tween toward the end of the animation, drag the slider up or enter a value between -1 and -100.

- To begin the motion tween rapidly and decelerate the tween toward the end of the animation, drag the slider down or enter a positive value between 1 and 100.

   By default, the rate of change between tweened frames is constant. Easing creates a more natural appearance of acceleration or deceleration by gradually adjusting the rate of change.

9 To rotate the selected item while tweening, choose an option from the Rotate menu:

- Choose None (the default setting) to apply no rotation.

- Choose Auto to rotate the object once in the direction requiring the least motion.

- Choose Clockwise (CW) or Counterclockwise (CCW) to rotate the object as indicated, and then enter a number to specify the number of rotations.

   Note: This rotation is in addition to any rotation you applied to the ending frame in step 4.

10 If you are using a motion path, select Orient to Path to orient the baseline of the tweened element to the motion path. See "Tweening motion along a path" on page 258.

11 Select Synchronization to ensure that the instance loops properly in the main movie.

Use the Synchronize command if the number of frames in the animation sequence inside the symbol is not an even multiple of the number of frames the graphic instance occupies in the movie.

12 If you are using a motion path, select Snap to attach the tweened element to the motion path by its registration point.

To create a motion tween using the Create Motion Tween command:

1 Select an empty keyframe and draw an object on the Stage, or drag an instance of a symbol from the Library window.

2 Choose Insert > Create Motion Tween.

If you drew an object in step 1, Flash automatically converts the object to a symbol and assigns it the name tween1. If you drew more than one object, additional objects are named tween2, tween3, and so on.

3 Click inside the frame where you want the animation to end, and choose Insert > Frame.

4 Move the object, instance, or type block on the Stage to the desired position. Adjust the size of the element if you want to tween its scale. Adjust the rotation of the element if you want to tween its rotation. Deselect the object when you have completed adjustments.

A keyframe is automatically added to the end of the frame range.

5 Select the keyframe at the end of the motion tween and choose Window > Panels > Frame. Motion Tweening should be selected automatically in the Frame panel.

6 If you modified the size of the item in step 4, select Scale to tween the size of the selected item.

7   Click and drag the arrow next to the Easing value or enter a value to adjust the rate of change between tweened frames:

- To begin the motion tween slowly and accelerate the tween toward the end of the animation, drag the slider up or enter a value between -1 and -100.

- To begin the motion tween rapidly and decelerate the tween toward the end of the animation, drag the slider down or enter a positive value between 1 and 100.

    By default, the rate of change between tweened frames is constant. Easing creates a more natural appearance of acceleration or deceleration by gradually adjusting the rate of change.

8   To rotate the selected item while tweening, choose an option from the Rotate menu:

- Choose None (the default setting) to apply no rotation.

- Choose Auto to rotate the object once in the direction requiring the least motion.

- Choose Clockwise (CW) or Counterclockwise (CCW) to rotate the object as indicated, and then enter a number to specify the number of rotations.

    Note: This rotation is in addition to any rotation you applied to the ending frame in step 4.

9   If you are using a motion path, select Orient to Path to orient the baseline of the tweened element to the motion path. See the following section.

10 Select Synchronize to ensure that the instance loops properly in the main movie.

    Use the Synchronize command if the number of frames in the animation sequence inside the symbol is not an even multiple of the number of frames the graphic instance occupies in the movie.

11 If you are using a motion path, select Snap to attach the tweened element to the motion path by its registration point.

Tweening motion along a path

Motion guide layers let you draw paths along which tweened instances, groups, or text blocks can be animated. You can link multiple layers to a motion guide layer to have multiple objects follow the same path. A normal layer that is linked to a motion guide layer becomes a guided layer.

To create a motion path for a tweened animation:

1 Create a motion-tweened animation sequence as described in "Tweening instances, groups, and type" on page 254.

   If you select Orient to Path, the baseline of the tweened element will orient to the motion path. If you select Snap, the registration point of the tweened element will snap to the motion path.

2 Do one of the following:

• Select the layer containing the animation and choose Insert > Motion Guide.

• Right-click (Windows) or Control-click (Macintosh) the layer containing the animation and choose Add Motion Guide from the context menu.

   Flash creates a new layer above the selected layer with a motion guide icon to the left of the layer name.

3 Use the Pen, Pencil, Line, Circle, Rectangle, or Brush tool to draw the desired path.

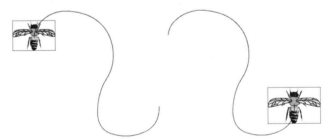

4 Snap the center to the beginning of the line in the first frame, and to the end of the line in the last frame.

   Note: Drag the symbol by its registration point for best snapping results.

5 To hide the motion guide layer and the line so that only the object's movement is visible while you work, click in the Eye column on the motion guide layer.

The group or symbol follows the motion path when you play the animation.

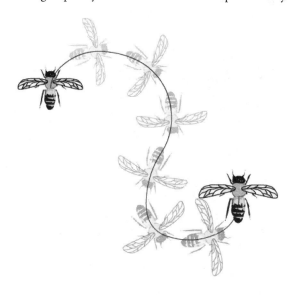

To link layers to a motion guide layer, do one of the following:

- Drag an existing layer below the motion guide layer. The layer is indented under the motion guide layer. All objects on this layer automatically snap to the motion path.

- Create a new layer under the motion guide layer. Objects you tween on this layer are automatically tweened along the motion path.

- Select a layer below a motion guide layer. Choose Modify > Layer and select Guided in the Layer Properties dialog box.

- Alt-click (Windows) or Option-click (Macintosh) the layer.

To unlink layers from a motion guide layer:

1 Select the layer you want to unlink.

2 Do one of the following:

- Drag the layer above the motion guide layer.

- Choose Modify > Layer and select Normal as the layer type in the Layer Properties dialog box.

- Alt-click (Windows) or Option-click (Macintosh) the layer.

Tweening shapes

By tweening shapes, you can create an effect similar to morphing, making one shape appear to change into another shape over time. Flash can also tween the location, size, and color of shapes.

Tweening one shape at a time usually yields the best results. If you tween multiple shapes at one time, all the shapes must be on the same layer.

Flash cannot tween the shape of groups, symbols, text blocks, or bitmap images. Use Modify > Break Apart to apply shape tweening to these elements. See "Breaking apart groups and objects" on page 199.

To control more complex or improbable shape changes, use shape hints, which control how parts of the original shape move into the new shape. See "Using shape hints" on page 262.

To tween a shape:

1 Click a layer name to make it the current layer and select an empty keyframe where you want the animation to start.

2 Create the image for the first frame of the sequence.

Use any of the drawing tools to create a shape.

3 Create a second keyframe the desired number of frames after the first frame.

4 Create the image for the last frame of the sequence. (You can tween the shape, color, or position of the image created in step 2.)

5 Choose Window > Panels > Frame.

6 For Tweening, select Shape.

7 Click and drag the arrow next to the Easing value or enter a value to adjust the rate of change between tweened frames:

- To begin the shape tween gradually and accelerate the tween toward the end of the animation, drag the slider down or enter a value between -1 and -100.

- To begin the shape tween rapidly and decelerate the tween toward the end of the animation, drag the slider up or enter a positive value between 1 and 100.

By default, the rate of change between tweened frames is constant. Easing creates a more natural appearance of transformation by gradually adjusting the rate of change.

8 Choose an option for Blend:

- Distributive creates an animation in which the intermediate shapes are smoother and more irregular.

- Angular creates an animation that preserves apparent corners and straight lines in the intermediate shapes.

Note: Angular is appropriate only for blending shapes with sharp corners and straight lines. If the shapes you choose do not have corners, Flash reverts to distributive shape tweening.

Using shape hints

To control more complex or improbable shape changes, you can use shape hints. Shape hints identify points that should correspond in starting and ending shapes. For example, if you are tweening a drawing of a face as it changes expression, you can use a shape hint to mark each eye. Then, instead of the face becoming an amorphous tangle while the shape change takes place, each eye remains recognizable and changes separately during the shift.

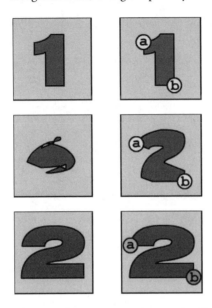

The same shape tween, without and with shape hints, respectively.

Shape hints contain letters (*a* through *z*) for identifying which points correspond in the starting and ending shape. You can use up to 26 shape hints.

Shape hints are yellow in a starting keyframe and green in an ending keyframe. When not on a curve, shape hints are red.

For best results when tweening shapes, follow these guidelines:

- In complex shape tweening, create intermediate shapes and tween them instead of just defining a starting and ending shape.

- Make sure that shape hints are logical. For example, if you are using three shape hints for a triangle, they must be in the same order on the original triangle and the triangle to be tweened. The order cannot be *abc* in the first keyframe and *acb* in the second.

- Shape hints work best if you place them in counterclockwise order beginning at the top left corner of the shape.

To use shape hints:

1 Select the first keyframe in a shape-tweened sequence.

2 Choose Modify > Transform > Add Shape Hint.

   The beginning shape hint appears as a red circle with the letter *a* somewhere on the shape.

3 Move the shape hint to a point that you want to mark.

4 Select the last keyframe in the tweening sequence.

   The ending shape hint appears somewhere on the shape as a green circle with the letter *a*.

5 Move the shape hint to the point in the ending shape that should correspond to the first point you marked.

6 Run the movie again to see how the shape hints change the shape tweening. Move the shape hints to fine-tune the tweening.

7 Repeat this process to add additional shape hints. New hints appear with the letters that follow (*b, c,* and so on).

While working with shape hints, you can also do the following:

• To see all shape hints, choose View > Show Shape Hints. The layer and keyframe that contain shape hints must be current for Show Shape Hints to be available.

• To remove a shape hint, drag it off the Stage.

• To remove all shape hints, choose Modify > Transform > Remove All Hints.

Creating frame-by-frame animations

Frame-by-frame animation changes the contents of the Stage in every frame and is best suited to complex animation in which an image changes in every frame instead of simply moving. Frame-by-frame animation increases file size more rapidly than tweened animation.

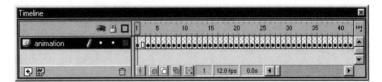

Use frame-by-frame animation when you need to change an image in each frame.

To create frame-by-frame animation:

1 Click a layer name to make it the current layer, and select a frame in the layer where you want the animation to start.

2 If the frame isn't already a keyframe, choose Insert > Keyframe to make it one.

3 Create the image for the first frame of the sequence.

You can use the drawing tools, paste graphics from the Clipboard, or import a file.

4 Click the next frame to the right in the same row and choose Insert > Keyframe, or right-click (Windows) or Control-click (Macintosh) and choose Insert Keyframe from the Frame pop-up menu.

This adds a new keyframe whose contents are the same as those of the first keyframe.

5 Alter the contents of this frame on the Stage to develop the next increment of the animation.

6 To complete your frame-by-frame animation sequence, repeat steps 4 and 5 until you have built the motion you want.

7 To test the animation sequence, choose Control > Play or click the Play button on the Controller.

It can be useful to play back animation as you create it.

Editing animation

After you create a frame or a keyframe, you can move it elsewhere in the current layer or to another layer, remove it, and make other changes. Only keyframes are editable. You can view tweened frames, but you can't edit them directly. You edit tweened frames by changing one of the defining keyframes or by inserting a new keyframe between the beginning and ending keyframes. You can drag items from the Library window onto the Stage to add the items to the current keyframe.

To display and edit more than one frame at a time, you use onion skinning.

To insert frames in the Timeline, do one of the following:

- To insert a new frame, choose Insert > Frame.

- To create a new keyframe, choose Insert > Keyframe, or right-click (Windows) or Control-click (Macintosh) the frame where you want to place a keyframe, and choose Insert Keyframe from the context menu.

- To create a new blank keyframe, choose Insert > Blank Keyframe, or right-click (Windows) or Control-click (Macintosh) the frame where you want to place the keyframe, and choose Insert Blank Keyframe from the context menu.

To delete or modify a frame or keyframe, do one of the following:

- To delete a frame, keyframe, or frame sequence, select the frame, keyframe, or sequence and choose Insert > Remove Frame, or right-click (Windows) or Control-click (Macintosh) the frame, keyframe, or sequence and choose Remove Frame from the context menu. Surrounding frames remain unchanged.

- To move a keyframe or frame sequence and its contents, drag the keyframe or sequence to the desired location.

- To extend the duration of a keyframe, Alt-drag (Windows) or Option-drag (Macintosh) the keyframe to the final frame of the new sequence.

- To copy a keyframe or frame sequence by dragging, Alt-click (Windows) or Option-click (Macintosh) and drag the keyframe to the new location.

- To copy and paste a frame or frame sequence, select the frame or sequence and choose Edit > Copy Frames. Select a frame or sequence that you want to replace, and choose Edit > Paste Frames.

- To convert a keyframe to a frame, select the keyframe and choose Insert > Clear Keyframe, or right-click (Windows) or Control-click (Macintosh) the keyframe and choose Clear Keyframe from the context menu. The cleared keyframe and all frames up to the subsequent keyframe are replaced with the contents of the frame preceding the cleared keyframe.

- To change the length of a tweened sequence, drag the beginning or ending keyframe left or right. To change the length of a frame-by-frame sequence, see "Creating frame-by-frame animations" on page 264.

- To add an item from the library to the current keyframe, drag the item from the Library window onto the Stage.

- To reverse an animation sequence, select the appropriate frames in one or more layers and choose Modify > Frames > Reverse. There must be keyframes at the beginning and end of the sequence.

Onion skinning

Normally, Flash displays one frame of the animation sequence at a time on the Stage. To help you position and edit a frame-by-frame animation, you can view two or more frames on the Stage at once. The frame under the playhead appears in full color, while surrounding frames are dimmed, making it appear as if each frame were drawn on a sheet of translucent onion-skin paper and the sheets were stacked one on top of another. Dimmed frames cannot be edited.

To simultaneously see several frames of an animation on the Stage:

 Click the Onion Skin button. All frames between the Start Onion Skin and End Onion Skin markers (in the Timeline header) are superimposed as one frame in the Movie window.

Onion Skin button

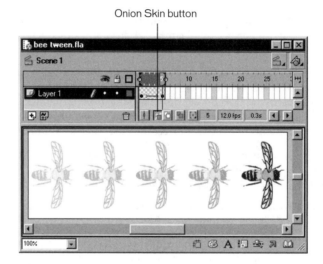

To control onion skinning display, do any of the following:

 • To display onion skinned frames as outlines, click the Onion Skin Outlines button.

• To change the position of either onion skin marker, drag its pointer to a new location. (Normally, the onion skin markers move in conjunction with the current frame pointer.)

 • To enable editing of all frames between onion skin markers, click the Edit Multiple Frames button. Usually onion skinning lets you edit only the current frame. However, you can display the contents of each frame between the onion skin markers normally, and make each available for editing, regardless of which is the current frame.

Note: Locked layers (those with a padlock icon) aren't displayed when onion skinning is turned on. To avoid a multitude of confusing images, you can lock or hide the layers you don't want onion skinned.

To change the display of onion skin markers:

 Click the Modify Onion Markers button and choose an item from the menu:

• Always Show Markers displays the onion skin markers in the Timeline header whether or not onion skinning is on.

• Anchor Onion Marks locks the onion skin markers to their current position in the Timeline header. Normally, the Onion Skin range is relative to the current frame pointer and the Onion Skin markers. By anchoring the Onion Skin markers, you prevent them from moving with the current frame pointer.

• Onion 2 displays two frames on either side of the current frame.

• Onion 5 displays five frames on either side of the current frame.

• Onion All displays all frames on either side of the current frame.

Moving an entire animation

If you need to move an entire animation on the Stage, you must move the graphics in all frames and layers at once to avoid realigning everything.

To move the entire animation to another location on the Stage:

1 Unlock all layers.

To move everything on one or more layers but nothing on other layers, lock or hide all the layers you don't want to move.

 2 Click the Edit Multiple Frames button in the Timeline.

3 Drag the onion skin markers so that they enclose all the frames you want to select, or click Modify Onion Markers and choose Onion All.

4 Choose Edit > Select All.

5 Drag the entire animation to the new location on the Stage.

CHAPTER 12
Creating Interactive Movies
. . . .

In simple animation, Flash plays the scenes and frames of a movie sequentially. In an interactive movie, your audience uses the keyboard, the mouse, or both to jump to different parts of a movie, move objects, enter information in forms, and perform many other interactive operations.

You create interactive movies by setting up actions—sets of instructions written in ActionScript that run when a specific event occurs. The events that can trigger an action are either the playhead reaching a frame, or the user clicking a button or pressing keys on the keyboard.

You set up actions in the Actions panel for a button, a movie clip, or a frame. Using the Actions panel controls in Normal Mode, you can insert actions without having to write any ActionScript; if you're proficient in ActionScript, you can write your own script. Instructions can be in the form of a single action, such as instructing a movie to stop playing, or a series of actions, such as first evaluating a condition and then performing an action. Many actions require little programming experience to set up. Other actions require some familiarity with programming languages and are intended for advanced development; for information on creating advanced actions, see the *ActionScript Reference Guide*.

About ActionScript

Flash uses the ActionScript scripting language to add interactivity to a movie. Similar to JavaScript, ActionScript is an object-oriented programming language. In object-oriented scripting, you organize information by arranging it into groups called classes. You can create multiple instances of a class, called objects, to use in your scripts. You can use ActionScript's predefined classes and create your own.

When you create a class, you define all the properties (characteristics) and methods (behaviors) of each object it creates, just as real-world objects are defined. For example, a person has properties such as gender, height, and hair color and methods such as talk, walk, and throw. In this example, "person" is a class and each individual person is an object, or an instance of that class.

Objects in ActionScript can contain data or they can be graphically represented on the Stage as movie clips.

For more information on these terms and their use, see the *ActionScript Reference Guide*.

Using the Actions panel

The Actions panel lets you create and edit actions for an object or frame using two different editing modes. You can select prewritten actions from the Toolbox list, drag and drop actions, and use buttons to delete or rearrange actions. In Normal Mode you can write actions using parameter (argument) fields that prompt you for the correct arguments. In Expert Mode you can write and edit actions directly in a text box, much like writing script with a text editor.

For information on choosing Actions panel options and switching between editing modes, see the corresponding topics in the *ActionScript Reference Guide.*

To display the Actions panel:

Choose Window > Actions.

Selecting a frame, button, or movie clip instance makes the Actions panel active. The Actions panel title changes to Object Actions if a button or movie clip is selected, and to Frame Actions if a frame is selected.

To select an actions editing mode:

1   With the Actions panel displayed, click the arrow in the upper right corner of the panel to display the pop-up menu.

2   Choose Normal Mode or Expert Mode from the pop-up menu.

Each script maintains its own mode. For example, if you script one instance of a button in Normal Mode and another in Expert Mode, switching between the selected buttons will switch the panel's mode.

Using the Actions panel in Normal Mode

In Normal Mode, you create actions by selecting actions from a list on the left side of the panel, called the Toolbox list. The Toolbox list contains Basic Actions, Actions, Operators, Functions, Properties, and Objects categories. The Basic Actions category contains the simplest Flash actions and is available only in Normal Mode. The selected actions are listed on the right side of the panel, in the Actions list. You can add, delete, or change the order of action statements; you can also enter parameters (arguments) for actions in the Parameters pane at the bottom of the panel.

In Normal Mode, you use the controls in the Actions panel to delete or change the order and parameters of statements. These controls are especially useful for managing frame or button actions that have several statements.

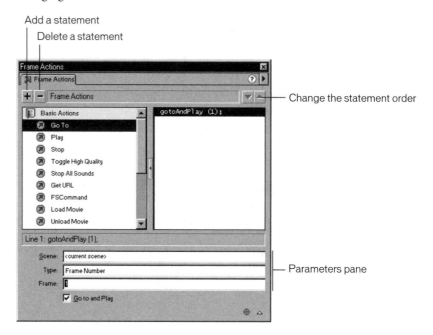

To select an action:

1 Click an Actions category in the Toolbox to display the actions in that category.

2 Double-click an action or drag it to the Actions list on the right.

To use the Parameters pane:

 1 Click the triangle in the lower right corner of the Actions panel to display the Parameters pane.

2 Select the action and enter new values in the parameters text boxes to change parameters of existing actions.

To insert a movie clip target path:

1 Click the Target Path button in the lower right corner of the Actions panel to display the Insert Target Path dialog box.

2 Select a movie clip from the display list.

For information on using a target path, see "Controlling other movies and movie clips" on page 295.

To move a statement up or down the list:

1 Select a statement in the Actions list.

2 Click the Up or Down Arrow buttons in the Actions panel.

To delete an action:

1 Select a statement in the Actions list.

2 Click the Delete (–) button.

To resize the Toolbox or Actions list, do one of the following:

• Drag the vertical splitter bar that appears between the Toolbox and Actions list.

• Double-click the splitter bar to collapse the Toolbox list; double-click the bar again to redisplay the list.

• Click the Left or Right Arrow button on the splitter bar to expand or collapse the list.

When the Toolbox list is hidden, you can still access its items using the Add (+) button in the upper left of the Actions panel.

Expert Mode

In Expert Mode, you create actions by entering ActionScript into the text box on the right side of the panel or by selecting actions from the Toolbox list on the left. You edit actions, enter parameters for actions, or delete actions directly in the text box, much as you would create script in a text editor.

Expert Mode lets advanced ActionScript users edit their scripts with a text editor, as they would JavaScript or VBScript. Expert Mode differs from Normal Mode in these ways:

- Selecting an item in the Add pop-up menu or Toolbox list inserts the item in the text-editing area at the pointer's position.

- No parameter text boxes appear.

- In the button panel, only the Add (+) button works.

- The Up and Down Arrow buttons remain inactive.

Toolbox list —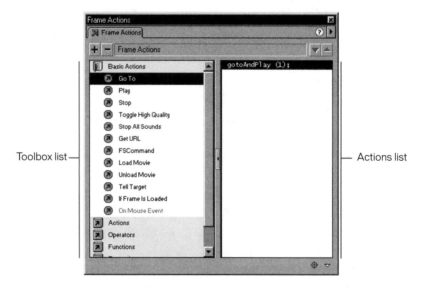— Actions list

For more information on using Export Mode, see the topic in the *ActionScript Reference Guide.*

Assigning actions to objects

You can assign an action to a button or a movie clip to make an action execute when the user clicks a button or rolls the pointer over it, or when the movie clip loads or reaches a certain frame. You assign the action to an instance of the button or movie clip; other instances of the symbol aren't affected. For a description of the actions you can add, see "Using basic actions for navigation and interaction" on page 283.

When you assign an action to a button or a movie clip, Flash automatically assigns a special action called a handler—the On Mouse Event action for buttons or the On Clip Event action for movie clips. A handler manages an event in a certain way and contains groups of ActionScript statements that run when a specific event occurs. Each handler begins with the word `on` or `onClipEvent` followed by the event to which the handler responds.

Events are actions that occur while a movie is playing—for example, a movie clip loading, the playhead entering a frame, or the user pressing a key on the keyboard. You can specify the mouse event or keyboard key that triggers the action; see "Setting mouse event options" on page 279. You can also specify the clip event that triggers the action; see the *ActionScript Reference Guide.*

Once you've assigned an action, it's recommended that you test whether it works. Only simple frame actions such as Go To and Play work in editing mode.

The following instructions describe how to set actions for objects using the Actions panel in Normal Mode. For information on using the Actions panel in Expert Mode, see the *ActionScript Reference Guide.*

To assign an action to a button or movie clip:

1 Select a button or movie clip instance and choose Window > Actions.

   If the selection is not a button instance, a movie clip instance, or a frame, or if the selection includes multiple objects, the Actions panel will be dimmed.

   (For information on assigning an action to a frame, see "Assigning actions to frames" on page 281.)

2 In the Toolbox list on the left side of the panel, click the Basic Actions category to display the basic actions.

   For a description of the actions you can add, see "Using basic actions for navigation and interaction" on page 283.

3 To assign an action, do one of the following:

- Double-click an action in the Basics Actions category.

- Drag an action from the Basic Actions category on the left to the Actions list on the right side of the panel.

- Click the Add (+) button and choose an action from the pop-up menu.

- Use the keyboard shortcut.

If you selected a movie clip, Flash automatically inserts the On Clip Event action and the action you selected in the Actions list. If you selected a button, Flash automatically inserts the On Mouse Event code to trigger any selected action.

4 To display the Parameters pane, click the triangle in the lower right corner of the Actions panel. Select the action and enter new values in the Parameters text boxes to change parameters of existing actions.

Parameters vary depending on the action you choose. For example, the default On Clip parameter is Load. See "Using basic actions for navigation and interaction" on page 283 for information on parameters for the most commonly used actions.

5 Repeat steps 3 and 4 to assign additional actions as necessary.

Setting mouse event options

Assigning an action to a button also automatically assigns a Mouse Event action to the button to handle, or manage, the action.

Each handler begins with the word on, followed by the event to which the handler responds.

For example:

```
on (release)
on (keyPress "<Space>")
on (rollOver)
```

The release parameter indicates that the user pressed and released the mouse button.

You can specify which mouse events trigger a button action using the Actions panel.

To set mouse event options:

1 Select the button to which you'll assign an action.

2 In the Toolbox list on the left side of the Actions panel, click the Basic Actions category to display the basic actions.

3 Choose from the following options:

• Select the On Mouse Event action.

• Select an action in the Basic Actions category.

4 In the Parameters pane, for Event, select a keyboard or mouse event that will trigger the action:

- Press triggers the action when the mouse button is pressed while the pointer is over the button.

- Release (the default) triggers the action when the mouse button is released while the pointer is over the button. This sets up standard clicking behavior.

- Release Outside triggers the action when the mouse button is released while the pointer is not over the button.

- Key Press triggers the action when the specified key is pressed. If you select this option, enter the key in the text box.

- Roll Over triggers the action when the pointer rolls over the button.

- Roll Out triggers the action when the pointer rolls outside the button.

- Drag Over triggers the action when the mouse button is pressed while the pointer is over the button, the pointer is rolled off the button, and then the pointer is rolled back over the button.

- Drag Out triggers the action when the mouse button is pressed over the button and the pointer then rolls off the button.

5 Assign any additional actions to the button.

For more information on mouse events, see the *ActionScript Reference Guide.*

To test frame actions:

1 Choose Control > Enable Simple Frame Actions.

2 Choose Control > Test Movie.

Assigning actions to frames

To make a movie do something when it reaches a keyframe, you assign a frame action to the keyframe. For example, to create a loop within a movie, you might add a frame action to Frame 20 that specifies "go to Frame 10 and play."

It's a good idea to place all of your frame actions in one layer to make it easier to track them. Frames with actions display a small *a* in the Timeline.

Frame with actions

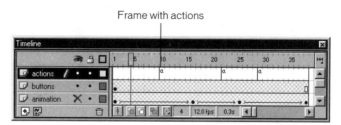

Once you've assigned an action, it's recommended that you test whether it works, using the Control > Test Movie command. Most actions won't work in editing mode.

For a description of the actions you can add, see "Using basic actions for navigation and interaction" on page 283.

The following instructions describe how to set actions for frames using the Actions panel in Normal Mode. For information on using the Actions panel in Expert Mode, see the *ActionScript Reference Guide*.

To assign an action to a keyframe:

1 Select a keyframe in the Timeline and choose Window > Actions.

If a selected frame is not a keyframe, the action is assigned to the previous keyframe. If the selection is not a frame, or if the selection includes multiple frames, the Actions panel will be dimmed.

(For information on assigning an action to a button or movie clip, see "Assigning actions to objects" on page 277.)

2 In the Toolbox list on the left side of the panel, click the Basic Actions category to display the basic actions.

3 To assign an action, do one of the following:

• Double-click an action in the Basic Actions category in the Toolbox list.

• Drag an action from the Toolbox list on the left to the Actions list on the right side of the panel.

• Click the Add (+) button, and choose a statement from the pop-up menu.

• Use the keyboard shortcut.

4 To display the Parameters pane, click the triangle in the lower right corner of the Actions panel. Select the action and enter new values in the Parameters text boxes to change parameters of existing actions.

Parameters vary depending on the action you choose.

5 Repeat steps 3 and 4 to assign additional actions as necessary.

To test a frame action in a scene:

Choose Control > Test Movie.

Using basic actions for navigation and interaction

The basic actions in the Actions panel let you control navigation and user interaction in a movie by selecting actions and having Flash write the ActionScript for you. The basic actions include the following:

- The Go To action jumps to a frame or scene.
- The Play and Stop actions play and stop movies.
- The Toggle High Quality action adjusts a movie's display quality.
- The Stop All Sounds action stops all sounds in the movie.
- The Get URL action jumps to a different URL.
- The FSCommand action controls the Flash Player that's playing a movie.
- The Load Movie and Unload Movie actions load and unload additional movies.
- The Tell Target action controls other movies and movie clips.
- The If Frame Is Loaded action checks whether a frame is loaded.
- The On Mouse Event action assigns a mouse event or keyboard key that triggers an action.

In addition, the Print action lets you designate frames of your movie as printable.

For information on the other actions available in ActionScript and on advanced interactivity, see the *ActionScript Reference Guide.*

Jumping to a frame or scene

To jump to a specific frame or scene in the movie, you use the Go To action. When the movie jumps to a frame, you can play the movie from the new frame (the default) or stop at the frame. The movie can also jump to a scene and play a specified frame or the first frame of the next or previous scene.

To jump to a frame or scene:

1 Select the frame, button instance, or movie clip instance to which you will assign the action.

2 Choose Window > Actions to display the Actions panel.

3 In the Toolbox list, click the Basic Actions category to display the basic actions, and select the Go To action.

   Flash inserts the Go To and Play action in the Actions list.

4 To keep playing the movie after the jump, leave the Go To and Play option (the default) selected in the Parameters pane. To stop the movie at a specified frame, deselect Go To and Play. The action changes to Go To and Stop.

5 In the Scene pop-up menu in the Parameters pane, specify the destination scene: Current or Named Scene to specify a frame within the scene, or Next or Previous to have the movie jump to the first frame of the scene.

6 In the Type pop-up menu in the Parameters pane, choose a destination frame:

- Next or Previous Frame.

- Frame Number, Frame Label, or Expression allow you to specify a frame. Expressions are any part of a statement that produces a value, such as 1+1.

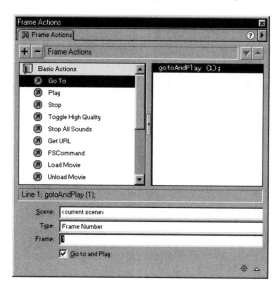

7 If you chose Frame Number, Frame Label, or Expression in step 6, for Frame, enter the frame by number, label, or an expression that evaluates to a frame number or label.

The following statement indicates the frame that is five frames ahead of the frame that contains the action:

```
gotoAndStop(_currentframe + 5);
```

For information on writing expressions, see the *ActionScript Reference Guide*.

Playing and stopping movies

Unless instructed otherwise, once a movie starts, it plays through every frame in the Timeline. You can stop or start a movie at specific intervals by using the Play and Stop actions. For example, you can stop a movie at the end of a scene before proceeding to the next scene. Once stopped, a movie must be explicitly started again, using the Play action.

The Play and Stop actions are most commonly used to control movie clips with buttons, or to control the main Timeline. The movie clip you want to control must have an instance name, must be targeted, and must be present in the Timeline. See "Controlling other movies and movie clips" on page 295.

To start or stop a movie:

1 Select the frame, button instance, or movie clip instance to which you will assign the action.

2 Choose Window > Actions to display the Actions panel.

3 In the Toolbox list, click the Basic Actions category to display the basic actions, and select the Stop action.

Flash inserts ActionScript similar to the following in the Actions list:

```
onClipEvent (load) {
    stop ();
}
```

where `onClipEvent (load)` indicates that when the movie loads, Flash should execute the instruction `stop` to stop the movie.

Note: Empty parentheses after an action indicate that it's a method (capability) that has no parameters or arguments.

To play a movie clip:

1 Select the movie clip you want to play, or select the button that controls the playback.

2 Choose Window > Actions to display the Actions panel.

3 In the Toolbox list, click the Basic Actions category to display the basic actions, and select the Play action.

Flash enters ActionScript similar to the following in the Actions list:

```
on (release) {
    play ();
}
```

where `on(release)` indicates that when the button is released, Flash should execute the instruction `play` to play the movie.

Adjusting movie display quality

Anti-aliasing requires a faster processor to smooth each frame of the movie before it is rendered on the viewer's screen, and thus it can slow playback. You can make a movie play faster by turning anti-aliasing off. To turn anti-aliasing for a movie on and off, you use the Toggle High Quality action. This action affects all movies playing back in the Flash Player. (You cannot adjust the movie display quality of an individual movie or movie clip in the Flash Player.)

A Toggle High Quality action assigned to a button lets the audience adjust the playback quality of the movie. The action switches anti-aliasing on or off. That is, clicking the mouse button once turns off anti-aliasing or turns it on if the movie already is low quality; clicking the mouse button again has the opposite effect.

For more information on choosing between appearance and playback speed, see the QUALITY parameter in "Editing Flash HTML settings" on page 353.

To adjust the movie speed or playback quality:

1 Select the frame, button instance, or movie clip instance to which you will assign the action.

Selecting a movie clip adjusts the movie speed; selecting a button adjusts the movie playback quality.

2 Choose Window > Actions to display the Actions panel.

3 In the Toolbox list, click the Basic Actions category to display the basic actions, and select the Toggle High Quality action.

Flash enters the following ActionScript similar in the Actions list:

```
toggleHighQuality ();
```

Stopping all sounds

To stop the audio track without interrupting the main movie Timeline, you use the Stop All Sounds action. (This action does not just suppress the volume.) The Stop All Sounds action affects all movies playing back in the Flash Player. Streaming sounds will resume playing when the sound's Timeline advances; attached sounds won't resume.

For more information on controlling sounds, see "Starting and stopping sounds at keyframes" on page 174.

To stop all sounds in a movie:

1 Select the frame, button instance, or movie clip instance to which you will assign the action.

2 Choose Window > Actions to display the Actions panel.

3 In the Toolbox list, click the Basic Actions category to display the basic actions, and select the Stop All Sounds action.

Flash enters the following ActionScript in the Actions list:

```
stopAllSounds ();
```

Jumping to a different URL

To load a document from a specific URL into a browser window, or to pass variables to another application at a defined URL, you use the Get URL action. (Variables store named values that can be retrieved for use in scripts.) For example, you can send variable data to a CGI script for processing in the same way as you would an HTML form. Only variables for the current movie are sent.

Typically, you would use the Get URL action to load a Web page, but you can also use it in a Flash projector to open a browser window automatically and display the specified URL.

Testing this action requires that the requested file be at the specified location and that absolute URLs have a network connection (for example, http://www.myserver.com/).

For information on passing variables, see the *ActionScript Reference Guide*.

To jump to a URL:

1 Select the frame, button instance, or movie clip instance to which you will assign the action.

2 Choose Window > Actions to display the Actions panel.

3 In the Toolbox list, click the Basic Actions category to display the basic actions, and select the Get URL action.

4 In the Parameters pane, enter the URL from which to get the document, following these guidelines:

- Use either a relative path such as mypage.html or an absolute path such as http:///www.mydomain.com/mypage.html.

  A relative path is a shorthand version of the full address that lets you describe one file's location in relation to another; it tells Flash to move up and down the hierarchy of nested files/folders/directories, starting from the file where you issued the Get URL instruction. An absolute path is the complete address that specifies the name of the server on which the file resides, the path (the nested hierarchy of directories, volumes, folders, and so on), and the name of the file itself.

- To get a URL based on the value of an expression, select Expression and enter an expression that evaluates to the URL's location.

  For example, the following statement indicates that the URL is the value of the variable dynamicURL:

  ```
  getURL(dynamicURL);
  ```

  For information on writing expressions, see the *ActionScript Reference Guide.*

5 For Window, specify the window or HTML frame into which the document will be loaded, as follows:

- Choose from the following reserved target names:

  _self specifies the current frame in the current window.

  _blank specifies a new window.

  _parent specifies the parent of the current frame.

  _top specifies the top-level frame in the current window.

- Enter the name of a specific window or frame as it is named in the HTML file.

- Select Expression and enter the expression that evaluates to the window's location.

6 For Variable, choose a method for sending variables for the loaded movie to the location listed in the URL text box:

- Choose Send Using Get to append a small number of variables to the end of the URL. For example, you use this option to send the values of the variables in a Flash movie to a server-side script.

- Choose Send Using Post to send variables separate from the URL, as longer strings in a separate header; this allows you to send more variables and lets you post information collected from a form to a CGI script on the server.

- Choose Don't Send to not pass any variables.

See the *ActionScript Reference Guide.*

Your code would look similar to the following:

```
getUrl ("page2.html", "blank");
```

where the Get URL action loads the HTML document "page2" into a new browser window.

Controlling the Flash Player

You use the FSCommand action to control the Flash stand-alone player.

You can also use this action to send messages to the application hosting the Flash Player—for example, JavaScript in a Web browser, Director, Visual Basic, Visual C++, and other programs that can host ActiveX controls. For more information about sending messages to other applications using the FSCommand, see the related topic in the *ActionScript Reference Guide*.

To control a movie playing as a projector:

1 Select the frame, button instance, or movie clip instance to which you will assign the action.

2 Choose Window > Actions to display the Actions panel.

3 In the Toolbox list, click the Basic Actions category to display the basic actions, and select FSCommand action.

4 In the Parameters pane, choose an option to control the stand-alone player from the Commands for Standalone Player pop-up menu:

• Choose Quit to close the movie projector.

• Choose Exec to start running an application from within the projector. In the Arguments text box, enter the path to the application.

• Choose Fullscreen [True/False] to control the projector view. In the Arguments text box, enter **True** for a full-screen view, or **False** for a normal view.

• Choose Allowscale [True/False] to control scaling of the movie. In the Arguments text box, enter **True** to scale the animation with the player, or enter **False** to display animation without scaling.

• Choose Showmenu [True/False] to control pop-up menu items. In the Arguments text box, enter **True** to display the full set of right-click menu items, or **False** to hide the menu bar.

You can also type the options in the Commands or Arguments text boxes, or enter them as expressions. For more information, see the *ActionScript Reference Guide*.

Loading and unloading additional movies

To play additional movies without closing the Flash Player, or to switch movies without loading another HTML document, use the Load Movie action.

The Unload Movie action removes a movie previously loaded by the Load Movie action.

These are some sample uses of the Load Movie action:

- Playing a sequence of banner ads that are SWF files, by placing a Load Movie action at the end of each SWF file to load the next movie.

- Developing a branching interface that lets the user choose among several different SWF files.

- Building a navigation interface with navigation controls in level 0 that load other levels. Loading levels produces smoother transitions than loading new HTML pages in a browser.

To load a movie:

1 Select the frame, button instance, or movie clip instance to which you will assign the action.

2 Choose Window > Actions to display the Actions panel.

3 In the Toolbox list, click the Basic Actions category to display the basic actions, and select the Load Movie action.

4 In the Parameters pane, for URL specify an absolute or relative URL for the SWF file to load.

   For use in the Flash Player or for testing in Flash, all the SWF files must be stored in the same folder and listed as file names without folder or disk drive specifications.

5 For Location, choose either Level or Target from the pop-up menu.

6 If you choose Level for Location, enter a level number as follows:

- To load the new movie in addition to existing movies, enter a level number that is not occupied by another movie. (To keep the movie and update the variables with new values, use the Load Variables action; for more information, see the *ActionScript Reference Guide.*)

- To replace an existing movie with the loaded movie, enter a level number that is currently occupied by another movie.

- To replace the original movie and unload every level, load a new movie into level 0.

The movie loaded first is loaded at the bottom level. The movie in level 0 sets the frame rate, background color, and frame size for all other loaded movies. Movies may then be stacked in levels above the movie in level 0.

For more information on levels and targets, see the movie clips chapter of the *ActionScript Reference Guide.*

7 If you choose Target for Location, specify a movie clip that will be replaced by a loaded movie.

The loaded movie inherits the position, rotation, and scale properties (attributes) of the targeted movie clip. The loaded movie's upper left corner is placed at the registration point of the target movie clip (the cross hairs location in symbol-editing mode).

8 For Variable, choose a method for sending variables for the loaded movie to the location listed in the URL text box:

- Choose Send Using Get to append a small number of variables to the end of the URL. For example, you would use this option to send the values of the variables in a Flash movie to a server-side script.

- Choose Send Using Post to send variables separate from the URL, as longer strings in a separate header. This method lets you send more variables and lets you post information collected from a form to a CGI script on the server. For example, you can send variables to a CGI script, which generates a SWF file as its CGI output.

- Choose Don't Send to not pass any variables.

See the Web applications chapter of the *ActionScript Reference Guide.*

In the following example, clicking a button loads a movie into the root directory at level 0, replacing any existing movie, and sends variables to the loaded movie using the Get method:

```
loadMovie ("someFile.cgi", 0, "GET");
```

where "someFile.cgi" outputs a Flash movie in SWF file format.

To unload a movie from a Flash movie window:

1 Select the frame, button instance, or movie clip instance to which you will assign the action.

2 Choose Window > Actions to display the Actions panel.

3 In the Toolbox list, click the Basic Actions category to display the basic actions, and select the Unload Movie action.

4 For Location, choose one of the following options from the pop-up menu:

- For a loaded movie, select Level and enter the level of the movie that you want to unload.

- To target a movie to unload, select Target and enter the path of the movie that you'll target to unload. To enter an expression that evaluates to a level or movie, select Expression and enter the expression. For example:

```
unloadMovie (3);
```

targets the movie on level 3 and unloads it.

To test a Load Movie or Unload Movie action:

1 If you're testing a Load Movie action, make sure that the movie being loaded is at the specified path. If the path is an absolute URL, an active network connection is required.

2 Choose Control > Test Movie.

Note: The Load Movie and Unload Movie actions do not work in editing mode.

Controlling other movies and movie clips

You can control a movie clip or a movie that was loaded with the Load Movie action by targeting the movie clip.

You assign actions to the frame, button, or movie clip that will control the movie clip (called the controller), and then target the movie or movie clip that receives the action (called the target movie clip). To control a movie or movie clip, you can use the Tell Target basic action. Alternatively, you can use the With action to perform multiple actions on the same target without having to address the targeted movie clip in each action.

To control a movie or movie clip, the controller requires the following:

- A target (Timeline) on which the action will occur must be specified. You can use the Insert Target Path dialog box to target a movie clip.

- The movie clip to be targeted must have an instance name—a unique name given to a movie clip instance that lets you target it in scripts. To name a movie clip instance, use the Instance panel (Window > Panels > Instance).

- A movie clip's Timeline must be on the Stage to be targeted. For example, if MovieClip A in frame 5 wants to tell MovieClip B what to do, MovieClip B must be on the Timeline in frame 5.

For information on the With action and controlling multiple Timelines or controlling movie clips in other ways, see the movie clips chapter of the *ActionScript Reference Guide*.

To control a movie clip:

1 Select the frame, button instance, or movie clip instance to which you will assign the action.

2 Choose Window > Actions to display the Actions panel.

3 In the Toolbox list, click the Basic Actions category to display the basic actions, and select the Tell Target action.

4 To specify the target movie clip to be controlled, click the Insert Target Path button in the lower right corner of the Actions panel.

The Insert Target Path dialog box appears, showing the movie clip hierarchy of the current clip. You use this dialog box to choose a target path for the Target text box in the Parameters pane.

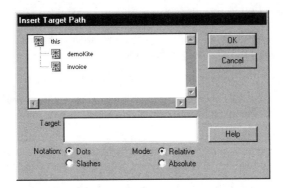

5 For Notation, use the default Dots (similar to JavaScript). Slash notation, available for those more familiar with Flash 4 notation, uses slashes to delimit the movie clip target path.

6 For Mode, choose how to display the hierarchy of movie clip instances:

- Relative (the default) displays only instances of movie clips that exist in the current frame of the current Timeline, and their children instances. The prefix `this` refers to the current Timeline.

- Absolute mode displays every movie clip instance in every frame of every scene of the entire movie. This mode always includes a leading slash or `_root` prefix (or `_level` to indicate a loaded movie level) to the inserted target path.

   Note: Absolute mode displays every instance in every frame, but because of the complexity of movie clip interactions, some instances may not be available when the Tell Target action is executed.

   You can freely switch between notations. However, changing between Relative and Absolute mode may deselect the movie clip.

7 Choose a movie clip from the tree view. The Target text box displays the path to that clip. Click OK.

8 In the Toolbox list of the Actions panel, select any additional actions that will instruct the target movie clip what to do.

Actions nested within the Tell Target block apply to the targeted Timeline. For example:

```
tellTarget (_root.plane){
    stop();
}
```

Checking whether a frame is loaded

To create a preloader to prevent certain actions from being triggered before the needed content has been downloaded by the viewer, use the If Frame Is Loaded action. A preloader is a simple animation that plays as the rest of a movie downloads. The If Frame Is Loaded action is helpful for verifying that a large file (such as a bitmap or sound) is loaded. You can also use the `_framesloaded` property (within an If action) to check whether the contents of a specific frame are available locally.

Using either the action or the property, you can start playing a simple animation while the rest of the movie downloads to a local computer. Both check whether the contents of a specific frame are available locally.

Typically, the If Frame Is Loaded action is used as a frame action, but it can also be used as a button action. To test an If Frame Is Loaded condition, use the Streaming option with the Test Movie command. The frames load as if streaming from a Web site. For more information, see "Testing movie download performance" on page 315.

To check whether a frame has been loaded:

1 Select the frame, button instance, or movie clip instance to which you will assign the action.

2 Choose Window > Actions to display the Actions panel.

3 In the Toolbox list, click the Basic Actions category to display the basic actions, and select the If Frame Is Loaded action.

4 In the Parameters pane, for Scene, select the scene containing the desired frame: Current Scene or a named scene.

5 For Type, choose Frame Number, Frame Label, or Expression.

6 For Frame, specify the frame to be loaded before the action is triggered as a frame number, frame label, or expression, according to your selection in step 5.

7 Select the action to occur when the particular frame has been loaded.

Flash enters ActionScript similar to the following in the Actions list:

```
ifFrameLoaded (100) {
    gotoAndPlay (10);
}
```

To use the If Frame Is Loaded action to play a short animation as a movie loads:

1 Create a short animation loop at the beginning of the movie. For example, you can create a loop that displays the message "Movie loading ..."

2 Create a frame action with the If Frame Is Loaded action that jumps out of the animation loop when all the frames are loaded and continues playing the movie.

For example, a 30-frame movie that has a 2-frame animation loop at the beginning requires the following action attached to Frame 1:

```
ifFrameLoaded (30) {
    gotoAndPlay (3);
```

To complete the example, attach the following action to Frame 2, to restart the movie at Frame 1:

```
gotoAndPlay (1);
```

When the frame specified in the If Frame Is Loaded action loads, the movie skips the second frame and continues playing the movie from the third frame.

To use the _framesloaded property in an action to play a short animation loop as a movie loads:

1 Create a short animation loop at the beginning of the movie. For example, you can create a loop that displays the message "Movie loading ..."

2 Create a frame action that jumps out of the animation loop after all the frames are loaded and continues playing the movie.

For example, a movie that has a two-frame animation loop at the beginning requires the following action attached to Frame 2:

```
if(_framesloaded==100) {
    gotoAndPlay (3);
} else {
    gotoAndPlay (1);
}
```

For more information on the _framesloaded property, see the *ActionScript Reference Guide.*

CHAPTER 13
Creating Printable Movies

Once you have set up interactivity in your Flash movie, you can set certain frames in the movie to be printable so that users can print them with the Flash Player. You can use the Flash Player printing feature to print catalogs, coupons, information sheets, receipts, invoices, or other documents in your Flash movies.

The Flash Player prints Flash content as vector graphics at the high resolutions available from printers and other output devices. Printing as vector graphics scales Flash artwork so that it prints clearly at any size without the pixelated effects that can occur when printing low-resolution bitmap images.

Printing movies from the Flash Player instead of from the browser gives Flash authors several advantages. You can do the following:

- Specify which frames in a Flash movie can be printed. This lets you create layouts appropriate to printing and protect material from unauthorized printing.

- Determine the print area of frames.

- Specify whether frames are printed as vectors (to take advantage of higher resolutions) or as bitmaps (to preserve transparency and color effects).

- Assign Print actions to print frames from movie clips, even if the movie clips are not visible. This lets you provide printable material without using valuable browser space.

Printing from the Flash Player

Users can print movies directly from the Flash Player in a browser in two ways: either using the Flash Player context menu and its Print command, or using the Print action. A Print action gives more control over how a Flash movie can be printed and eliminates the need to use the Flash Player context menu.

The Print action can print frames in any Timeline, including the main Timeline or the Timeline of any movie clip or loaded movie level. The Print action also lets you specify a print area and lets you print color effects, including transparency.

The Flash Player context menu is more limited in its printing: it only prints frames in the main Timeline and does not let you print transparency or color effects.

Note: Flash Player versions earlier than 4.0.25 (Windows) or 4.0.20 (Macintosh) do not support direct printing of frames.

Preparing movies for printing

To set up printing from the Flash Player, you can set which frames to print and set their print area. To best control what users can print out, keep the following in mind as you set up movies and movie clips for printing:

- Adjust the page layout in any frames that you'll designate as printable to match the desired printed output. The Flash Player prints all shapes, symbols, bitmaps, text blocks, and text fields. Levels in a Flash movie are not composited on print output.

- The Flash Player printer driver uses the HTML settings for dimension, scale, and alignment in the Publish Settings dialog box. Use these settings to control the print layout.

- The selected frames print as they appear in the movie clip symbol. You can let users print a movie clip that is not visible in a browser by setting the movie clip's _visible property to false using the Actions panel. Changing the property of a movie clip with the Set Property action, tweening, or any transformation tool does not affect how a movie clip prints.

- For a movie clip to be printable, it must be on the Stage or work area and it must be given an instance name.

- All elements must be fully loaded to print. You can use the _framesloaded property or the If Frame Is Loaded action to check whether the printable content is loaded. For more information, see "Checking whether a frame is loaded" on page 297.

Supported printers

The Flash Player can print to both PostScript and non-PostScript printers. For a list of supported Flash Player printing platforms, see "Flash Web Printing for eBusiness" on the Macromedia Web site (http://www.macromedia.com/software/flash/open/webprinting/faq.html.

Designating printable frames

All frames in the specified Timeline print by default. You may want to limit the number of frames that can print—for example, if you have a lengthy animation of dozens of frames. You can designate specific frames in a movie as printable in order to print only those frames; unspecified frames won't print.

To specify frames as printable, you label the frames.

To designate printable frames:

1 Open or make active the movie that you want to publish.

2 If the Frame panel isn't visible onscreen, choose Modify > Frame.

3 Select the desired frame in the Timeline that you want to make printable.

4 In the Frame panel, for Label enter **#p** to specify the frame as printable.

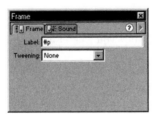

5 Repeat steps 3 and 4 for each frame you want to designate as printable.

Specifying a print area

By default, the movie's Stage determines the print area. Any object that extends off the Stage is clipped and does not print. Loaded movies use their own Stage size for the print area, not the main movie's Stage size.

As an alternative to using a movie's Stage size, you can set three different print areas:

- For either the Flash Player context menu or the Print action, you can designate the movie's bounding box as the print area for all frames by selecting an object in one frame as the bounding box. This option is useful, for example, if you want to print a full-page data sheet from a Web banner.

- With the Print action, you can use the composite bounding box of all printable frames in a Timeline as the print area—for example, to print multiple frames that share a registration point. To use the composite bounding box, select the Max option in the Print action parameters. See "Adding a Print action" on page 304.

- With the Print action, you can change the print area for each frame, scaling objects to fit the print area—for example, to have objects of different sizes in each frame fill the printed page. To change the bounding box per frame, use the Frame option in the Print action parameters. See "Adding a Print action" on page 304.

To specify a print area:

1 Open the movie whose frames you will set to print.

2 Choose a frame that you have not specified to print with a #p frame label.

   To organize your work, you can select the next frame after one labeled #p.

3 Create a shape on the Stage the size of the desired print area.

   You can also choose a frame with any object of the appropriate print area size to use that frame's bounding box.

4 Select the frame in the Timeline that contains the shape you'll use for the bounding box.

5 If the Frame panel is not visible onscreen, choose Modify > Frame.

6 In the Frame panel, enter #b to specify the selected shape as the bounding box for the print area.

   You can enter only one #b label per Timeline. This option is the same as selecting the Movie bounding box option with the Print action.

Changing the printed background color

The Flash Player prints the background color set in the Movie Properties dialog box. You can change the background color for only the frames to be printed by placing a colored object on the lowest layer of the Timeline being printed.

To change the printed background color:

1 Place a filled shape that covers the Stage on the lowest layer of the Timeline that will print.

2 Select the shape and choose Modify > Movie. Select a color for the printing background.

This changes the entire movie's background color, including that of movie clips and loaded movies.

3 Choose from the following options:

- To print that color as the movie's background, make sure that the frame in which you placed the shape is designated to print. For instructions, see "Designating printable frames" on page 301.

- To maintain a different background color for nonprinting frames, repeat steps 2 and 3. Then place the shape on the lowest layer of the Timeline, in all frames that are not designated to print. For instructions, see the following section.

Disabling printing

If you don't want any frames in the main Timeline to be printable, you label a frame as !#p to make it nonprintable. Labeling a frame as !#p makes the entire movie nonprintable and dims the Print command in the Flash Player context menu. You can also remove the Flash Player context menu.

If you disable printing, you can still print frames using the browser Print command. Because this command is a browser feature, you cannot control or disable it using Flash.

To disable printing in the Flash Player context menu by dimming the Print command:

1 Open or make active the movie that you want to publish.

2 If the Frame panel isn't visible onscreen, choose Modify > Frame.

3 Select the first keyframe in the main Timeline.

4 In the Frame panel, for Label enter **!#p** to specify the frame as nonprinting.

You need to specify only one !#p label to dim the Print command in the context menu.

Note: Alternatively, you can select a blank frame and label it #p to prevent printing from the Flash Player context menu.

To disable printing by removing the Flash Player context menu:

1 Open or make active the movie that you want to publish.

2 Choose File > Publish Settings.

3 Select the HTML tab and deselect Display Menu.

4 Click OK.

For more information on publishing options, see "Publishing Flash movies" on page 319.

Adding a Print action

You can add a Print action to a button or other element in your movie to let users print the movie. You assign the Print action to a button, frame, or movie clip. If you assign a Print action to a frame, the action executes when the playhead reaches the designated frame.

The Print action lets you print frames in other movie clips in addition to the main Timeline. Each Print action sets only one Timeline for printing, but the action lets you specify any number of frames within the Timeline to print. If you attach more than one Print action to a single button or frame, the Print dialog box appears for each action executed.

To assign a Print action to a button, frame, or movie clip:

1 Open the movie whose frames you will set to print.

2 Select the desired keyframe in the Timeline that you want to be able to print and make sure that it is labeled #p. See the instructions in "Designating printable frames" on page 301.

   If you don't specify which frames to print, all frames in the movie print by default.

3 Select the frame, button instance, or movie clip instance to which you will assign the Print action.

   Each Print action sets only one Timeline to be printable.

4 Choose Window > Actions to display the Actions panel.

5 In the Toolbox list, click the Actions category to display the actions, and double-click to select the Print action.

   Flash inserts the Print action in the Actions list.

6 For Print, choose to print the frame as vectors or as a bitmap:

• As Vectors prints the frame at a higher quality, but without transparency.

   Objects containing transparency or color effects cannot be printed as vector data. (The printer cannot interpret the alpha channel that defines the effect as vector data.)

• As Bitmap prints transparency in an alpha channel or color effect.

   This option prints at the highest available resolution of the printer.

7 To specify which movie Timeline to print, choose a Location option:

• For Level, specify the level number of the main Timeline or loaded movie. To use an expression to evaluate to the level, select Expression and enter an expression. For more information on levels, see "Loading and unloading additional movies" on page 292.

• For Target, enter the path to the target movie, or click the Target Path button in the lower right corner and use the Insert Target Path dialog box to locate and select the target movie. To use an expression to evaluate to the target, select Expression and enter an expression.

8 To set the printing boundaries, select a Bounding Box option:

- Movie uses the bounding box of an object in the frame labeled #b as the print area for all frames as set in "Specifying a print area" on page 302. For example, choose this option to print a full-page data sheet from a Web banner.

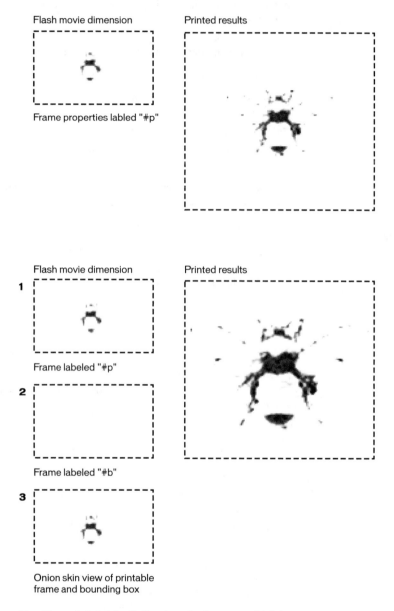

Flash movie dimension

Printed results

Frame properties labled "#p"

Flash movie dimension

Printed results

1

Frame labeled "#p"

2

Frame labeled "#b"

3

Onion skin view of printable frame and bounding box

Top: Frame labeled #p (left) prints the Stage area (right).
Bottom: Frame labeled #p (1) and frame labeled #b (2), with onion skin view (3), print the object's bounding box (right).

- Max uses the composite bounding box of all printable frames in a Timeline as the print area.

- Frame uses the bounding box of the objects in each printable frame of a Timeline as the print area, changing the print area for each frame and the scaling objects to fit the print area. For example, use Frame if you have different-sized objects in each frame and you want each object to fill the printed page.

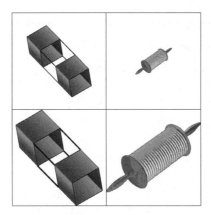

Frame option sets the bounding box of each frame as the print area (top), scaling artwork to fit (bottom).

Note: Choosing the Max or Frame bounding box options in the Print action overrides any frames labeled #b for the movie's bounding box.

Printing from the Flash Player context menu

You can use the Print command in the Flash Player context menu to print frames from any Flash movie.

The context menu's Print command cannot print transparency or color effects and cannot print frames from other movie clips; for these printing capabilities, use the Print action instead. See "Adding a Print action" on page 304.

To print movie frames using the Flash Player context menu Print command:

1 Open the movie whose frames you will print.

   The command prints the frames labeled #b using the Stage for the print area or the specified bounding box. See "Designating printable frames" on page 301 and "Specifying a print area" on page 302.

   If you haven't designated specific frames to print, all frames in the movie's main Timeline print.

2 Choose File > Publish Preview > Default or press F12 to view your Flash movie in a browser.

3 Right-click (Windows) or Control-click (Macintosh) in the Flash movie in the browser window to display the Flash Player context menu.

4 Choose Print from the Flash Player context menu to display the Print dialog box.

5 In Windows, choose the print range to select which frames to print:

• Choose All to print all frames in the movie if no frames are labeled.

• Choose Pages and enter a range to print the labeled frames in that range.

• Choose Selection to print the current frame.

6 On the Macintosh, in the Print dialog box, select the pages to print:

• Choose All to print the current frame if no frames are labeled or to print all labeled frames.

• Choose From and enter a range to print the labeled frames in that range.

7 Select other print options, according to your printer's properties.

8 Click OK (Windows) or Print (Macintosh).

About publishing a movie with printable frames

You can publish a Flash movie with printable frames to the Web using the Publish command to generate the necessary Flash HTML templates. For more information, see "Publishing Flash movies" on page 319.

Users must have the Flash Player 4.0.25 (Windows) or 4.0.20 (Macintosh) or later to take advantage of any print functionality you have added and to be able to print the designated frames in Flash. You can set up a detection scheme to check for the proper Flash Player version. See "Screening traffic to your Web site" on page 361.

CHAPTER 14
Publishing and Exporting

When you're ready to deliver your movie to an audience, you must publish or export the Flash FLA file to another format for playback.

The Flash Publish feature is designed for presenting animation on the Web. The Publish command creates the Flash Player (SWF) file and an HTML document that inserts your Flash Player file in a browser window.

The Export Movie command lets you create Flash content that can be edited in other applications and export a movie directly into a single format. For example, you can export an entire movie as a Flash Player file; as a series of bitmap images; as a single frame or image file; and as moving and still images in various formats, including GIF, JPEG, PNG, BMP, PICT, QuickTime, or AVI.

With the Publish command, you can do the following:

- Choose the formats in which you want the authoring file delivered and adjust any settings for the particular file format. Flash automatically publishes the authoring file in the selected formats, creates additional files based on the selected settings, and stores the settings with the movie file for reuse.

  The Export Movie options generally match those for publishing, but they do not save the settings for reuse.

- Create alternative file formats—GIF, JPEG, PNG, and QuickTime—and the HTML needed to display them in the browser window. Alternative formats enable a browser to display your movie's animation and interactivity for users who don't have the Flash Player installed.

- Create Generator templates to easily update content on a Web site, such as graphics and text, without having to replace files individually. For example, in Flash you can use Generator data as variables to provide immediate or customized feedback to visitors to your Flash Web site, make production of your Flash Web site more efficient, and create artwork, such as scrolling lists, that you can't create in Flash alone. See "About Generator and Flash" on page 318.

As an alternative to using the Publish command, if you're proficient in HTML, you can create your own HTML document with any HTML editor and include the tags required to display a Flash movie. See "About HTML publishing templates" on page 347.

If you have Macromedia Dreamweaver, you can add a Flash movie to your Web site easily. Dreamweaver generates all the needed HTML code. See your Dreamweaver documentation for more information.

Before you publish your movie, it's important to test how the movie works using the Test Movie and Test Scene commands. For more information, see "Testing movie download performance" on page 315.

Playing Flash movies

The Flash Player format (SWF) is the main file format for distributing Flash content, and the only format that supports all the interactive functionality of Flash.

You can play a Flash Player movie in the following ways:

- In Internet browsers such as Netscape Navigator and Internet Explorer that are equipped with the Flash Player

- With the Flash Xtra in Director and Authorware

- With the Flash ActiveX control in Microsoft Office and other ActiveX hosts

- As part of a QuickTime movie

- As a type of stand-alone application called a projector

The Flash Player file format is an open standard that is supported by other applications. See the Macromedia Web site at http://www.macromedia.com for the latest information.

Optimizing movies

The larger your movie file, the longer the download time and the slower the movie will be. You can take a number of steps to prepare your movie for optimal playback. As part of the publishing process, Flash automatically performs some optimizing on movies, including detecting duplicate shapes on export and placing them in the file only once, and converting nested groups into single groups.

Before exporting a movie, you can optimize it further using various strategies to reduce the movie size. As you make changes, test your movie on a variety of different computers, operating systems, and Internet connections.

To optimize movies in general:

- Use symbols, animated or otherwise, for every element that appears more than once.

- Whenever possible, use tweened animations, which take up less file space than a series of keyframes.

- For animation sequences, use movie clips instead of graphic symbols.

- Limit the area of change in each keyframe; make the action take place in as small an area as possible.

- Avoid animating bitmap elements; use bitmap images as background or static elements.

- For sound, use MP3, the smallest sound format, whenever possible.

To optimize elements and lines:

- Group elements as much as possible.

- Use layers to separate elements that change over the course of the animation from those that do not.

- Use Modify > Curves > Optimize to minimize the number of separate lines that are used to describe shapes.

- Limit the number of special line types such as dashed, dotted, ragged, and so on. Solid lines require less memory. Lines created with the Pencil tool require less memory than brush strokes.

To optimize text and fonts:

- Limit the number of fonts and font styles. Use embedded fonts sparingly, because they increase file size.

- For Embed Fonts options, select only the characters needed instead of including the entire font.

To optimize colors:

- Use the Effect panel (Window > Panels > Effect) to create many different-colored instances of a single symbol.

- Use the Mixer panel (Window > Panels > Mixer) to match the color palette of the movie to a browser-specific palette.

- Use gradients sparingly. Filling an area with gradient color requires about 50 bytes more than filling it with solid color.

- Use alpha transparency sparingly; it can slow playback.

Testing movie download performance

To locate where a movie may pause during downloading, you can test a scene or an entire movie using the Test Scene or Test Movie command, or you can open an existing SWF file. If required data has not downloaded by the time the movie reaches a frame, the movie pauses until the data arrives.

To view downloading performance graphically, you can display the Bandwidth Profiler in the Flash Player to see how much data is sent for each frame in the movie according to the defined modem speed. In simulating the speed of downloading, the Bandwidth Profiler uses estimates of typical Internet performance, not the exact speed of the modem. For example, a 28.8 Kbps modem can theoretically download data at 3.5 Kbytes/second. But if you choose 28.8 from the Control menu, Flash sets the actual rate to 2.3 Kbytes/second to simulate typical Internet performance more accurately.

You can also generate a report to find frames that are slowing playback, and then optimize or eliminate some of the content in those frames. To generate a report, you use the Select Generate Report option in the Publish Settings dialog box.

To change the settings for the Flash Player file created by Test Movie and Test Scene, you choose File > Publish Settings. See "Previewing and testing movies" on page 74.

To test downloading performance:

1 Do one of the following:

• Choose Control > Test Scene or Control > Test Movie.

   Flash displays the Output window to help you trouble-shoot problems in your ActionScript. You can use the Trace action to display comments in the Output window for help with debugging. For more information, see the related topics in the *ActionScript Reference Guide*.

• Choose File > Open, and select a SWF file.

   If you test a scene or movie, Flash publishes the current selection as a SWF file using the settings in the Publish Settings dialog box. (See "Publishing Flash movies" on page 319.) The SWF file opens in a new window and begins playing immediately.

2 In the Flash Player's Debug menu, choose a downloading speed to determine the downloading rate that Flash simulates: 14.4 Kbps, 28.8 Kbps, 56 Kbps. To enter your own settings, choose Customize.

3 In the Flash Player, choose View > Bandwidth Profiler to display a graph of the downloading performance:

• The left side of the profiler displays information on the movie, its settings, and state. The Movie section indicates the dimensions, frame rate, size in KB and bytes, duration, and preloaded frames by number of seconds.

• The right section of the profiler shows the Timeline header and graph. In the graph, each bar represents an individual frame of the movie. The size of the bar corresponds to that frame's size in bytes. The lower red line beneath the Timeline header indicates whether a given frame streams in real-time with the current modem speed set in the Control menu. If a bar extends above the red line, the movie must wait for that frame to load.

4 Choose View > Show Streaming to turn the streaming bar off or on.

The streaming bar indicates the number of frames loaded along with the frame currently playing.

5 Click a bar on the graph to display settings for the corresponding frame in the left window and stop the movie.

6 Adjust the view of the graph as desired:

• Choose View > Streaming Graph to display which frames will cause pauses.

This default view displays alternating light and dark gray blocks representing each frame. The side of each block indicates its relative byte size. The first frame stores a symbol's contents, so is often larger than other frames.

• Choose View > Frame by Frame Graph to display the size of each frame.

This view helps you see which frames are contributing to streaming delays. If any frame block extends above the red line in the graph, then the Flash Player halts playback until the entire frame downloads.

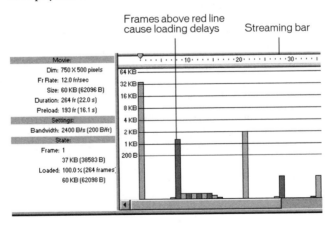

Bandwidth Profiler showing streaming bar and Frame-by-Frame Graph view

7 Close the test window to return to the normal authoring environment.

Once you've set up a test environment incorporating the Bandwidth Profiler, you can open any SWF directly in test mode. The file opens in a player window, using the Bandwidth Profiler and other selected viewing options.

For more information on debugging your movies, see the troubleshooting topic in the *ActionScript Reference Guide*.

To generate a report listing the amount of data in the final Flash Player file by file:

1 Choose File > Publish Settings.

2 Select Generate Size Report.

3 Click Publish.

Flash generates a text file with the same name as the exported movie plus the .txt extension. The report lists the amount of data in the final Flash Player file by frame.

```
Movie Report
------------

Frame #    Frame Bytes    Total Bytes    Page
-------    -----------    -----------    ----------------
   1          38583          38583       Scene 1
   2              2          38585       2
   3              2          38587       3
   4              2          38589       4
   5              2          38591       5
   6              2          38593       6
   7             10          38603       7
   8           1441          40044       8
   9             29          40073       9
  10             29          40102       10
  11             29          40131       11
  12             29          40160       12
  13             29          40189       13
  14             29          40218       14
  15             19          40237       15
  16             10          40247       16
  17              2          40249       17
  18              2          40251       18
  19              2          40253       19
  20              2          40255       20
  21           2109          42364       21
  22              2          42366       22
  23              2          42368       23
  24              2          42370       24
  25              2          42372       25
  26              2          42374       26
  27             10          42384       27
```

About Generator and Flash

Generator extends the Flash authoring environment by letting designers work in Flash to build rich media content and deliver the final product in a variety of animated or static formats.

Any object created in Flash—including library elements, symbols, animations, Timelines, and publishing output—can be turned into a Generator object by using symbols and Generator variables. (Generator variables are text enclosed by curly brackets, for example, {text}.) Using Generator, you can choose the best visual display of information for your viewers—including scrolling lists, charts and graphs (basic, pie, stock, scatter), tables, a variety of different graphic formats, sound, and movies—to create real-time, custom multimedia Web experiences.

If you have Generator 2 installed, in Flash you can create templates that contain variable Generator elements (graphics, text, and sound) to be replaced with content provided by a data source (text files, databases, and so on). This generated content can be played back in the client's browser as a Flash Player movie, or as a JPEG, PNG, GIF, animated GIF, or QuickTime file.

In Flash, you can use Generator in the following ways:

- You can specify how a Flash movie interacts with Generator—including the default frame rate, frame size, and background color—in the Generator panel of the Publish Settings dialog box. See "Publishing Generator templates" on page 327.

- You can modify Flash HTML templates to work with Generator. See "Customizing HTML publishing templates" on page 348.

- You can update Generator name/value pairs using the Movie Explorer. Name/value pairs are variable names coupled with values, such as URL parameters. For more information on the Movie Explorer, see "Using the Movie Explorer" on page 98.

For more information on Generator, visit http://www.macromedia.com/generator or see your Generator 2 documentation.

Publishing Flash movies

Publishing a Flash movie on the Web is a two-step process. First, you prepare all required files for the complete Flash application with the Publish Settings command. Then you publish the movie and all its files with the Publish command. To prepare Flash content for use in other applications, you use the Export command; see "Exporting movies and images" on page 339.

The Publish Settings command lets you choose formats and specify settings for the individual files included in the movie—including GIF, JPEG, or PNG—and then store these settings with the movie file.

Depending on what you specified in the Publish Settings dialog box, the Publish command then creates the following files:

- The Flash movie for the Web (the SWF file).

- Alternate images in a variety of formats that appear automatically if the Flash Player is not available (GIF, JPEG, PNG, and QuickTime).

- The supporting HTML document required to display a movie (or an alternate image) in a browser and control browser settings.

- Stand-alone projectors for both Windows and Macintosh systems and QuickTime videos from Flash movies (EXE, HQX, or MOV files, respectively).

To alter or update a Flash Player movie created with the Publish command, you must edit the original Flash movie and then use the Publish command again to avoid discarding any authoring information. Importing a Flash Player movie into Flash strips some of the authoring information.

To set publishing options for a Flash movie's files:

1 Specify where you will publish the Flash movie files:

• Create the folder where you want to save the published files, and save your Flash movie file.

• Browse to and open an existing folder, and save your Flash movie file.

2 Choose File > Publish Settings.

3 Select the option for each file format you want to create.

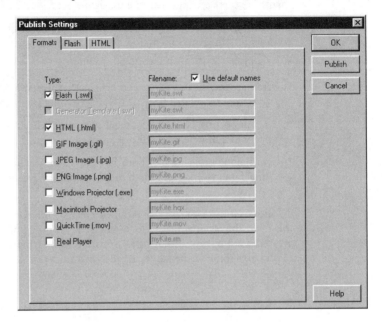

The HTML format is selected automatically, because an HTML file is required to display your Flash movie in a browser. In addition, if the selected format has settings, a corresponding tab appears above the current panel in the dialog box. Choosing an image format such as GIF, JPEG, or PNG automatically adds the required HTML code to display the image if the Flash Player is not available.

For more information on publishing settings for individual file formats, see the sections that follow.

4 For Filename, choose from the following options:

- Use the default file names.

- Deselect Use Default Name. Then enter your own file name.

  You can browse to where you will publish the files and publish each file in a different location (for example, if you want to save the SWF file in one location and the HTML file in another location). On Windows, use backslashes to specify the directory/folder/file hierarchy; on the Macintosh, use colons (:). For a relative path, use ..\to indicate the path to the hard drive; for an absolute path, specify the drive name. For example:

  For example, in Windows, specify an absolute path as `C:\Folder\filename.swf` where `C:` is the drive name, `\Folder` specifies the folder name, and `filename.swf` is the name of the file.

  On the Macintosh, specify an absolute path as `HardDrive name:Folder:filename.swf`.

5 To create a projector, select Windows Projector or Macintosh Projector.

  Although you can create a Macintosh projector using the Windows versions of Flash, you must also use a file translator such as BinHex to make the resulting file appear as an application file in the Macintosh Finder. The Windows version of Flash names a Macintosh projector file with the .hqx extension.

6 Enter a unique name for Filename, or select Use Default Name to create each file using the Flash file's name with the extension appropriate for that format.

7 Click the tab for the format options you want to change. Specify publish settings for each format, as described in the following sections.

8 When you have finished setting options, do one of the following:

- To generate all the specified files, click Publish to generate all the specified files, or click OK.

- To save the settings with your file and close the dialog box without publishing, click OK.

To publish a Flash movie:

1 If necessary, set the publishing options for the files, as described in the previous procedure.

2 Choose File > Publish to create the files in the formats and location specified in the Publish Settings dialog box.

Publishing a Flash Player movie

When publishing a Flash Player movie, you can set image and sound compression options, and an option to protect your movie from being imported. Use the controls in the Flash panel of the Publish Settings dialog box to change the following settings.

To publish a Flash Player movie:

1 Choose File > Publish Settings and click the Flash tab.

2 Choose a Load Order to set the order in which Flash loads a movie's layers for displaying the first frame of your movie: Bottom Up or Top Down.

This option controls which parts of the movie Flash draws first over a slow network or modem connection.

3 Select Generate Size Report to generate a report listing the amount of data in the final Flash Player file by file. See "Testing movie download performance" on page 315.

4 To allow debugging the published SWF file, select any of the following options:

- Omit Trace Actions makes Flash ignore the Trace action in the current movie to prevent the Output window from opening and display comments.

For more information, see the related topic in the *ActionScript Reference Guide.*

- Protect from Import prevents others from importing the Flash SWF file and converting it back into a Flash movie.

- Debugging Permitted activates the Debugger and allow debugging a Flash movie remotely. If you select this option, you can choose to password-protect your movie file.

- If desired, select Password to enter a password to prevent unauthorized users from debugging a Flash movie that has Debugging permission. If you add a password, others must enter the password before they can debug the file. To remove the password, clear the Password field.

For more information on the Debugger, see the related topic in the *ActionScript Reference Guide.*

5 To control bitmap compression, adjust the JPEG Quality slider or enter a value.

Lower image quality produces smaller files; higher image quality produces larger files. Try different settings to determine the best trade-off between size and quality; 100 provides the highest quality and least compression.

6 If you did not specify a sample rate and compression for individual sounds in the Sound Properties dialog box or to override your settings, select an option:

• Click Set Audio Stream to set the exported stream rate and compression for all movie sounds; then use the Sound Properties dialog box to set the audio stream. A stream sound begins playing as soon as enough data for the first few frames has been downloaded; a stream sound is synchronized to the Timeline for playing on a Web site.

• Click Set Audio Event to set the exported rate and compression for all movie sounds; then use the Sound Properties dialog box to set the audio event. An event sound must download completely before it begins playing and continues playing until explicitly stopped.

• Select Override Sound Settings to override the settings in the Sound Properties dialog box for individual sounds and create a larger high-fidelity audio movie for local use and a smaller low-fidelity version for the Web.

For instructions on changing these settings, see "Compressing sounds for export" on page 175.

7 Choose a Flash version. Not all Flash 5 features work in movies published as earlier Flash versions.

8 To save the settings with the current file, click OK.

Publishing HTML for Flash Player files

Playing a Flash movie in a Web browser requires an HTML document that activates the movie and specifies browser settings. This document is generated automatically by the Publish command, from HTML parameters in a template document.

HTML parameters determine where the Flash movie appears in the window, the background color, the size of the movie, and so on, and set attributes for the OBJECT and EMBED tags. You can change these and other settings in the HTML panel of the Publish Settings dialog box. Changing these settings overrides options you've set in your movie.

Your settings are inserted in a template document. The template document can be any text file that contains the appropriate template variables—including a plain HTML file, one that includes code for special interpreters such as ColdFusion or Active Server Pages (ASP), or a template included with Flash (for more information, see "About HTML publishing templates" on page 347).

You can also customize a template (see "Customizing HTML publishing templates" on page 348), or manually enter HTML parameters for Flash using any HTML editor (see "Editing Flash HTML settings" on page 353).

To publish HTML for displaying the Flash file:

1 Choose File > Publish Settings.

   The HTML file type is selected by default.

2 Enter a unique name for Filename, or select Use Default Name to create a file with the Flash file name plus the .html extension.

3 Click the HTML panel to display its settings.

4 Choose an installed template to use from the Template pop-up menu; click the Info button to the right to display a description of the selected template.

   The menu lists all of the template files in the Macromedia Flash 5/HTML folder. The basic templates simply display the movie in a browser, and more advanced templates contain code for browser detection and other features. If you don't choose a template, Flash uses the Default.html template, or if that template isn't present, Flash uses the first template in the list.

   Flash saves the modified template using the Flash movie's file name plus the template's file extension. For example, if you select a template named Standard.asp for use with a Flash movie named MyMovie.swf, the resulting file would be named MyMovie.asp.

5 Choose a Dimensions option to set the values of the WIDTH and HEIGHT attributes in the OBJECT and EMBED tags:

- Choose Match Movie (the default) to use the size of the movie.

- Choose Pixels to enter the number of pixels in the Width and Height field.

- Choose Percent to use a percentage relative to the browser window.

6 Select Playback options to control the movie's play and features, as follows:

- Paused at Start pauses the movie until a user clicks a button in the movie or chooses Play from the shortcut menu. By default, the option is deselected and the movie begins to play as soon as it is loaded (the PLAY parameter is true).

- Loop repeats the movie when it reaches the last frame. Deselect this option to stop the movie when it reaches the last frame. (The LOOP parameter is on by default.)

- Display Menu displays a shortcut menu when users right-click (Windows) or Control-click (Macintosh) the movie. Deselect this option to display only About Flash in the shortcut menu. By default, this option is on (the MENU parameter is true).

- For Windows only, select Device Font to substitute anti-aliased (smooth-edged) system fonts for fonts not installed the on the user's system. Using device fonts increases the legibility of type at small sizes and can decrease the movie's file size. This option only affects movies containing static text (text that you created when authoring a movie and that does not change when the movie is displayed) set to display with device fonts. For more information, see "Using device fonts" on page 216.

  Select Quality to determine the trade-off between processing time and applying anti-aliasing to smooth each frame before it is rendered on the viewer's screen, as follows. This option sets the QUALITY parameter's value in the OBJECT and EMBED tags.

- Low favors playback speed over appearance and does not use anti-aliasing.

- Auto Low emphasizes speed at first but improves appearance whenever possible. Playback begins with anti-aliasing turned off. If the Flash Player detects that the processor can handle it, anti-aliasing is turned on.

- Auto High emphasizes playback speed and appearance equally at first but sacrifices appearance for playback speed if necessary. Playback begins with anti-aliasing turned on. If the actual frame rate drops below the specified frame rate, anti-aliasing is turned off to improve playback speed. Use this setting to emulate the View > Antialias setting in Flash.

- Medium applies some anti-aliasing, but does not smooth bitmaps. It produces a better quality than the Low setting, but lower quality than the High setting.

- High (the default) favors appearance over playback speed and always uses anti-aliasing. If the movie does not contain animation, bitmaps are smoothed; if the movie has animation, bitmaps are not smoothed.

- Best provides the best display quality and does not consider playback speed. All output is anti-aliased and bitmaps are always smoothed.

7 For the Windows version of Internet Explorer 4.0 with the Flash ActiveX control, choose a Window Mode option for transparency, positioning, and layering. This option specifies the ALIGN attribute for the OBJECT, EMBED, and IMG tags.

- Window plays a Flash Player movie in its own rectangular window on a Web page, for the fastest animation. The option sets the WMODE parameter of the OBJECT tag to WINDOW.

- Opaque Windowless moves elements behind Flash movies (for example, with dynamic HTML) to prevent them from showing through, setting the WMODE parameter to OPAQUE.

- Transparent Windowless shows the background of the HTML page on which the movie is embedded through all transparent areas of the movie, but may slow animation. The option sets WMODE to TRANSPARENT.

8 Choose an HTML Alignment option to position the Flash movie window within the browser window:

- Default centers the movie in the browser window and crops edges if the browser window is smaller than the movie.

- Left, Right, Top or Bottom aligns movies along the corresponding edge of the browser window and crop the remaining three sides as needed.

9 Choose a Scale option to place the movie within specified boundaries, if you've changed the movie's original width and height. The Scale option sets the SCALE parameter in the OBJECT and EMBED tags.

- Default (Show All) display the entire movie in the specified area without distortion while maintaining the original aspect ratio of the movies. Borders may appear on two sides of the movie.

- No Border scales the movie to fill the specified area and keeps the movie's original aspect ratio without distortion, cropping if needed.

- Exact Fit displays the entire movie in the specified area without preserving the original aspect ratio, which may cause distortion.

10 Choose a Flash Alignment option to set how the movie is placed within the movie window and how it is cropped, if necessary. This option sets the SALIGN parameter of the OBJECT and EMBED tags.

- For Horizontal alignment, choose Left, Center, or Right.

- For Vertical alignment, choose Top, Center, or Bottom.

11 Select Show Warning Messages to display error messages if tag settings conflict—for example, if a template has code referring to an alternate image that has not been specified.

12 To save the settings with the current file, click OK.

Publishing Generator templates

Generator lets you add dynamic content, such as text, graphics, and sound, to a Flash movie. You can specify publishing options in the Generator panel of the Publish Settings dialog box.

To publish a Generator template with the Flash file:

1 Choose File > Publish Settings.

2 Select the Generator Template type. Enter a unique name for Filename, or select Use Default Name to create a file with the Flash file name plus the .swf extension.

3 Click the Generator panel to display its settings.

4 For Dimensions, enter a Width and Height in pixels to specify the movie's width and height when the file is converted to a file or stream; or select Match Movie to make the published movie the same size as the original Flash movie and maintain its aspect ratio.

5 Choose a Background color for the scenes of your movie, to override the background color set with the Modify > Movies command, as follows:

• Set a Web-safe color name, for example, black. A Web-safe palette uses the 216 colors that are common to the Windows and Macintosh system palettes.

• Set a Web hexadecimal value (for example, #3434aa).

• Set a regular hexadecimal value (for example, 0x232356).

6 Specify a Frame Rate to set how quickly the frames of the current movie appear when an animation is played back, overriding the frame rate set with the Modify > Movies command.

The rate is specified in frames per second (fps). If you specify a frame rate of 10 fps, each frame of the animation appears on the screen for 1/10 of a second; a 100-frame animation plays for 10 seconds.

7 Choose a Load Order to set the order in which Flash loads a movie's layers for displaying the first frame of your movie: Bottom Up or Top Down.

This option controls which parts of the movie Flash draws first over a slow network or modem connection.

8 Choose Data Encoding to set the encoding system to use when reading all data sources referenced in the template file.

Default uses the encoding method of the system from which the template is served. You should use the same character encoding system for all the data sources. For more information, see the *Using Generator 2* guide included with the Generator product.

9 Select Create External Font Files to have Generator create font files.

The Generator Enterprise Edition caches these font files to speed performance when many fonts are used in a movie.

10 Select External Media to specify the name of the Generator template containing the symbols and include its library in the selected file.

This option lets you access symbols as if they resided in the selected file. If the same symbol is defined in both the external media file and the current file, the external media file's symbol is used.

11 Select Parameters to define variables; then enter the variable name and its value.

This option lets you test templates locally as you develop them or test how variables will work when processed.

12 To save the settings with the current file, click OK.

Publishing GIF files

GIF files provide an easy way to export drawings and simple animations for use in Web pages. Standard GIF files are simply compressed bitmaps.

An animated GIF (sometimes referred to as a GIF89a) offers a simple way to export short animation sequences. Flash optimizes an animated GIF, storing only frame-to-frame changes.

Flash exports the first frame in the movie as a GIF, unless you mark a different keyframe for export by entering the frame label #Static. Flash exports all the frames in the current movie to an animated GIF unless you specify a range of frames for export by entering the frame labels #First and #Last in the appropriate keyframes.

Flash can generate an image map for a GIF to maintain URL links for buttons in the original movie. Place the frame label #Map in the keyframe in which you want to create the image map. If you don't create a frame label, Flash creates an image map using the buttons in the last frame of the movie. You can create an image map only if the $IM template variable is present in the template you select. See "Creating an image map" on page 351.

To publish a GIF file with the Flash file:

1 Choose File > Publish Settings.

2 Select the GIF Image type. Enter a unique name for Filename, or select Use Default Name to create a file with the Flash file name plus the .gif extension.

3 Click the GIF panel to display its settings.

4 For Dimensions, enter a Width and Height in pixels for the exported bitmap image, or select Match Movie to make the GIF the same size as the Flash movie and maintain the aspect ratio of your original image.

5 Choose a Playback option to determine whether Flash creates a still (Static) image or an animated GIF (Animation). If you choose Animation, select Loop Continuously or enter the number of repetitions.

6 Choose an option to specify a range of appearance settings for the exported GIF:

- Optimize Colors removes any unused colors from a GIF file's color table. This option reduces the file size by 1000 to 1500 bytes without affecting image quality, but slightly increases the memory requirements. This option has no effect on an adaptive palette. (An adaptive palette analyzes the colors in the image and creates a unique color table for the selected GIF.)

- Interlace makes the exported GIF display in a browser incrementally as it downloads. An interlaced GIF provides the user with basic graphic content before the file has completely downloaded and may download faster over a slow network connection. Do not interlace an animated GIF.

- Smooth applies anti-aliasing to an exported bitmap to produce a higher-quality bitmap image and improve text display quality. However, smoothing may cause a halo of gray pixels to appear around an anti-aliased image placed on a colored background, and it increases the GIF file size. Export an image without smoothing if a halo appears or if you're placing a GIF transparency on a multicolored background.

- Dither Solids applies dithering to solid colors as well as gradients. See Dither options in step 8.

- Remove Gradients, turned off by default, converts all gradients fills in the movie to solid colors using the first color in the gradient. Gradients increase the size of a GIF and often are of poor quality. If you use this option, choose the first color of your gradients carefully to prevent unexpected results.

7 Choose a Transparent option to determine the transparency of the movie's background and the way alpha settings are converted to GIF:

- Opaque to make the background a solid color.

- Transparent to make the background transparent.

- Alpha to set partial transparency. Then enter a Threshold value between 0 and 255 to make all colors below the value completely transparent (invisible) and colors above the threshold partially transparent. A value of 128 corresponds to 50% alpha (transparent).

8 Choose a Dither option to specify how pixels of available colors are combined to simulate colors not available in the current palette. Dithering can improve color quality, but it increases the file size. Choose from the following options:

- None turns off dithering and replaces colors not in the basic color table with the solid color from the table that most closely approximates the specified color. Not dithering can produce smaller files but unsatisfactory colors.

- Ordered provides good-quality dithering with the smallest increase in file size.

- Diffusion provides the best-quality dithering but increases file size and processing time more than ordered dithering. It also only works with the Web 216 color palette selected.

9 Choose a Palette Type to define the image's color palette:

- Web 216 uses the standard 216-color browser-safe palette to create the GIF image, for good image quality and the fastest processing on the server.

- Adaptive analyzes the colors in the image and creates a unique color table for the selected GIF. This option is best for systems displaying thousands or millions of colors; it creates the most accurate color for the image but results in a file size larger than a GIF created with the Web 216 palette. To reduce the size of a GIF with an adaptive palette, use the Max Colors option in step 10 to decrease the number of colors in the palette.

- Web Snap Adaptive is the same as the Adaptive palette option except that it converts very similar colors to the Web 216 color palette. The resulting color palette is optimized for the image, but when possible, Flash uses colors from Web 216. This produces better colors for the image when the Web 216 palette is active on a 256-color system.

- Custom to specify a palette that you have optimized for the selected image. This option has the same processing speed as the Web 216 palette. To use this option, you should know how to create and use custom palettes. To choose a custom palette, click the Ellipsis (...) button to the right of the Palette box at the bottom of the dialog box and select a palette file. Flash supports palettes saved in the ACT format, exported by Macromedia Fireworks and other leading graphics applications; for more information, see "Importing and exporting color palettes" on page 150.

10 If you selected the Adaptive or Web Snap Adaptive palette in step 9, enter a value for Max Colors to set the number of colors used in the GIF image. Choosing a smaller number of colors can produce a smaller file but may degrade the colors in the image.

11 To save the settings with the current file, click OK.

Publishing JPEG files

The JPEG format lets you save an image as a highly compressed, 24-bit bitmap. Generally, GIF is better for exporting line art, while JPEG is better for images that include continuous tones like photographs, gradients, or embedded bitmaps.

Flash exports the first frame in the movie as a JPEG, unless you mark a different keyframe for export by entering the frame label #Static.

To publish a JPEG file with the Flash file:

1 Choose File > Publish Settings.

2 Select the JPEG Image type. Enter a unique name for Filename, or select Use Default Name to create a file with the Flash file name plus the .jpg extension.

3 Click the JPEG panel to display its settings.

4 For Dimensions, enter a Width and Height in pixels for the exported bitmap image, or select Match Movie to make the JPEG the same size as the Flash movie and maintain the aspect ratio as your original image.

5 For Quality, drag the slider or enter a value to control the amount of JPEG file compression used.

   Lower image quality produces smaller files, while higher image quality produces larger files. Try different settings to determine the best trade-off between size and quality.

Note: You can set the bitmap export quality per object using the Bitmap Properties dialog box to change the object's compression setting. Selecting the default compression option in the Bitmap Properties dialog box applies the Publish Settings' JPEG Quality option. See "Setting bitmap properties" on page 165.

6 Select Progressive to display Progressive JPEG images incrementally in a Web browser, to make images appear faster when loaded over a slow network connection.

   This option is similar to interlacing in GIF and PNG images.

7 To save the settings with the current file, click OK.

Publishing PNG files

PNG is the only cross-platform bitmap format that supports transparency (an alpha channel). It is also the native file format for Macromedia Fireworks.

Flash exports the first frame in the movie as a PNG, unless you mark a different keyframe for export by entering the frame label #Static.

To publish a PNG file with the Flash file:

1 Choose File > Publish Settings.

2 Select the PNG Image type. Enter a unique name for Filename, or select Use Default Name to create a file with the Flash file name plus the .png extension.

3 Click the PNG panel to display its settings.

4 For Dimensions, enter a Width and Height in pixels for the exported bitmap image, or select Match Movie to make the PNG the same size as the Flash movie and maintain the aspect ratio as your original image.

5 Choose a Bit Depth to set the number of bits per pixel and colors to use in creating the image:

• Choose 8-bit for a 256-color image.

• Choose 24-bit for thousands of colors.

• Choose 24-bit with Alpha for thousands of colors with transparency (32 bits).

The higher the bit depth, the larger the file.

6 Choose Options to specify appearance settings for the exported PNG:

- Optimize Colors removes any unused colors from a PNG file's color table. This option reduces the file size by 1000 to 1500 bytes without affecting image quality, but slightly increases the memory requirements. This option has no effect on an adaptive palette.

- Interlace makes the exported PNG display in a browser incrementally as it downloads. An interlaced PNG provides the user with basic graphic content before the file has completely downloaded and may download faster over a slow network connection. Do not interlace an animated PNG.

- Smooth applies anti-aliasing to an exported bitmap to produce a higher-quality bitmap image and improve text display quality. However, smoothing may cause a halo of gray pixels to appear around an anti-aliased image placed on a colored background, and it increases the PNG file size. Export an image without smoothing if a halo appears or if you're placing a PNG transparency on a multicolored background.

- Dither Solids applies dithering to solid colors and gradients. See Dither options in step 7.

- Remove Gradients, turned off by default, converts all gradient fills in the movie to solid colors using the first color in the gradient. Gradients increase the size of a PNG and often are of poor quality. If you use this option, choose the first color of your gradients carefully to prevent unexpected results.

7 Choose a Dither option to specify how pixels of available colors are mixed to simulate colors not available in the current palette. Dithering can improve color quality, but it increases the file size. Choose from the following options:

- None turns off dithering and replaces colors not in the basic color table with the solid color from the table that most closely approximates the specified color. Not dithering can produce smaller files but unsatisfactory colors.

- Ordered provides good-quality dithering with the smallest increase in file size.

- Diffusion provides the best-quality dithering but increases file size and processing time more than ordered dithering. It also only works with the Web 216 color palette selected.

8 Choose Palette Type to define the color palette for the PNG image:

- Web 216 uses the standard 216-color browser-safe palette to create the PNG image, for good image quality and the fastest processing on the server.

- Adaptive analyzes the colors in the image and creates a unique color table for the selected PNG. This option is best for systems displaying thousands or millions of colors; it creates the most accurate color for the image but results in a file size larger than a PNG created with the Web 216 palette.

- Web Snap Adaptive is the same as the Adaptive palette option except that it converts very similar colors to the Web 216 color palette. The resulting color palette is optimized for the image, but when possible, Flash uses colors from Web 216. This produces better colors for the image when the Web 216 palette is active on a 256-color system.

  To reduce the size of a PNG with an adaptive palette, use the Max Colors option to decrease the number of palette colors, as described in the next step.

- Custom to specify a palette that you have optimized for the selected image. This option has the same processing speed as the Web 216 palette. To use this option, you should know how to create and use custom palettes. To choose a custom palette, click the Ellipsis (...) button to the right of the Palette box at the bottom of the dialog box and select a palette file. Flash supports palettes saved in the ACT format, exported by Macromedia Fireworks and other leading graphics applications; for more information, see "Importing and exporting color palettes" on page 150.

9 If you selected the Adaptive or Web Snap Adaptive palette in step 8, enter a value for Max Colors to set the number of colors used in the PNG image. Choosing a smaller number of colors can produce a smaller file but may degrade the colors in the image.

10 Choose Filter Options to select a line-by-line filtering method to make the PNG file more compressible, and experiment with the different options for a particular image:

- None turns off filtering.

- Sub transmits the difference between each byte and the value of the corresponding byte of the prior pixel.

- Up transmits the difference between each byte and the value of the corresponding byte of the pixel immediately above.

- Average uses the average of the two neighboring pixels (left and above) to predict the value of a pixel.

- Path computes a simple linear function of the three neighboring pixels (left, above, upper left), and then chooses as a predictor the neighboring pixel closest to the computed value.

- Adaptive analyzes the colors in the image and creates a unique color table for the selected PNG. This option is best for systems displaying thousands or millions of colors; it creates the most accurate color for the image but results in a file size larger than a PNG created with the Web 216 palette. You can reduce the size of a PNG created with an adaptive palette by decreasing the number of colors in the palette.

11 To save the settings with the current file, click OK.

Publishing QuickTime 4 movies

The QuickTime Publish option creates movies in the QuickTime 4 format, copying the Flash movie onto a separate QuickTime track. The Flash movie plays in the QuickTime movie exactly as it does in the Flash Player, retaining all of its interactive features. If the Flash movie also contains a QuickTime movie, Flash copies it to its own track in the new QuickTime file. For more information on QuickTime movies, see your QuickTime documentation.

To publish a QuickTime 4 movie with the Flash file:

1 Choose File > Publish Settings.

2 Select the QuickTime Image type. Enter a unique name for Filename, or select Use Default Name to create a file with the Flash file name plus the .mov extension.

3 Click the QuickTime panel to display its settings.

4 For Dimensions, enter a Width and Height in pixels for the exported QuickTime movie, or select Match Movie to make the QuickTime movie the same size as the Flash movie and keep its aspect ratio.

5 Choose an Alpha option to control the transparency (alpha) mode of the Flash track in the QuickTime movie without affecting any alpha settings in the Flash movie:

• Alpha Transparent to make the Flash track transparent and show any content in tracks behind the Flash track.

• Copy to make the Flash track opaque and mask all content in tracks behind the Flash track.

• Auto to make the Flash track transparent if it is on top of any other tracks, but opaque if it is the bottom or only track in the movie.

6 Choose a Layer option to control where the Flash track plays in the stacking order of the QuickTime movie:

• Top to place the Flash track always on top of other tracks in the QuickTime movie.

• Bottom to place the Flash track always behind other tracks.

• Auto to place the Flash track in front of other tracks if Flash objects are in front of video objects within the Flash movie, and behind all other tracks if Flash objects are not in front.

7 Select Streaming Sound to have Flash export all of the streaming audio in the Flash movie to a QuickTime sound track, recompressing the audio using the standard QuickTime audio settings. To change these options, click Audio Settings; see your QuickTime documentation for more information.

8 Choose Controller to specify the type of QuickTime controller used to play the exported movie—None, Standard, or QuickTime VR.

9 Select Playback options to control how QuickTime plays a movie:

• Looping repeats the movie when it reaches the last frame.

• Paused at Start pauses the movie until a user clicks a button in the movie or chooses Play from the shortcut menu. By default, the option is deselected and the movie begins to play as soon as it is loaded.

• Play Every Frame displays every frame of the movie without skipping to maintain time and does not play sound.

10 Choose File Flatten (Make Self-Contained) to combine the Flash content and imported video content into a single QuickTime movie. Deselecting this option makes the QuickTime movie refer to the imported files externally; the movie won't work properly if these files are missing.

11 To save the settings with the current file, click OK.

Previewing the publishing format and settings

To preview your Flash movie with the publishing format and settings you've selected, you can use the Publish Preview command. This command exports the file and opens the preview in the default browser. If you preview a QuickTime movie, Publish Preview launches the QuickTime Movie Player. If you preview a projector, Flash launches the projector.

To preview a file with the Publish Preview command:

1 Define the file's export options using the Publish Settings command; see "Publishing Flash movies" on page 319.

2 Do one of the following:

• Choose File > Publish Preview, and from the submenu choose the file format you want to preview.

• Press F12 to export and preview the default format.

Using the current Publish Settings values, Flash creates a file of the specified type in the same location as the Flash movie file. This file remains in this location until you overwrite or delete it.

Using the stand-alone player

The stand-alone player plays Flash Player movies exactly as they appear in a Web browser or an ActiveX host application. The stand-alone player is installed along with Flash (named FlashPla.exe in Windows and FlashPlayer on the Macintosh). When you double-click a Flash Player file, the operating system starts the stand-alone player, which in turn runs the movie.

You can control movies in the stand-alone player using menu commands and the FScommand action. For example, to make the stand-alone player take over the whole screen, you assign the FScommand action to a frame or button and then select the Fullscreen command with the True argument. For more information, see "Controlling other movies and movie clips" on page 295.

To control movies from the stand-alone player, choose from the following options:

- Open a new or existing file by choosing File > New or File > Open.

- Change your view of the movie by choosing View > Magnification, and from the submenu choose Show All, Zoom In, Zoom Out, or 100%.

- Control movie playback by choosing Control > Play, Rewind, Loop, Step Forward or Step Backward.

Exporting movies and images

To prepare Flash content for use in other applications or to export the contents of the current Flash Movie in a particular file format, you use the Export Movie and Export Image commands. The Export commands do not store export settings separately with each file, as does the Publish command. (Use Publish to create all the files you need to put a Flash movie on the Web. See "Publishing Flash movies" on page 319.)

The Export Movie command lets you export a Flash movie to a still-image format and create a numbered image file for every frame in the movie. You can also use Export Movie to export the sound in a movie to a WAV file (Windows only).

To export the content of the current frame or the currently selected image to one of the still-image formats, or to a single-frame Flash Player movie, you use the Export Image command.

- When you export a Flash image as a vector-graphic file (in the Adobe Illustrator format), you preserve its vector information. You can edit these files in other vector-based drawing programs, but you can't import these images into most page-layout and word-processing programs.

- When you save a Flash image as a bitmap GIF, JPEG, PICT (Macintosh), or BMP (Windows) file, the image loses its vector information and is saved with pixel information only. You can edit Flash images exported as bitmaps in image editors such as Adobe Photoshop, but you can no longer edit them in vector-based drawing programs.

To export a movie or image:

1 If you are exporting an image, select the frame or image in the current movie that you want to export.

2 Choose File > Export Movie or File > Export Image.

3 Enter a name for the output file.

4 Choose the file format from the Format pop-up menu.

5 Click Save.

   If the format you selected requires more information, an Export dialog box appears.

6 Set the export options for the format you selected, as described in the following sections.

   The export options and publish settings are identical for Flash movies and Generator templates. For information on other export formats, see the following section.

7 Click OK, then click Save.

About export file formats

You can export Flash movies and images in more than a dozen different formats, as shown in the table that follows. Movies are exported as sequences, and images as individual files. PNG is the only cross-platform bitmap format that supports transparency (as an alpha channel). Some nonbitmap export formats do not support alpha (transparency) effects or mask layers.

For more information on a specific file format, see the sections that follow.

File type	Extension	Windows	Macintosh
"Adobe Illustrator" on page 341	.ai	✔	✔
Animated GIF, GIF Sequence, and GIF Image	.gif	✔	✔
"Bitmap (BMP)" on page 342	.bmp	✔	
DXF Sequence and AutoCAD DXF Image	.dxf	✔	✔
Enhanced Metafile	.emf	✔	
EPS (Version 6.0 or earlier)	.eps	✔	✔
FutureSplash Player	.spl	✔	✔
Generator template	.swt	✔	✔
"JPEG Sequence and JPEG Image" on page 343	.jpg	✔	✔
PICT Sequence (Macintosh)	.pct		✔
"PNG Sequence and PNG Image" on page 344	.png	✔	✔
"Publishing QuickTime 4 movies" on page 336	.mov	✔	✔
"QuickTime Video (Macintosh)" on page 345	.mov		✔
"WAV audio (Windows)" on page 345	.wav	✔	
"Windows AVI (Windows)" on page 346	.avi	✔	
"Windows Metafile" on page 346	.wmf	✔	

Adobe Illustrator

The Adobe Illustrator format is ideal for exchanging drawings between Flash and other drawing applications such as FreeHand. This format supports very accurate conversion of curve, line style, and fill information. Flash supports import and export of the Adobe Illustrator 88, 3.0, 5.0, and 6.0 formats. (See "Adobe Illustrator files" on page 159.) Flash does not support the Photoshop EPS format or EPS files generated using Print.

Versions of the Adobe Illustrator format before 5 do not support gradient fills, and only version 6 supports bitmaps.

The Export Adobe Illustrator dialog box lets you choose the Adobe Illustrator version—88, 3.0, 5.0, or 6.0.

To make exported Flash files compatible with Adobe Illustrator 8.0 or later, use the Macromedia Flashwriter for Adobe Illustrator plug-in, included in the Flash product.

Animated GIF, GIF Sequence, and GIF Image

This option lets you export files in the GIF format. The settings are the same as those available on the GIF tab in the Publish Settings dialog box, with the following exceptions:

Resolution is set in dots per inch (dpi). You can enter a resolution or click Match Screen to use the screen resolution.

Include lets you choose to export the minimum image area or specify the full document size.

Colors lets you set the number of colors that can be used to create the exported image—black-and-white; 4-, 8-, 16-, 32-, 64-, 128- or 256- bit color; or Standard Color (the standard 216-color, browser-safe palette).

You can also choose to interlace, smooth, make transparent, or dither solid colors. For information on these options, see "Publishing GIF files" on page 328.

Animation is available for the Animated GIF export format only and lets you enter the number of repetitions, where 0 repeats endlessly.

Bitmap (BMP)

This format lets you create bitmap images for use in other applications. The Bitmap Export options dialog box has these options:

Dimensions sets the size of the exported bitmap image in pixels. Flash ensures that the size you specify always has the same aspect ratio as your original image.

Resolution sets the resolution of the exported bitmap image in dots per inch (dpi) and has Flash automatically calculate width and height based on the size of your drawing. To set the resolution to match your monitor, select Match Screen.

Color Depth specifies the bit depth of the image. Some Windows applications do not support the newer 32-bit depth for bitmap images; if you have problems using a 32-bit format, use the older 24-bit format.

Smooth applies anti-aliasing to the exported bitmap. Anti-aliasing produces a higher-quality bitmap image, but it may create a halo of gray pixels around an image placed on a colored background. Deselect this option if a halo appears.

DXF Sequence and AutoCAD DXF Image

This 3D format lets you export elements of your movie as AutoCAD DXF release 10 files, so that they can be brought into a DXF-compatible application for additional editing.

This format has no definable export options.

Enhanced Metafile (Windows)

Enhanced Metafile Format (EMF) is a graphics format available in Windows 95 and Windows NT that saves both vector and bitmap information. EMF supports the curves used in Flash drawings better than the older Windows Metafile format. However, many applications do not yet support this newer graphics format.

This format has no definable export options.

EPS 3.0 with Preview

You can export the current frame as an EPS 3.0 file for placement in another application, such as a page layout application. An EPS (encapsulated PostScript®) file can be printed by a PostScript printer. As an option, you can include a bitmap preview with the exported EPS file for applications that can import and print the EPS files (such as Microsoft Word and Adobe PageMaker®), but that can't display them on-screen.

Flash has no definable exporting options for EPS files.

FutureSplash Player

This file format was used by Flash prior to its acquisition by Macromedia. The export options match the Flash publish settings options. See "Publishing a Flash Player movie" on page 322.

JPEG Sequence and JPEG Image

The JPEG export options match the JPEG Publish Settings options with one exception: the Match Screen export option makes the exported image match the size of the movie as it appears on your screen. (The Match Movie publishing option makes the JPEG image the same size as the movie and maintains the aspect ratio of the original image.)

For more information, see "Publishing JPEG files" on page 331.

PICT (Macintosh)

PICT is the standard graphics format on the Macintosh and can contain bitmap or vector information. Use the Export PICT dialog box to set the following options:

Dimensions sets the size of the exported bitmap image specified in pixels. Flash ensures that the size you specify always has the same aspect ratio as your original image.

Resolution sets the resolution in dots per inch (dpi) and has Flash automatically calculate width and height based on the size of your drawing. To set the resolution to match your monitor, select Match Screen. Bitmap PICT images usually look best onscreen with 72-dpi resolution.

Color Depth designates whether the PICT file is object-based or bitmap. Object-based images generally look better when printed, and scaling doesn't affect their appearance. Bitmap PICT images normally look best displayed onscreen and can be manipulated in applications such as Adobe Photoshop®. You can also choose a variety of color depths with bitmap PICT files.

Include Postscript is available only for an object-based PICT file to include information that optimizes printing on a PostScript printer. This information makes the file larger and may not be recognized by all applications.

PNG Sequence and PNG Image

These export settings are similar to the PNG Publish Settings options, with the following exceptions:

Dimensions sets the size of the exported bitmap image to the number of pixels you enter in the Width and Height fields.

Resolution lets you enter a resolution in dots per inch (dpi). To use the screen resolution and maintain the aspect ratio of your original image, select Match Screen.

Colors is the same as the Bit Depth option in the PNG Publish Settings tab and sets the number of bits per pixel to use in creating the image. For a 256-color image, choose 8-bit; for thousands of colors, choose 24-bit; for thousands of colors with transparency (32 bits) choose 24-bit with Alpha. The higher the bit depth, the larger the file.

Include lets you choose to export the minimum image area or specify the full document size.

Filter options match those in the PNG Publish Settings tab.

In addition, you can choose Interlace to make the exported PNG display in a browser incrementally as it downloads; Smooth to apply anti-aliasing to an exported bitmap to produce a higher-quality bitmap image and improve text display quality; and Dither Solid Colors to apply dithering to solid colors and gradients.

For information on these options, see "Publishing PNG files" on page 332.

QuickTime

The QuickTime export option creates a movie with a Flash track in the QuickTime 4 format. Any layers in the Flash project are exported as a single Flash track. This export format lets you combine the interactive features of Flash with the multimedia and video features of QuickTime in a single QuickTime 4 movie, which can be viewed by anyone with the QuickTime 4 plug-in.

These export options are identical to QuickTime publish options. See "Publishing QuickTime 4 movies" on page 336.

QuickTime Video (Macintosh)

The QuickTime Video format converts the Flash project into a sequence of bitmaps embedded in the file's video track. The Flash content is exported as a bitmap image without any interactivity. This format is useful for editing Flash content in a video-editing application.

The Export QuickTime Video dialog box contains the following options:

Dimensions specifies a width and height in pixels for the frames of a QuickTime movie. By default, you can specify only the width or the height, and the other dimension is automatically set to maintain the aspect ratio of your original movie. To set both the width and the height, deselect Maintain Aspect Ratio.

Format selects a color depth. Options are black-and-white; 4-, 8-, 16-, or 24-bit color; and 32-bit color with alpha (transparency).

Smooth applies anti-aliasing to the exported QuickTime movie. Anti-aliasing produces a higher-quality bitmap image, but it may cause a halo of gray pixels to appear around images when placed over a colored background. Deselect the option if a halo appears.

Compressor selects a standard QuickTime compressor. See your QuickTime documentation for more information.

Quality controls the amount of compression applied to your movie. The effect depends on the compressor selected.

Sound Format sets the export rate for sounds in the movie. Higher rates yield better fidelity and larger files. Lower rates save space.

WAV audio (Windows)

The WAV Export Movie option exports only the sound file of the current movie to a single WAV file. You can specify the sound format of the new file.

Choose Sound Format to determine the sampling frequency, bit rate, and stereo or mono setting of the exported sound. Select Ignore Event Sounds to exclude events sounds from the exported file.

Windows AVI (Windows)

This format exports a movie as a Windows video, but discards any interactivity. The standard Windows movie format, Windows AVI is a good format for opening a Flash animation in a video-editing application. Because AVI is a bitmap-based format, movies that contain long or high-resolution animations can quickly become very large.

The Export Windows AVI dialog box has the following options:

Dimensions specifies a width and height in pixels for the frames of an AVI movie. Specify only the width or the height; the other dimension is automatically set to maintain the aspect ratio of your original movie. Deselect Maintain Aspect Ratio to set both the width and the height.

Video Format selects a color depth. Many applications do not yet support the Windows 32-bit image format. If you have problems using this format, use the older 24-bit format.

Compress Video displays a dialog box for choosing standard AVI compression options.

Smooth applies anti-aliasing to the exported AVI movie. Anti-aliasing produces a higher-quality bitmap image, but it may cause a halo of gray pixels to appear around images when placed over a colored background. Deselect the option if a halo appears.

Sound Format lets you set the sample rate and size of the sound track, and whether it will be exported in mono or stereo. The smaller the sample rate and size, the smaller the exported file, with a possible trade-off in sound quality. For more information on exporting sound to the AVI format, see "Compressing sounds for export" on page 175.

Windows Metafile

Windows Metafile format is the standard Windows graphics format and is supported by most Windows applications. This format yields good results for importing and exporting files. It has no definable export options. See "Enhanced Metafile (Windows)" on page 342.

About HTML publishing templates

Flash HTML templates let you control what movie goes on a Web page and how it looks and plays back in the Web browser. A Flash template is a text file that contains both unchanging HTML code and template code or variables (which differ from ActionScript variables). When you publish a Flash movie, Flash replaces the variables in the template you selected in the Publish Settings dialog box with your HTML settings, and produces an HTML page with your movie embedded.

Flash includes various templates, suitable for most users' needs, that eliminate the need to edit an HTML page with the Flash movie. For example, one template simply places a Flash movie on the generated HTML page so that users can view it through a Web browser if the plug-in is installed. Another template does the same thing except it first detects whether the plug-in has been installed, and if not, installs it.

You can easily use the same template, change the settings, and publish a new HTML page. If you're proficient in HTML, you can also create your own templates using any HTML editor. Creating a template is the same as creating a standard HTML page, except that you replace specific values pertaining to a Flash movie with variables that begin with a dollar ($) sign.

Flash HTML templates have these characteristics:

- A one-line title that appears on the Template pop-up menu

- A longer description that appears when you click the Info button

- Template variables beginning with $ that specify where parameters values should be substituted when Flash generates the output file

  Note: Use \ $ if you need to use a $ for another purpose in the document.

- HTML OBJECT and EMBED tags that follow the tag requirements of Microsoft Internet Explorer and Netscape Communicator/Navigator, respectively. To display a movie properly on an HTML page, you must follow these tag requirements. Internet Explorer opens a Flash movie using the OBJECT HTML tag; Netscape uses the EMBED tag. For more information, see "Using OBJECT and EMBED" on page 353.

Customizing HTML publishing templates

If you're familiar with HTML, you can modify HTML template variables to create an image map, a text report, or a URL report, or to insert your own values for some of the most common Flash OBJECT and EMBED parameters (for Internet Explorer and Netscape Communicator/Navigator, respectively).

Flash templates can include any HTML content for your application, or even code for special interpreters such as Cold Fusion, ASP, and the like.

To modify an HTML publishing template:

1 Using an HTML editor, open the Flash HTML template you want to change, located in the Macromedia Flash 5/HTML folder.

2 Edit the template as needed. To use the default values, leave the variables empty.

   For information on variables supported in Flash, see the following table.

   For information on creating an image map or a text or URL report, or to insert your own values for OBJECT and EMBED parameters, see the sections for those topics, following this procedure.

3 When you have finished editing the variables, save the template in the Macromedia Flash 5/HTML folder.

   Flash saves the modified template with the Flash movie's file name and the template extension. For example, saving a template named Standard.asp for publishing a Flash movie named MyMovie.swf produces a template named MyMovie.asp.

4 To apply the template settings to your Flash movie, choose File > Publish Settings, select the HTML panel, and select the template you modified.

   Flash changes only the template variables in the template selected in the Publish Settings dialog box.

5 Choose your remaining publishing settings, and click OK. For more information, see "Publishing Flash movies" on page 319.

The following tables lists the template variables that Flash recognizes. For a definition of all the tags these variables work with, see "Editing Flash HTML settings" on page 353.

Parameter	Template Variable
Template title	$TT
Template description start	$DS
Template description finish	$DF
Width	$WI
Height	$HE
Movie	$MO
HTML alignment	$HA
Looping	$LO
Parameters for OBJECT	$PO
Parameters for EMBED	$PE
Play	$PL
Quality	$QU
Scale	$SC
Salign	$SA
Wmode	$WM
Devicefont	$DE
Bgcolor	$BG
Movie text (area to write movie text)	$MT
Movie URL (location of movie URLs)	$MU
Image width (unspecified image type)	$IW
Image height (unspecified image type)	$IH
Image file name (unspecified image type)	$IS
Image map name	$IU
Image map tag location	$IM
QuickTime width	$QW
QuickTime height	$QH

Parameter	Template Variable
QuickTime file name	$QN
GIF width	$GW
GIF height	$GH
GIF file name	$GS
JPEG width	$JW
JPEG height	$JH
JPEG file name	$JN
PNG width	$PW
PNG height	$PH
PNG file name	$PN
Generator variables OBJECT tag	$GV
Generator variables EMBED tag	$GE

Creating an image map

Flash can generate an image map using any image and maintain the function of buttons that link to URLs, even if another image is substituted. On encountering the $IM template variable, Flash inserts the image map code in a template. The $IU variable identifies the name of the GIF, JPEG, or PNG file.

To create an image map:

1 In your Flash movie, specify the keyframe you'll use for the image map and label it **#Map** in the Frame panel (Windows > Panels > Frame).

   You can use any keyframe with buttons that have attached Get URL actions.

   If you don't create a frame label, Flash creates an image map using the buttons in the last frame of the movie. This option generates an embedded image map, not an embedded Flash movie.

2 In an HTML editor, open the HTML template you'll modify. Flash stores HTML templates in the Macromedia Flash 5/HTML folder.

3 Save your template.

4 Choose File > Publish Settings, click the Format tab, and select a format for the image map—GIF, JPEG, or PNG.

5 Click OK to save your settings.

As an example, inserting the following code in a template:

```
$IM
<IMG SRC=$IS usemap=$IU WIDTH=$IW HEIGHT=$IH BORDER=0>
```

might produce this code in the HTML document created by the Publish command:

```
<MAP NAME="mymovie">
<AREA COORDS="130,116,214,182" HREF="http://www.macromedia.com">
</MAP>
<IMG SRC="mymovie.gif" usemap="#mymovie" WIDTH=550 HEIGHT=400
BORDER=0>
```

Creating a text report

The $MT template variable causes Flash to insert all the text from the current Flash movie as a comment in the HTML code. This is useful for indexing the content of a movie and making it visible to search engines.

Creating a URL report

The $MU template variable makes Flash generate a list of the URLs referred to by actions in the current movie and insert it at the current location as a comment. This enables link verification tools to see and verify the links in the movie.

Using shorthand template variables

The $PO (for OBJECT tags) and $PE (for EMBED tags) template variables are useful shorthand elements. Both variables cause Flash to insert into a template any nondefault values for some of the most common Flash OBJECT and EMBED parameters, including PLAY ($PL), QUALITY ($QU), SCALE ($SC), SALIGN ($SA), WMODE ($WM), DEVICEFONT ($DE), and BGCOLOR ($BG). See the sample template in the following section for an example of these variables.

Sample template

The Default.html template file in Flash, shown here as a sample, includes many of the commonly used template variables.

```
$TTFlash Only (Default)
$DS
Use an OBJECT and EMBED
tag to display Flash.
$DF
<HTML>
<HEAD>
<TITLE>$TI</TITLE>
</HEAD>
<BODY bgcolor="$BG">

<!-- URLs used in the movie-->
$MU
<!-- text used in the movie-->
$MT

<OBJECT classid="clsid:D27CDB6E-AE6D-11cf-96B8-444553540000"

 codebase="http://download.macromedia.com/pub/shockwave/cabs/
flash/swflash.cab#version=5,0,0,0"
 ID=$TI WIDTH=$WI HEIGHT=$HE>
 $PO
<EMBED $PE WIDTH=$WI HEIGHT=$HE
 TYPE="application/x-shockwave-flash"
PLUGINSPAGE="http://www.macromedia.com/shockwave/download/
index.cgi?P1_Prod_Version=ShockwaveFlash"></EMBED>
</OBJECT>

</BODY>
</HTML>
```

Editing Flash HTML settings

An HTML document is required to play a Flash movie in a Web browser and specify browser settings. If you are experienced with HTML, you can change or enter HTML parameters manually in an HTML editor, or create your own HTML files to control a Flash movie.

For information on having Flash create the HTML document automatically when you publish a movie, see "Publishing Flash movies" on page 319. For information on customizing HTML templates included in Flash, see "Customizing HTML publishing templates" on page 348.

Using OBJECT and EMBED

To display a Flash Player movie in a Web browser, an HTML document must use the OBJECT and EMBED tags with the proper parameters.

For OBJECT, four settings (HEIGHT, WIDTH, CLASSID, and CODEBASE) are attributes that appear within the OBJECT tag; all others are parameters that appear in separate, named PARAM tags. For example:

```
<OBJECT CLASSID="clsid:D27CDB6E-AE6D-11cf-96B8-444553540000"
WIDTH="100"
HEIGHT="100" CODEBASE="http://active.macromedia.com/flash5/cabs/
swflash.cab#version=5,0,0,0">
<PARAM NAME="MOVIE" VALUE="moviename.swf">
<PARAM NAME="PLAY" VALUE="true">
<PARAM NAME="LOOP" VALUE="true">
<PARAM NAME="QUALITY" VALUE="high">
</OBJECT>
```

For the EMBED tag, all settings (such as HEIGHT, WIDTH, QUALITY, and LOOP) are attributes that appear between the angle brackets of the opening EMBED tag. For example:

```
<EMBED SRC="moviename.swf" WIDTH="100" HEIGHT="100" PLAY="true"
LOOP="true" QUALITY="high"
PLUGINSPAGE="http://www.macromedia.com/shockwave/download/
index.cgi?P1_Prod_Version=ShockwaveFlash">
</EMBED>
```

To use both tags together, position the EMBED tag just before the closing OBJECT tag, as follows:

```
<OBJECT CLASSID="clsid:D27CDB6E-AE6D-11cf-96B8-444553540000"
WIDTH="100"
HEIGHT="100" CODEBASE="http://active.macromedia.com/flash5/cabs/
swflash.cab#version=5,0,0,0">
<PARAM NAME="MOVIE" VALUE="moviename.swf">
<PARAM NAME="PLAY" VALUE="true">
<PARAM NAME="LOOP" VALUE="true">
<PARAM NAME="QUALITY" VALUE="high">

<EMBED SRC="moviename.swf" WIDTH="100" HEIGHT="100" PLAY="true"
LOOP="true" QUALITY="high"
PLUGINSPAGE="http://www.macromedia.com/shockwave/download/
index.cgi?P1_Prod_Version=ShockwaveFlash">
</EMBED>

</OBJECT>
```

Note: If you use both the OBJECT and the EMBED tags, use identical values for each attribute or parameter to ensure consistent playback across browsers. The parameter swflash.cab#version=5,0,0,0 is optional, and you can omit it if you don't want to check for version number.

The following tag attributes and parameters describe the HTML created by the Publish command. You can refer to this list as you write your own HTML to insert in Flash movies. Unless noted, all items apply to both OBJECT and EMBED tags. Optional entries are noted. When customizing a template, you can substitute a template variable listed here for the value. See "Customizing HTML publishing templates" on page 348.

SRC

Value

movieName.swf

Template variable: $MO

Description
Specifies the name of the movie to be loaded. EMBED only.

MOVIE

Value
movieName.swf

Template variable: $MO

Description
Specifies the name of the movie to be loaded. OBJECT only.

CLASSID

Value

`clsid:D27CDB6E-AE6D-11cf-96B8-444553540000`

Description

Identifies the ActiveX control for the browser. The value must be entered exactly as shown. `OBJECT` only.

WIDTH

Value

n or *n%*

Template variable: `$WI`

Description

Specifies the width of the movie in either pixels or percentage of browser window.

HEIGHT

Value

n or *n%*

Template variable: `$HE`

Description

Specifies the height of the movie in either pixels or percentage of browser window.

Because Flash movies are scalable, their quality won't degrade at different sizes if the aspect ratio is maintained. (For example, the following sizes all have a 4:3 aspect ratio: 640 pixels by 480 pixels, 320 pixels by 240 pixels, and 240 pixels by 180 pixels.)

CODEBASE

Value

`http://active.macromedia.com/flash5/cabs/`
`swflash.cab#version=5,0,0,0"`

Description

Identifies the location of the Flash Player ActiveX control so that the browser can automatically download it if it is not already installed. The value must be entered exactly as shown. `OBJECT` only.

PLUGINSPAGE

Value

```
http://www.macromedia.com/shockwave/download/
index.cgi?P1_Prod_Version=ShockwaveFlash
```

Description

Identifies the location of the Flash Player plug-in so that the user can download it if it is not already installed. The value must be entered exactly as shown. `EMBED` only.

SWLIVECONNECT

Value

`true` | `false`

Description

(Optional) Specifies whether the browser should start Java when loading the Flash Player for the first time. The default value is `false` if this attribute is omitted. If you use JavaScript and Flash on the same page, Java must be running for the FSCommand to work. However, if you are using JavaScript only for browser detection or another purpose unrelated to FSCommand actions, you can prevent Java from starting by setting `SWLIVECONNECT` to `false`. You can also force Java to start when you are not using JavaScript with Flash by explicitly setting `SWLIVECONNECT` to `true`. Starting Java substantially increases the time it takes to start a movie; set this tag to `true` only when necessary. `EMBED` only.

Use the Exec FSCommand actions to start Java from a stand-alone projector. See "Controlling the Flash Player" on page 291.

PLAY

Value

`true` | `false`

Template variable: `$PL`

Description

(Optional) Specifies whether the movie begins playing immediately on loading in the browser. If your Flash movie is interactive, you may want to let the user initiate play by clicking a button or performing some other task. In this case, set the `PLAY` attribute to `false` to prevent the movie from starting automatically. The default value is `true` if this attribute is omitted.

LOOP

Value

true | false

Template variable: $LO

Description

(Optional) Specifies whether the movie repeats indefinitely or stops when it reaches the last frame. The default value is true if this attribute is omitted.

QUALITY

Value

low | high | autolow | autohigh | best

Template variable: $QU

Description

(Optional) Specifies the level of anti-aliasing to be used during playback of your movie. Because anti-aliasing requires a faster processor to smooth each frame of the movie before it is rendered on the viewer's screen, choose a value based on whether speed or appearance is your top priority:

- Low favors playback speed over appearance and never uses anti-aliasing.

- Autolow emphasizes speed at first but improves appearance whenever possible. Playback begins with anti-aliasing turned off. If the Flash Player detects that the processor can handle it, anti-aliasing is turned on.

- Autohigh emphasizes playback speed and appearance equally at first but sacrifices appearance for playback speed if necessary. Playback begins with anti-aliasing turned on. If the actual frame rate drops below the specified frame rate, anti-aliasing is turned off to improve playback speed. Use this setting to emulate the View > Antialias setting in Flash.

- Medium applies some anti-aliasing and does not smooth bitmaps. It produces a better quality than the Low setting, but lower quality than the High setting.

- High favors appearance over playback speed and always applies anti-aliasing. If the movie does not contain animation, bitmaps are smoothed; if the movie has animation, bitmaps are not smoothed.

- Best provides the best display quality and does not consider playback speed. All output is anti-aliased and all bitmaps are smoothed.

The default value for Quality is high if this attribute is omitted.

BGCOLOR

Value

#*RRGGBB* (hexadecimal RGB value)

Template variable: $BG

Description

(Optional) Specifies the background color of the movie. Use this attribute to override the background color setting specified in the Flash file. This attribute does not affect the background color of the HTML page.

SCALE

Value

showall | noborder | exactfit

Template variable: $SC

Description

(Optional) Defines how the movie is placed within the browser window when WIDTH and HEIGHT values are percentages.

- Default (Show all) makes the entire movie visible in the specified area without distortion, while maintaining the original aspect ratio of the movie. Borders may appear on two sides of the movie.

- No Border scales the movie to fill the specified area, without distortion but possibly with some cropping, while maintaining the original aspect ratio of the movie.

- Exact Fit makes the entire movie visible in the specified area without trying to preserve the original aspect ratio. Distortion may occur.

The default value is showall if this attribute is omitted (and WIDTH and HEIGHT values are percentages).

ALIGN

Value

L | R | T | B

Template variable: $HA

Description

Specifies the ALIGN attribute for the OBJECT, EMBED, and IMG tags and determines how the Flash movie window is positioned within the browser window.

- Default centers the movie in the browser window and crops edges if the browser window is smaller than the movie.

- Left, Right, Top, and Bottom align the movie along the corresponding edge of the browser window and crop the remaining three sides as needed.

SALIGN

Value

L | R | T | B | TL | TR | BL | BR

Template variable: $SA

Description

(Optional) Specifies where a scaled Flash movie is positioned within the area defined by the WIDTH and HEIGHT settings. See "SCALE" on page 358 for more information about these conditions.

- L, R, T, and B align the movie along the left, right, top or bottom edge, respectively, of the browser window and crop the remaining three sides as needed.

- TL and TR align the movie to the top left and top right corner, respectively, of the browser window and crop the bottom and remaining right or left side as needed.

- BL and BR align the movie to the bottom left and bottom right corner, respectively, of the browser window and crop the top and remaining right or left side as needed.

If this attribute is omitted, the movie is centered in the browser window. Cropping may occur or borders may appear on any side, as needed.

BASE

Value

base directory or URL

Description

(Optional) Specifies the base directory or URL used to resolve all relative path statements in the Flash Player movie. This attribute is helpful when your Flash Player movies are kept in a different directory from your other files.

MENU

Value

true | false

Template variable: $ME

Description

(Optional) Specifies what type of menu is displayed when the viewer right-clicks (Windows) or Command-clicks (Macintosh) the movie area in the browser.

- True displays the full menu, allowing the user a variety of options to enhance or control playback.

- False displays a menu that contains only the About Flash option.

The default value is true if this attribute is omitted.

WMODE

Value

Window | Opaque | Transparent

Template variable: $WM

Description

(Optional) Lets you take advantage of the transparent movie, absolute positioning, and layering capabilities available in Internet Explorer 4.0. This tag works only in Windows with the Flash ActiveX control.

- Window plays the movie in its own rectangular window on a Web page.

- Opaque makes the movie hide everything behind it on the page.

- Transparent makes the background of the HTML page show through all the transparent portions of the movie, and may slow animation performance.

The default value is Window if this attribute is omitted. Object only.

Configuring a Web server for Flash

When your files are accessed from a Web server, the server must properly identify them as Flash Player files in order to display them. If the MIME type is missing or not properly delivered by the server, the browser may display error messages or a blank window with a puzzle piece icon.

Your server may already be configured properly. To test server configuration, see TechNote #12696 on the Macromedia Flash Support Center, http://www.macromedia.com. If your server is not properly configured, you (or your server's administrator) must add the Flash Player MIME types to the server's configuration files and associate the following MIME types with the Flash Player file extensions:

- MIME type application/x-shockwave-flash has the .swf file extension.
- MIME type application/futuresplash has the .spl file extension.

If you are administering your own server, consult your server software documentation for instructions on adding or configuring MIME types. If you are not administering your own server, contact your Internet service provider, webmaster, or server administrator to add the MIME type information.

If your site is on a Macintosh server, you must also set the following parameters: Action: Binary; Type: SWFL; and Creator: SWF2.

Screening traffic to your Web site

When publishing Flash content on the Web, you can configure a Web server to make it easier to play Flash movies, using a script-based detector to determine whether a user has the Flash Player plug-in or ActiveX control installed. Called the Macromedia Flash Dispatcher, this detector is included in the Macromedia Flash (SWF) Deployment Kit, in the Macromedia Flash 5/Goodies folder.

The Dispatcher is a combination of JavaScript, VBScript, and Flash data that screen incoming traffic to your Web site. The Dispatcher detects whether the user's Web browser has the Flash plug-in or ActiveX control installed, and if so, what version. You can configure the Dispatcher to load a document with Flash content, load alternate content, or oversee the updating or installation of the player.

For more information, see the ReadMe file and documentation included with the Flash (SWF) Deployment Kit in Macromedia Flash 5/Goodies folder.

INDEX

D

debugging files, protecting with password 322
default color palette 149
Default compression option, for sounds 177
Default Layout command, for panels 80
deleting
    frames or keyframes 87, 267
    layers 205
    lines 130
    objects 189
    scenes 88
Deselect All command 184
DEVICE FONT parameter, publish settings 325
device fonts 210, 216
dimensions, publishing Flash movie 325
Disable Timeline Docking preference 111
display, speeding 110
distributing objects to top, bottom, left, right,
        or center 197
dithering colors, GIF files 330, 333
dot syntax 296
Down state, for buttons 233
download performance 315
dragging objects 187
Draw Border and Background option
    for dynamic text 220
    for input text 221
drawing 113
    adjusting anchor points 124
    adjusting line segments 124
    anchor points 118
    brush strokes 125
    click accuracy tolerance 133
    converting lines to fills 131
    curve points and corner points 122
    curves, with Pen tool 121
    erasing lines or shapes 130
    expanding shapes 131
    modifying shapes 131
    optimizing curves 129
    ovals and rectangles 117
    overlapping shapes 115
    Pen tool 118
    Pencil tool 116
    precise lines and curves 118
    reshaping lines and shapes 126
    rounded rectangles 117

drawing *(continued)*
    showing anchor points on shapes 126
    smoothing curves 133
    snapping line end points 133
    snapping objects 132
    softening fill edges 131
    straight lines 117, 119
    straightening and smoothing lines 128
    tolerance for redrawing geometric shapes 133
    tolerance for straightening lines 133
    tools overview 114
duplicating, symbols 232
dynamic text 218
    HTML formatting for 219
    rich text formatting for 219
    setting options 220

E

Easing option
    for motion tweening 255, 257
    for shape tweening 261
Edit Center command 198
Edit Envelope
    for sounds 173
    units in 173
    zooming in 173
Edit in New Window command 239
Edit in Place command 238
Edit Multiple Frames button 269
Edit Selected command 186
Edit Symbol command 239
editable text boxes 218
    rich text formatting in 219
editing
    imported bitmap images 164
    layers 204
    reshaping lines and shapes 126
    softening edges of an object 131
    symbols 238
    text 222
Effects menu, in Sound panel 170
Effects panel 241
Embed Fonts option
    for dynamic text 220
    for input text 221
EMBED parameter 353
empty symbols, creating 229

R

Radial Gradient option 140
Raw compression, for sound 178
Recognize Lines preference 133
Recognize Shapes preference 133
Rectangle tool 117
    Round Rectangle modifier 117
registering images from frame to frame 268
registration point, moving 198
relative path 289
Remove Frame command 87, 267
Remove Gradients option 329, 333
renaming layers 204
rendering settings 110
reshaping
    lines and shapes 126
    type 223
resizing objects 191
restoring transformed objects 195
Reverse command, for animation 267
Revert command 76
reverting to the last saved version of a file 76
RGB colors, importing and exporting 150
rich text formatting, in editable text boxes 219
Right Channel option, for sound 170
Rotate command 192
Rotate option, for motion tweening 255, 257
rotating
    and scaling simultaneously 193
    by 90° 192
    by dragging 192
    clockwise or counterclockwise 192
    objects 192
    with Transform panel 192
Ruler Units menu 74
rulers 104
    changing units of 104
    setting units 74
    showing 104

S

SALIGN parameter 359
    publish settings 326
Sample Rate
    for ADPCM sound compression 177
    for raw sound compression 178
Save As command 76

Save command 76
saving movies 76
Scale and Rotate command 193
Scale command 191
Scale option, for motion tweening 255, 256
SCALE parameter 358
    publish settings 326
scaling
    and rotating simultaneously 193
    by dragging 191
    objects 191
    with Transform panel 191
Scene panel 88
scenes 88
    changing order of 89
    creating 88
    deleting 88
    duplicating 89
    pasting into 188
    previewing 75
    renaming 89
    selecting everything on every layer of 184
    viewing 88
Seconds button, in Edit Envelope 173
Selectable option
    for dynamic text 220
    for text 216
selecting
    adding to a selection 184
    connected lines 183
    deselecting 184
    everything between two keyframes 184
    everything in a scene 184
    hiding selection edges 186
    layers 204
    locking groups or symbols 184
    objects 182
    text and text blocks 222
    with a freehand selection area 185
    with a selection marquee 183
    with a straight-edged selection area 185
    with the Lasso tool 185
selection highlights, for objects 182
Send Backward command 190
Send to Back command 190
shape hints 264
    with shape tweening 262

T

tangent handles, adjusting 124
target path, inserting 275
targeting
    loaded movies 296
    movie clips 295
    printable frames 305
Tell Target action 295
templates
    creating 348
    sample 352
    selecting 324
    shorthand variables 352
    variables 349
Test button, in Sound Properties dialog box 176
Test Movie command 76, 237
Test Scene command 76, 237
testing
    download performance 315
    frame actions 282
    loading and unloading movies 294
    sounds 176
text 209
    alignment 215
    anti-aliasing 110
    bold and italic style 213
    breaking apart 199
    character options 214
    converting to lines and fills 223
    creating 211
    creating font symbols 217
    device fonts 210
    dynamic text options 220
    editable text boxes 218
    editing 222
    embedded fonts 210
    fill color 213
    fixed-width text block 211
    Font panel 213
    importing with Clipboard 188
    input text options 221
    linking to a URL 223
    making selectable 216
    margins 215
    reshaping type 223
    resizing a text block 211
    selecting 222

text *(continued)*
    selecting a font 213
    selecting device fonts 216
    selecting font size 213
    setting font and paragraph attributes 212
    transforming type 222
    widening text block 211
text blocks, selecting 183, 222
text boxes
    creating 218
    dynamic 218
    editable 218
    input 218
    rich text formatting in 219
text report, in HTML file 351
Text tool 211
TGA files, importing 155
TIFF files, importing 155
Time In control, for sounds 173
Time Out control, for sounds 173
Timeline 82
    animation frames in 251
    Center Frame button 84
    centering the playhead in 84
    changing frame display 84
    changing layer height 203
    changing layer order 205
    changing number of layers displayed 203
    changing the appearance of 83
    controlling 295
    converting keyframes into frames 87, 267
    copying and pasting frames 87, 267
    creating keyframes in 250
    deleting frames or keyframes 87, 267
    disable docking preference 111
    docking to the application window 83
    dragging 83
    dragging frames 87, 267
    editing 266, 269
    editing frames 86
    hiding layers in 202
    inserting frames 87, 266
    layer name fields in 83
    locking layers in 205
    onion skinning frames 268
    playhead 84
    Preview in Context option 85

V

values 285
Variable option
 for dynamic text 220
 for input text 221
variables 288
 sending to URL 288
 sending with loaded movie 292
 template 349
vector graphics
 compared to bitmaps 68
 creating from imported bitmap images 161
 importing with Clipboard 188
 printing 299

W

WAV sounds
 exporting 345
 importing 168
Web 216 color palette 330
Web servers, configuring for Flash Player 361
Web Snap Adaptive color palette 330
Web-safe color palette 149
weight, for lines 138
WIDTH parameter 355
 publish settings 325
Windows Metafile files
 exporting 346
 importing 154
With action 295
WMODE parameter 360
 publish settings 326
Word Wrap option
 for dynamic text 220
 for input text 221
work area 70
Work Area command 103

Z

zoom buttons, in Edit Envelope 173
zooming 102